Political Relationship
and Narrative Knowledge

Critical Studies in Education and Culture Series

Wittgenstein: Philosophy, Postmoodernism, Pedagogy
Michael Peters and James Marshall

Policy, Pedagogy, and Social Inequality: Community College Student Realities in Post-Industrial America
Penelope E. Herideen

Psychoanalysis and Pedagogy
Stephen Appel, editor

The Rhetoric of Diversity and the Traditions of America Literary Study: Critical Multiculturalism in English
Lesliee Antonette

Becoming and Unbecoming White: Owning and Disowning a Racial Identity
Christine Clark and James O'Donnell

Critical Pedagogy: An Introduction, 2nd Edition
Barry Kanpol

Michel Foucault: Materialism and Education
Mark Olssen

Revolutionary Social Transformation: Democratic Hopes, Political Possibilities, and Critical Education
Paula Allman

Critical Reflection and the Foreign Language Classroom
Terry A. Osborn

Community in Motion: Theatre for Development in Africa
L. Dale Byam

Nietzsche's Legacy for Education: Past and Present Values
Michael Peters, James Marshall, and Paul Smeyers, editors

Ritual, Ceremonies, and Cultural Meaning in Higher Education
Kathleen Manning

Political Relationship and Narrative Knowledge

A CRITICAL ANALYSIS OF SCHOOL AUTHORITARIANISM

Peter B. Armitage

Critical Studies in Education and Culture Series
Edited by Henry A. Giroux

BERGIN & GARVEY
Westport, Connecticut • London

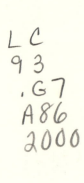
Library of Congress Cataloging-in-Publication Data

Armitage, Peter B., 1939–
  Political relationship and narrative knowledge : a critical analysis of school
authoritarianism / Peter B. Armitage.
      p. cm.—(Critical studies in education and culture series, ISSN 1064-8615)
  Includes bibliographical references and index.
  ISBN 0-89789-690-4 (alk. paper)
  1. Politics and education—Great Britain. 2. Authoritarianism—Great Britain.
3. Critical theory. 4. Critical pedagogy. I. Title. II. Series.
LC93.G7A86 2000
370.11'5—dc21   99–055885

British Library Cataloguing in Publication Data is available.

Library of Congress Catalog Card Number: 99–055885
ISBN: 0-89789-690-4
ISSN: 1064-8615

First published in 2000

Bergin & Garvey, 88 Post Road West, Westport, CT 06881
An imprint of Greenwood Publishing Group, Inc.
www.greenwood.com

Printed in the United States of America

The paper used in this book complies with the
Permanent Paper Standard issued by the National
Information Standards Organization (Z39.48–1984).

10 9 8 7 6 5 4 3 2 1

For my parents, Hugh and Hazel Armitage

Contents

Series Foreword

Educational reform has fallen upon hard times. The traditional assumption that schooling is fundamentally tied to the imperatives of citizenship designed to educate students to exercise civic leadership and public service has been eroded. The schools are now the key institution for producing professional, technically trained, credentialized workers for whom the demands of citizenship are subordinated to the vicissitudes of the marketplace and the commercial public sphere. Given the current corporate and right wing assault on public and higher education, coupled with the emergence of a moral and political climate that has shifted to a new Social Darwinism, the issues which framed the democratic meaning, purpose, and use to which education might aspire have been displaced by more vocational and narrowly ideological considerations.

The war waged against the possibilities of an education wedded to the precepts of a real democracy is not merely ideological. Against the backdrop of reduced funding for public schooling, the call for privatization, vouchers, cultural uniformity, and choice, there are the often ignored larger social realities of material and power and oppression. On the national level, there has been a vast resurgence of racism. This is evident in the passing of anti-immigration laws such as Proposition 187 in California, the dismantling of the welfare state, the demonization of black youth that is taking place in the popular media, and the remarkable attention provided by the media to forms of race talk that argue for the intellectual inferiority of blacks or dismiss calls for racial justice as simply a holdover from the "morally bankrupt" legacy of the 1960s.

Poverty is on the rise among children in the United States, with 20 percent of all children under the age of eighteen living below the poverty line.

Unemployment is growing at an alarming rate for poor youth of color, especially in the urban centers. While black youth are policed and disciplined in and out of the nation's schools, conservative and liberal educators define education through the ethically limp discourses of privatization, national standards, and global competitiveness.

Many writers in the critical education tradition have attempted to challenge the right wing fundamentalism behind educational and social reform in both the United States and abroad while simultaneously providing ethical signposts for a public discourse about education and democracy that is both prophetic and transformative. Eschewing traditional categories, a diverse number of critical theorists and educators have successfully exposed the political and ethical implications of the cynicism and despair that has become endemic to the discourse of schooling and civic life. In its place, such educators strive to provide a language of hope that inextricably links the struggle over schooling to understanding and transforming our present social and cultural dangers.

At the risk of overgeneralizing, both cultural studies theorists and critical educators have emphasized the importance of understanding theory as the grounded basis for "intervening into contexts and power . . . in order to enable people to act more strategically in ways that may change their context for the better."[1] Moreover, theorists in both fields have argued for the primacy of the political by calling for and struggling to produce critical public spaces, regardless of how fleeting they may be, in which "popular cultural resistance is explored as a form of political resistance."[2] Such writers have analyzed the challenges that teachers will have to face in redefining a new mission for education, one that is linked to honoring the experiences, concerns, and diverse histories and languages that give expression to the multiple narratives that engage and challenge the legacy of democracy.

Equally significant is the insight of recent critical educational work that connects the politics of difference with concrete strategies for addressing the crucial relationships between schooling and the economy, and citizenship and the politics of meaning in communities of multicultural, multiracial, and multilingual schools.

Critical Studies in Education and Culture attempts to address and demonstrate how scholars working in the fields of cultural studies and the critical pedagogy might join together in a radical project and practice informed by theoretically rigorous discourses that affirm the critical but refuse the cynical, and establish hope as central to a critical pedagogical and political practice but eschew a romantic utopianism. Central to such a project is the issue of how pedagogy might provide cultural studies theorists and educators with an opportunity to engage pedagogical practices that are not only transdisciplinary, transgressive, and oppositional, but also connected to a wider project designed to further racial, economic, and political democracy.[3] By taking seriously the relations between culture and power, we further the possibilities of resistance, struggle, and change.

Critical Studies in Education and Culture is committed to publishing work that opens a narrative space that affirms the contextual and the specific while simultaneously recognizing the ways in which such spaces are shot through with issues of power. The series attempts to continue an important legacy of theoretical work in cultural studies in which related debates on pedagogy are understood and addressed within the larger context of social responsibility, civic courage, and the reconstruction of democratic public life. We must keep in mind Raymond Williams's insight that the "deepest impulse (informing cultural politics) is the desire to make learning part of the process of social change itself."[4] Education as a cultural pedagogical practice takes place across multiple sites, which include not only schools and universities but also the mass media, popular culture, and other public spheres, and signals how within diverse contexts, education makes us both subjects of and subject to relations of power.

This series challenges the current return to the primacy of market values and simultaneous retreat from politics so evident in the recent work of educational theorist, legislators, and policy analysts. Professional relegitimation in a troubled time seems to be the order of the day as an increasing number of academics both refuse to recognize public and higher education as critical public spheres and offer little or no resistance to the ongoing vocationalization of schooling, the continuing evisceration of the intellectual labor force, and the current assaults on the working poor, the elderly, and women and children.[5]

Emphasizing the centrality of politics, culture, and power, *Critical Studies in Education and Culture* will deal with pedagogical issues that contribute in imaginative and transformative ways to our understanding of how critical knowledge, democratic values, and social practices can provide a basis for teachers, students, and other cultural workers to redefine their role as engaged and public intellectuals. Each volume will attempt to rethink the relationship between language and experience, pedagogy and human agency, and ethics and social responsibility as part of a larger project for engaging and deepening the prospects of democratic schooling in a multiracial and multicultural society. *Critical Studies in Education and Culture* takes on the responsibility of witnessing and addressing the most pressing problems of public schooling and civic life, and engages culture as a crucial site and strategic force for productive social change.

Henry A. Giroux

NOTES

1. Lawrence Grossberg, "Toward a Genealogy of the State of Cultural Studies," in Cary Nelson and Dilip Parameshwar Gaonkar, eds., *Disciplinarity and Dissent in Cultural Studies* (New York: Routledge, 1996), 143.

2. David Bailey and Stuart Hall, "The Vertigo of Displacement," *Ten 8*, 2:3 (1992), 19.

3. My notion of transdisciplinary comes from Mas'ud Zavarzadeh and Donald Morton, "Theory, Pedagogy, Politics: The Crisis of the 'Subject' in the Humanities," in Mas'ud Zavarzadeh and Donald Morton, eds., *Theory Pedagogy Politics: Texts for Change* (Urbana: University of Illinois Press, 1992), 10. At issue here is neither ignoring the boundaries of discipline-based knowledge nor simply fusing different disciplines, but creating theoretical paradigms, questions, and knowledge that cannot be taken up within the policed boundaries of the existing disciplines.

4. Raymond Williams, "Adult Education and Social Change," in *What I Came to Say* (London: Hutchinson-Radus, 1989), 158.

5. The term "professional legitimation" comes from a personal correspondence with Professor Jeff Williams of East Carolina University.

Acknowledgments

I wish to thank my former tutor at London University, Tony Green, for his support and congenial relationship, even though we disagreed on many matters. I also thank Professor David Cooper of Durham University, who practiced availability and gave valuable advice despite his heavy workload. I would also like to thank Dr. Eric Bredo of the University of Virginia for comments, two of which will need another book.

My greatest debt is to my wife, Sheila Armitage. I could not have completed this book without her unfailing support.

Introduction

It has been claimed that "periods of advance" in education occur when there is a close link between theory and practice (Simon 1994, 6). Theory and practice should be united in a narrative critical education science, which is partly what I do in this study. However, theoreticians work with the language of deductive logic and science, while "practitioners work with narrative knowledge" (Polkinghorne 1988, x). So a problem which evolved from an engagement with practice concerned the two different kinds of language arising from two different ways of organizing reality.

The research sprang from critical reflection on the problematic, political practices of my school and teaching situation. I had taught for one year full-time in a British grammar school from 1971 to 1972 when the school amalgamated with a secondary modern to form a comprehensive. I followed the political practices and episodes of the amalgamation in relation to their political and educational significance and the ongoing story in order to understand what we were doing and where we were going. It then seemed that the amalgamation resulted in an ineffective and underperforming school as I saw it, and I tried to introduce practical and constructive changes. The most significant effect of the amalgamation may have been the slide from a small school into a large, bureaucratic organization and a situation where the size of the structure dominated the individual. The decisions taken by the authorities seemed to be based on common sense and political expediency rather than critical, educational analysis and strategic choice. Another problem seemed to be the divorce of educational practice from educational theory; another was a weak political public sphere for political communication to promote change. So I critically analyzed the political practices and took political action to promote change for the sake of good education for all, whatever that should mean.

What was to be done? I took political action for educational reasons, and this developed unexpectedly into an unfolding story. I focused on a practical problem, brought it up for discussion with my colleagues and then communicated persistently to solve it. What I confronted was political *resistance*, even to participation by communication. This was both politically and educationally significant. A major obstacle to improvement could have been the English practice of head teacher power whereby the head has total power leading to relationships of domination, reification and resistance. So the problem became: How do you overcome resistance to change when the people doing the resisting are in authority and power? I worked the problem by "communicative action" from a position of subordination, and this is how, in retrospect, I generated the data for this study. It is necessary to communicate and make relationships so that teachers can learn to understand each other adequately and develop a "public sphere" where opinions can be expressed and the intersubjective, political nature of humanity realized. This was the theory I found I was working with after having read Carl Rogers (1961). The practice of silence and distorted communication in a private world was a theory I rejected. This led in due course to the practical discovery that action produces reaction, and thus a story unfolded which led to an understanding of the real and "messy" political practices of the school, rather than the superficial realities of a "smooth-running" bureaucratic system. I had uncovered the meaningful practices of power characterized by domination and resistance.

This leads to the practical questions of this research. What were the actual practices of the school authorities? What were the theories and import behind these practices? How could the practices and processes be changed to better practices? What theories embodied in practice produce practices which work for educational ends? Hence, the significance of this study is the light it throws on how authoritarian, ideological practices cause arrested development and prevent healthy change and growth.

I accomplish three tasks to answer the above questions. First, I narrate a political and ideological battle in an educational situation in order to understand the meaningful choices made by agents and to evaluate the problem of the political and practical mind-set of a school in a "theoretically informed" and "reconstituted" analysis. This will entail theoretical understanding as informing practical understanding. I aim at a retrospective, narrative explanation of the sequence of events and teleological causes which led to the ending. Second, I enact a Habermasian critical education science and critical praxis to demonstrate its importance for the solution of educational problems by unifying theory and practice in education and by ideological critique. Third, I diagnose the practical and ideological problems of a school and critically examine them from theoretical perspectives. These perspectives include theoretical claims concerning the nature of human relationships, communication, politics, depth hermeneutic and ideological analysis, modern culture and organization, distorted communication, creativity and knowledge.

I turn now to the narrative history of the school political conflict. I narrate and analyze the background and amalgamation of two schools into a comprehensive school in Chapter 1 and record the social and political events, practical actions and choices in relation to their educational significance. I interpret the "everyday hermeneutics" and events and the origins of the micro-political problem situation that developed, and narrate major events such as a meeting on mixed ability teaching and a conflict with the chairman of governors, a debate on the new house system of organization, a dialogue with the housemaster responsible for the system and the rejection of change or the discussion of change by the head teacher. This is in order to configure the meaning of the events into a pattern of practice. I then summarize the theory of a critical education science as a theoretical justification for the action research in situation which characterizes a new theory of educational practice which I attempt to introduce to solve problems. I conclude that schools should recognize the significance of micro-political relationships in school organization.

I continue the story in Chapter 2 and interpret a political process to promote political and educational change resulting from the deadlocked discussion and immobility in Chapter 1. I initiated action by sending a letter criticizing the practices of the head teacher to the City Education Authority. I record the actions and reactions and the development of the political conflict which resulted, and the nature of the real political order and relationships. I then record the exchange of letters with the authority and the continuation of deadlock even though the head teacher had retired abruptly. I narrate an opaque situation. I evaluate the situation politically with educational interests and educational theory as a standard of reference. The process revealed a conflict between the practical, commonsense approach of educational traditionalists and my "theoretically informed" approach, centered on the irrational and ideological practices of the house system as I saw it. I then introduce a number of theoretical understandings in order to gain a "critical foothold" on the practical problems of the events in progress. I start with a theory critical of the neglect of the human bond in modern culture. This is followed by a theory critical of relationships of domination and resistance and the practices which promote it. I then explain a "self-defining" theory of communication in negotiatory and transactional relationships rather than one-sided ones. Since this lacks an emotional dimension, I introduce the theoretical sociology of the emotions and a theory of internal communication and emotional development. Finally, I conclude various approaches to "theory as practice" with a critical theory of the scientific organization of schools and an alternative derived from practice. I conclude by relating the theories to the concrete evaluation situation.

In Chapter 3, I continue the story of political action and reaction in the pursuit of change on my part after the deadlock and immobility described in Chapters 1 and 2. I narrate and analyze the new situation with a new head teacher. I then initiate further action to change the situation by meeting with the governors of the school and presenting them with an analysis of the situation since the amalgamation. When this partially failed, I then tested the system of political communication a second time by approaching the governors. This resulted in a medical inspection and a disciplinary tribunal for criticizing a head teacher. I then introduce critical understandings of culture as symbolic analysis and as a process of interpretation for a theoretical perspective.

I continue narrating the story and interpret the tribunal or trial evidence in Chapter 4 to understand the political situation as revealed in the trial. In Chapter 5, the story unfolds further with a recording and analysis of the tribunal's findings and its perspective on the political order of relationships in the school and education authority. The mind-set of the educational system is uncovered and revealed.

In Chapter 6, further insight into the story is revealed by two policy documents which stand in contrast between a social theoretical view of school practices and a natural scientific view and provide perspective on the narrative conflict. I then analyze the issues of secrecy and revelation as a theoretical perspective on the narrative practice as recorded, including its ethical and political dimensions. This is followed with an analysis of the nature of discourse, practice and politics. I then summarize the nature of power and two critical theories of politics as they relate to the practical interests of the narrative as it has unfolded, to gain further insight into the nature of a school in situation.

The story develops a stage further in Chapter 7. After I had resigned from the school I took the issues to the Department of Education and Science to test the meaning of political democracy in Britain and to seek a satisfactory end to the narrative from my point of view. I record and analyze an attempt at communication between the micro and macro levels of the system and how and why it failed.

In Chapter 8, I first examine Habermas's critical theory of modern culture in order to put the school situation I have described in a wider context of understanding. He has explained the developing story of Western culture from a historical and therefore narrative perspective as well as a sociological perspective. The purpose of the theory is to explain the constitution of modern culture as a failed project of the Enlightenment concept of reason. The system and cultural life world were coupled in simple societies, but as modern society developed, the system "cut loose from," "turned back on" and dominated the lifeworld of language and culture. Thus, authority became authoritarian and one-sided rather than consensual and dialogical. The dominant paradigm of knowledge has become scientific knowledge, the reasoning assumes, and has excluded the importance and significance of historical knowledge and the self-reflection of the cognitive and knowing subject. Next, I analyze Habermas's theory of bureaucratic systems oppression and I present an understanding of the scientific, formal, abstract method of organizing schools in order to show the practical effects of systems theory in the common, everyday cultural reality of present-day school organizations. I then explain a theory of distorted communication and its cultural implications. I put the practical problems in relation to a theory of systems domination, distorted communication and a theory of emancipation which is Habermas's story for the future. Finally, I explain Weber's theory of the Protestant Ethic and the spirit of capitalism as an example of "singular causal imputation."

Finally, in Chapter 9, I come to the end of the narrative and ask the question, "Why did this situation develop?" in order to provide a narrative explanation of the quasi-causes of the events. The aim is to provide narrative knowing and narrative truth.

This leads me to explain why I use the narrative form in this study. It was demanded of me by practical reality. *Narrative Knowing and the Human Sciences* by Donald Polkinghorne (1988) has illuminated this study in its final stages. I use the narrative form because it is "meaning-making" (36). The realm of meaning is linguistic. Bodily action is meaningful and actions are organized in time by the narrative form. Polkinghorne summarizes his argument that "narrative is a scheme by means of which human beings give meaning to their experience of temporality and personal actions" (11). Narrative language arises from speech and all speech is from a body which is the primary source of meaning. The body experiences time directly and through the language system creates meaning as "display." The experience of time is "multilayered" and at its lowest level is united and continuous rather than split up. The time dimension of reality is expressed in the narrative form which sequences time. Intermediary between action as expression rather than mechanical is the organizing device of the plot, which gathers together events into a story from a beginning to a middle and an end.

If you want to understand the *how* and the *why* in politics you must first understand the *who* and the *what* (Lawrence 1992, 3) which meant that in order to understand how the system worked and why it wasn't changing it was necessary to examine who was making the policy decisions and what the policy consisted of, even if the policy was only silently expressed. If a school can critically analyze and understand the ideological forces which prevent educational development, it can move a long way toward providing successful education and prevent educational failure, assuming understanding can be followed by communication and transformation.

This study originated theoretically from a critical view of current political practices articulated by Bernard Crick in his *In Defence of Politics* (1962). He defends a view of action and political action as the meaningful action of an agent, a free decision because we are bodies in situation and only have direct access to our own meanings. Politics is freedom. Micro-politics is a politics of action and meaning. When practitioners reflect on their practice, they use the narrative form. When meaningful actions are joined together with other meaningful actions, a plot develops and from the plot a story with a beginning, a middle and an end. Life is a dramatic narrative. Shakespeare is more important than Newton or Darwin. This view of politics is not the norm in educational organizations, but I believe it should be, and I have acted on that belief.

The practical argument of this thesis is based on the case analysis of a single school. I claim that political understanding and a critical attitude toward political practices and the political process is necessary for educational change and improvement, in order to produce quality in education by solving practical problems in situation. Educational and political practices are interconnected. I argue that in order to achieve educational change, you need to get political change from a system of domination and resistance to an ethical, democratic system of participation and reciprocity. In order to achieve this, people in authority need to understand the limits of the "authority of authority." This thesis entails the view that the individual educator in practical relationship is the key figure in school change, and improvement and the macro system should be adapted and connected to the micro function for it to work.

I claim that the practical creation of an Arendtian and Habermasian public sphere works in practice as well as in theory, and that practical common sense is inadequate for effective education and must be informed by theoretical analysis and insight. The practice is difficult because socially deterministic ideologies are in conflict with educational values, and the school is a battleground between ideology and education and between social determinism and individual and democratic freedom. So if you want to improve schooling, you need to challenge the problem of ideological thinking which keeps things as they are and resists change. This is no easy task because ideology is based in people's most fundamental ideas and feelings—hence changing ideology is synonymous with changing people's beliefs and intentions. Politics is frequently understood as ideology and unalterable, and the resistance to change has commonsense ideology as its source. I seek to show how this is a mistaken view of politics, and it is the ignorance and misunderstanding of politics as the "master-science" which contributes to educational problems of failure, a claim I model in a detailed, political narrative and real conflicts of interest and struggles for power.

This leads to some comment on the nature of social theory. Charles Taylor has theorized "social theory as practice." It is worth lingering on the distinction he makes between theory in the physical sciences and theory in the social and human sciences. The objects of the physical sciences are "independent," but the objects of the social sciences are not independent but are about themselves, and therefore the relationship of theory to practice is very different. Thus, social scientific theories are "theories about practice," which means they are conjoined to the practices themselves. Social scientific theories are born out of "pre-theoretical" practices. Any social practice is based on certain "self-understandings" and "self-descriptions" which can be theorized. Old social theories and common sense are not untheoretical but constitute social practices. The theories are "constitutive" of the practices, so if a theory can be made to work on a self-understanding it can have a "transformative" effect (Taylor 1985).

The social scientific theories which I use in this research are related to the social practices of the active participants in the narrative, and their aim is to transform the understanding of practices by reconstituting the understanding implicit in them. For example, a problem of communication could be transformed by a theoretical attitude to communication, negotiation and transactive human relationships. A theory of communication is a criticism of inadequate communication and intervenes in a social and political order based on silence and distorted communication and hidden relationships of power.

This is a study in micro-sociolgy. Sociological research used to be predominantly theorized from a macro-perspective to the neglect of the micro, but the macro- and the micro-perspectives are equally important. What is more, in everyday practice they should be connected. The mechanism for this is an "abductive" part and whole analysis in context conducted by the individual in relationship. This book is conducive to such a view since I use the narrative form and hence human communication and relationships are the data for the study. I use an "intensive-extensive design" (Scheff 1990, 195). I start with the data in order to discover the sequence of social events leading to causal connections between the episodes of the narrative, and from this I derive a theory. I use the data as "empirical markers" for theoretical concepts and hence connect theory with practice in context. Ultimately, this study is about the "micro-foundations of society" that is with human actions embodied in everyday social encounters in the interests of community and social solidarity. The micro approach to society has been explained by Anthony Giddens in *The Constitution of Society* (1984) and this study rests on his theoretical position.

The micro case study is a study in political culture, not a study in social psychology or sociology or philosophy. Culture is the "distinctive" "symbolic-expressive dimension of social life" (Wuthnow, Hunter, Bergesen, and Kurzweil 1984, 259). It is a "behavioral phenomenon" which is "observable" and analyzable (19). Its basic unit is the speech act and consists of specific "communicative behavior." Culture is closely related to language and includes a moral dimension. To study culture is to relate specific speech and symbolic acts to the broader social environment in which they occur. It is to treat the culture as a whole and not as fragmented into parts (240–263).

The term "ideology" is one of my central concepts. An ideology is a "weapon in a political battle fought out on the terrain of language." (Thompson 1990, 28) It is a weapon of domination and domination is a particular type of power relation (292). This is a critical conception rather than a scientific or neutral one.

The practical, broadly conceived, merges with the ethical and the moral (Carr 1986, 73). I reject a static approach to understanding a school as a structure for important understanding is obtained by viewing a school as a process in order to capture its dynamics and identity over time, since social practices are constituted in time (Rosaldo 1989, 107).

I shall briefly state a view of good education because the significance of this study is how to produce practices for good education and to overcome problems that prevent educational development. I take education as the concern of "empowering" individuals as persons, and define persons as centers of thought and consciousness and as agents of themselves (Langford 1973). The nature of a good education has been articulated by Mary Warnock, and I put it here because it confirms my own experience (Warnock 1973, 112–122). Warnock argues that good education means the development of the imagination, which she defines as the connection between feeling and thought and the ability to form a network of intellectual interconnections for understanding the world. The imagination is the human faculty to see significance in the world. She argues that this involves specialization of some kind in academic and practical subjects in order to learn to communicate. She sees the inability to communicate as a crucial educational obstacle and the less academically inclined can learn that through practical subjects, if that is their inclination. What is relevant is that thought and communication are interrelated and that necessarily includes thinking about political relationships in everyday life.

I want to warn the reader that there are two competing views of education, one which I oppose and the other which I support (Fay 1987, 86–97). The one I oppose is derived from the natural and physical sciences. This views education as instrumental. The purpose of education is to use knowledge to understand the world as a mechanism of cause and effect so that if you understand the causes that drive a process, you can control them and get what you want. The other view, my view, is the social scientific view which briefly is that education is concerned to use knowledge to change the view persons have of the world; not to manipulate it by controlling causes, but to understand it. The two views conflict on what it means to be a person and the conflict runs deep. The former is more materialistic and the latter more symbolic.

The philosophical underpinning of this study is existentialist. The individual self is not a "substance" but rather a "narrative." That means that in order to explain human behavior and practices, it is necessary to understand the "meaning" and "significance" of an action, a choice or a decision. So the research is executed in the narrative form (Cooper 1990, 74). Rather like Mr. Pickwick in *Pickwick Papers*, I discovered that the actions I recorded, which included my own, developed into a narrative which required explanation. Existentialism is a reaction to Western empiricism and rationalism which is regarded as too abstract to capture the reality of the individual person. The individual is embodied in situation, and philosophy should start from the lived emotional experience of the person. Existentialism gives a place to emotion and feeling in social and personal life. Emotions are intentional, meaningful and social. They are basic and prior to intellectual understanding. Emotions are accountable and give significance and meaning to existence. Thus, the reader will understand the dynamics of this study through the embodied acts of individual agents in situation and will take belief, action and emotion seriously.

Political Relationship
and Narrative Knowledge

Chapter 1

The Making of a Comprehensive School: The Significance of Micro-Political Relationships

I am convinced that we must think, not *behind* the symbols, but starting from symbols, . . . that they constitute the *revealing* substrate of speech which lives among men. In short, the symbol *gives rise to* thought.
—Ricoeur, quoted by Thompson 1981a, 6

THE PROBLEMATIC AMALGAMATION OF BOREHAM GRAMMAR SCHOOL AND CROSSLINKS SECONDARY MODERN

I begin by narrating the meaningful decisions, actions and events that shaped the political culture of a comprehensive school amalgamation, in order to interpret them analytically as they unfolded over time from the perspective of educational and social theory.

The grammar and secondary modern schools of the tripartite system of education in England existed in very different cultures. The grammar school was selective of pupils and teachers and pursued a predominantly academic curriculum and prepared pupils for a university education. The secondary modern was non-selective and prepared the pupils for the world of semi-skilled work. The grammar school had more prestige. The tripartite system of education provides the historical and cultural background to this study.

The historical background is relevant to the situation at the amalgamated school. The 1941 Norwood Report set out the "essentially ideological underpinning" behind the inherited tripartite system of education. There were to be three types of schools corresponding to three types of children.

Some (a few) were capable of abstract thought and interested in ideas, in "learning for its own sake"—for these grammar schools would be provided. Others (also a few) were more interested and adept at the application of ideas to technology—for these there would be (selective) technical schools. The great majority, however, were more concerned with practical activities and the immediate environment—for these the new type of secondary "modern" schools should be provided. (Simon 1991, 61)

It turned out that the theory legitimized the system and was therefore borne out in practice. It resulted in "educational fatalism" by ideological means. Simon writes:

Teachers (of course with exceptions) became convinced that the mass of the children could achieve little, and lowered their sights accordingly. Children themselves assimilated a negative self-image, and this affected their level of aspiration and so their achievement; the theory was inevitably used to convince parents of the innate failings of their own children. A whole ethos of failure developed which profoundly affected attitudes to education, and therefore the process itself. What was being constructed in terms of the educational system was, in fact, a near perfect means of social control—or, in another sense, of buttressing the existing social order. (159)

The amalgamation was designed to change this system and institute a comprehensive system.

When the Boreham grammar school and the Crosslinks secondary modern school were amalgamated in 1972, the governors appointed Brian Fellows, the acting head of Boreham grammar, to head the new school. This was a meaningful, symbolic act. It seemed that their intention was to build the new school on the historical, publically recognized strength and prestige of the academic tradition of the grammar school. Significantly, the governors didn't advertise the availability of the position nationally, which they could have done in order to attract a candidate with comprehensive qualifications and experience, and someone interested in reforming and modernizing an educational institution. Maybe they should have had an outsider for internal political reasons as much as anything else. Brian Fellows had been a student at the Boreham school and taught there for around 30 years (that is, his school days and most of his adult life had been spent in one institution). He was, therefore, not a person likely to make profound changes, and it was the supposed need for educational reform that had brought about the amalgamation. One possible meaning and interpretation of the appointment is that there was no serious effort to think through the ideas on which the new school would rest and no serious effort to change ideas and strategies of education, since the head held a traditionalist ideology of education. There had been an outpouring of books and theories on education during the 1960s, a serious rethinking of educational ideas, but on the work site they were irrelevant. The formal organization was to rest on a traditional ideology in a changing situation. That seemed to be the message sent by the governors. Moreover, the second deputy head had also been a pupil at the Boreham and had longevity similar to the head. Personality, culture and policy were joined in these appointments.

The head teacher has autocratic powers in the English educational system. He leads and controls the curriculum, teaching methods and the educators. His personality and cultural style are reflected in the school. This situation poses a problem of political power, because if someone with so much power acts in misguided ways, how can he be opposed? The head, however, has to perform and his authority is not automatic (Ball 1987, 82–87). In the micro-political model of the school, conflict and domination constitute the micro-politics of the school and the distinction between the formal and the informal breaks down, as Ball has argued (278).

In order to demonstrate his lack of bias toward the Crosslinks school, the other half of the amalgamation, the new head's actions seemed to discriminate against the academic, grammar school tradition. One of his long-standing grammar school colleagues, whose life was school teaching, was not given a house teacher position in the new school, an act which seemed to signify the head's political independence from his grammar school colleagues. If he had given a house position to a member of the Boreham, the ties of loyalty which held the Crosslinks teachers together would have been lessened and there would have been an academic element present in the pastoral system. It could have been politically significant by amalgamating two schools pastorally as well as academically. As it was, the political significance was apparently that the Boreham teachers gave up any hope of having a significant leadership presence in the new school. This is a practical judgment based on a strategic view of education (Carr and Kemmis 1986, 39).

A second political decision was that the new school adopted the historical Crosslinks house system. The academically oriented grammar school teachers were appointed to the academic heads of department posts and the Crosslinks teachers took the pastoral posts; that is, the two kinds of teachers were treated as equally valuable. The reasoning seemed to have been political considerations without regard to academic consequences, since it created equality between appointments from the previous halves of the old schools. The decision was problematic.

The reasoning behind the various decisions which were made at the time of the amalgamation was based on traditional assumptions without consideration of the need to innovate and attempt to create a modern system of education. The school was dominated by a need to maintain the political status quo, and not rethink educational practices and introduce educational and cultural change. These early decisions reverberated through this narrative, having a cumulative effect.

The initial decisions were critical for the school since they indicated a direction, and the head teacher is the leader, the "critical reality definer" and "licensed authority." He is responsible for the "definition of the school" and the education which takes place there. To say that the head is the "critical reality definer" is to say that his judgment matters to everyone in the institution, and if it is wrong or unrealistic or ineffective, the institution cannot succeed. On the one hand, it would have been more rational to appoint someone recently qualified in educational theory, since it was criticism of the grammar school tradition and the previous system which had led to the changes in the first place. On the other hand, there was really no one available with comprehensive experience, since the new system was still to be thought out. There was a dilemma for the governors and the government of the school since a new form of educational organization was being instituted. There was a new "paradigm" of education so that everyone was inexperienced by definition. However, apparently this important factor was not recognized, and this was a reason why the school was founded on weakness. There was no plan or policy for the new system. What everyone needed was reeducating and in-service training.

A further major decision was not only the adoption of the Crosslinks house system but the appointment of *all* the senior ex-Crosslinks housemasters to be the housemasters in the new school. The political, ideological symbolism should not be underestimated. None of the new house teachers appeared to have had much to do with ordinary and advanced-level academic courses. Their claim to expertise came from a supposed superior ability to manage children with discipline problems and from a different background in teaching to that of the ex-grammar school teachers, a child-centered rather than an adult-centered philosophy. It was cause for the admitted decline in examination results over the following years. The new school became a predominantly Crosslinks affair. Their ex-teachers, following the amalgamation, controlled the leadership positions to set the symbolic tone and cultural atmosphere of the school, and the atmosphere they set was to lower the standards to the least successful. They appeared to communicate an egalitarian ideology of equality of results and "levelling down." The above two actions effectively doomed the school to mediocrity, from which it did not recover. Everything was geared to saving the face of the least able and the least interested; to failure and not success. It was an ideological and narrow politics which dominated educational considerations. If the system of politics and government had been different at the time, criticisms would have been voiced and debate would have ensued, thus preventing costly educational mistakes with long-term consequences. The Crosslinks house teachers as a whole were not academically inclined by the standards of the grammar school and their appointment put the academic side of the school at a political disadvantage, and hence a non-academic, sociological type of education came to be dominant. An academic education is a thinking education and if an academic education is devalued, as it was, then thinking and understanding itself is devalued (Peters 1966, 30–35). I shall interpret the significance of the following events as the lack of critical thought which characterized the way the school was administered from its very beginnings.

What really happened, as I interpret the situation in retrospect, was that the academic culture was effectively weakened, but nothing desirable and strong was put in its place. The policy of the school was never stated, only implied. A culture of silence and distorted communication was introduced. That in itself was a failure since schools are places where policy is essential (Ball 1990, 3–21). Without a policy, there is an intellectual void. Policy is both intention and practice. The unstated policy was equality, which should have been equality of opportunity for all, but what was lacking was a concept of quality and the recognition of individual differences. The meaning of quality was given an individualistic interpretation, meaning that any improvement in an individual was worthy of public recognition. The concept of education was ideological since it was based on traditional assumptions and common sense but not on reason.

There was a cultural event, instituted by the head teacher, known as "bright tie day" in the summer term before the amalgamation in September. It was relevant to the "everyday hermeneutics" of the new school and communicated a cultural message. A teacher from the Crosslinks side had suggested that on Fridays, to celebrate the end of the week, we should all wear bright ties. This symbolic idea, which carried implications for the new culture of the school, was instituted, and teachers, some of whom were not noted for their adherence to teen-age color fashions (what would have happened if it had been long hair day?), and on the contrary had throughout their working lives worn sober, grey suits and ties remarkable for their lack of color, duly turned up in bright ties. It was of course ironical that the bright ties symbolized a cheerfulness the ex-grammar school teachers did not feel. To some it indicated a triumph over the evil grammar school system which had apparently blighted so many lives, and perhaps this was the only rationale the new school had. We were no longer to be an "intellectual forcing house" but concerned with the whole person. The bright tie saga did spark off a muted public argument when one teacher angrily condemned the whole thing as "childish." This provoked the comment that the opposition were kill-joys who lacked a sense of humor, and authority implicitly ordered everybody in the hierarchy to keep silent and stay in their place. The institution of bright ties faded away and those whose taste was for somber colors stuck to them.

This event was significant because it was an attempt to promote harmony and cooperation between two very different cultural groups who represented different traditions and ideologies. It symbolized the way the new head teacher intended to manage the new school, which was by avoiding conflict and issues at all costs and assuming consensus. The culture became a culture of secrecy and silence. According to Dennis Moore, the district inspector, the amalgamation was a "nasty political battle" and the policy was to quiet things down and pretend that differences didn't exist. The bright tie day was a trivial event which distracted attention from the serious educational issues of the amalgamation, which were not mentioned or discussed. The serious decisions such as the implemention of the house system were taken in secrecy and not opened to public debate and criticism. The system was undemocratic and power was centralized and teachers didn't know exactly how it worked or who the governors were. The head teacher and governors were responsible for the decisions that were made and the policy rationale they adopted was inadequate to the new situation.

The policy of "melting differences" is an implicit statement that the authorities saw themselves as managing an organizational bureaucracy. Formal organization assumes consent whereas the micro-political model embraces the concept of conflict as the basis of organization (Ball 1987, 8). Hence, Moore was saying that "political activity" was not allowed and talk is considered dangerous because politics is driven by talk. The idea to bring out here is that the theory of organization which Dennis Moore was working with was inadequate. Schools are not organized bureaucracies but are "anarchic" institutions (12–13).

Bernard Crick claims, in *In Defence of Politics*, that the nature of politics is freedom in action. That is, the relationship between political persons is freedom of interaction. It is a theoretical claim that is compatible with a micro-political theory of organization and incompatible with a scientific organizational theory. Crick distinguishes between real politics, which he praises, and misunderstandings, which he criticizes. He criticizes confusing politics with democracy, ideology, technology and false friends described as the non-political conservative, the apolitical liberal, and the anti-political socialist (Crick 1962, 79–82). This will become important as the story develops because it was the relationship between Dennis Moore and myself which became distorted by conflicting understandings that propelled the story forward.

I claim it was the absence of true, rational politics as analyzed by Crick which was the major cause of the educational ineffectiveness and powerlessness of the school because, without politics, the problems of the school could not be addressed. The solution is in the problem. The central role of the governors and the head teacher is to govern the school. They can do this politically or by some other form of government such as tyranny, dictatorship, authoritarian coercion, oligarchy or a combination of them all. Crick argues that political rule is better than other forms of rule because it is tied to moral considerations and realistically confronts the problem of diversity. Boreham and Crosslinks were two very different schools, culturally and historically. At the amalgamation the Boreham history was denied and the past was ignored. This denial and ignoring of history was a problem which resulted in a lack of reality. Above all, there must be unity and no conflict. As Moore said at the tribunal, it was essential to "melt differences" since there had been conflict on the governing body. This statement symbolized the unrealistic attitude of the authorities. It was an impractical suggestion since modern society is increasingly pluralistic. A comprehensive school implies pluralism. Differences are normal and can create a productive tension and dialogue. The policy of "melting differences" was an ideological operation since it allowed an unstated ideology to be put in place without opposition. It also implied that the new ideology was based on unity of opinion and was legitimized (Thompson 1990, 60). Ball argues that schools are "arenas of ideological dispute." Talk is normal, not pathological.

An unspoken political ideology of the school was the avoidance of political conflict and thus the need to confront political problems. Yet, conflict is basic to the organization of a school since educational ideas are contested (Ball 1987, 17–26). The method of critique of ideology in order to produce emancipatory knowledge is applicable to the avoidance of conflict. Suppressed conflict is socially harmful since it does not remove the reasons for conflict but only denies them. It then requires a continuous effort to enforce an ideology against the possibility that anyone should question it. Conflict between the old grammar school academic tradition and the Crosslinks tradition was inevitable. But, by bringing it out into the open where it could have been managed in a productive way, differences of opinion could have been reconciled and issues settled in a political way. The failure to accept conflict as a reality of the institution was a political failure which related to educational failure. It was an insupportable educational judgment.

The staff of the grammar school walked over to the common room of the Crosslinks school, 200 yards away in another building, at the appointed time on the appointed day of the amalgamation for an inaugural meeting of the joint staff of the new school. The tone was set by two older members of the grammar school staff of naturally traditional, academic sympathies who walked with backs straight, eyes looking ahead, poised with military bearing, who unemotionally and exactly correctly set off from one school to the other in acceptance of the inevitable, however much regret and sadness they felt inside for the passing of the old ways. It was the lack of expressed emotion and therefore communication that was striking because without emotion and communication there could be no change. One can do one's public duty but withhold inner cooperation if one's feelings reject the ideas which one is asked to accept. A main characteristic of the amalgamation was the silence and almost total lack of communication. The authorities should have initiated and encouraged communication as part of their democratic role. Then there would have been debate and criticism and the way the school should be managed would have been given serious attention. As a consequence of a critical atmosphere, the serious mistakes which were made could have been foreseen. A modern society needs to be integrated by communication and hence the need for a Habermasian communicative ethics and politics.

The symbolic walk across the field by the two older teachers was remarkable for what didn't follow. The eyes straight ahead unswervingly were to look straight past and through the eyes they might have met had somebody had the wit to spark off an introduction. But it was the introduction that was studiously avoided. It was like a formal military organization. As a result there was no communication, therefore no relationship and no bond. The Habermasian rationalization process was bypassed. As a consequence of that, the amalgamation was rooted in lack of cooperation and communication and the school was secretly divided at the heart. Everybody knew this and accepted it. There was no Habermasian discourse. Where was the leadership to initiate it? Leadership, policy and discourse are inseparable. This was an uneducational practice which critique is designed to prevent.

Another event of significance was the issue or lack of issue over whether the school should have a house system or a year system. This was a subject around which, had a public debate ensued and been encouraged, there might have been fierce argument and natural and legitimate differences between people would have been forced out into the open where they are ultimately less harmful. But the people in authority in the Crosslinks school had apparently persuaded the decision-takers that the house system was much superior to the year system. The grammar school staff capitulated on this issue without a debate. They should have raised this issue in its early stages and they failed to do so. As a consequence, the Crosslinks ideology of education, based on the refusal to recognize significant differences, became the dominant ideology, without a debate. Thus, the politics of the school was conducted in silence. In effect, a formal bureaucracy was instituted in which talk was outlawed.

The Boreham school had two good history teachers, one of them outstanding as an eloquent story teller, and they both left at the amalgamation, leaving the new history department to Crosslinks teachers. This was a political and symbolic blow to the quality of education in the school since the strength of the academic side had been seriously depleted and the Crosslinks side of the school had the political strength to dominate the educational philosophy of the school unopposed. The battle for the educational philosophy and soul of the school had been lost from the beginning.

An amalgamation required a symbolic and memorable occasion such as a visit from the chief education officer to give an appropriate speech setting out the aims and philosophy of comprehensive education. But, here was another significant failure. There were no speeches or public figures called in to initiate and legitimate change. This should have taken place. The introduction of comprehensive education was an event of historical meaning and importance. It required fresh thinking and a new outlook. There was a growing literature on modern and comprehensive education but it was not mentioned on the work site. Practice was entirely divorced from theory. The absence of any theoretical discussion within the school was yet another reason for an unsuccessful school.

Another symbolic event of the amalgamation was a putting match between the head teacher of the Boreham grammar school and the deputy head teacher of the Crosslinks school. It took place on the old grammar school lawn which had always been reserved for teachers, and was sacred ground for generations of pupils. At that time, the pursuit of an academic, intellectual education was the educational ideology which was clearly and strictly followed. The lawn had always been sacred since it was reserved for teachers, but now a putting course was started and the two head teachers surrounded by jubilant, excited boys were setting the spirit of the times. Why was this match arranged? Was it an alternative to bright tie day? In the future we were to be happy together, to be all one with the bad old days behind us. It almost seemed to mean that boys would no longer be boys, that they would love their teachers in the future, and teachers and pupils would work together in mutual good will and harmony forever. Did the putting game symbolize a new approach to education, that classroom learning would be entertaining, and easy, that from now on we should live a life without problems and difficulties? Was education to become fun, not work? This event symbolized the lack of seriousness with which the new schooling system was introduced. It was a waste of time and did nothing for education. All the problems of the new school were to be addressed by not addressing them. They would be avoided and the people who had the most power to do something were to use that power to prevent serious change and improved education.

There was also talk during the amalgamation about the question of the naming of the school because, of course, a name has symbolic and emotional significance to the people who know it and know it over a period of time. Once a school has a good and well-known name, it is difficult to break it easily. And a school is generally particular about the name of the school, meaning its reputation. Apart from appointments, the name was one area where the insiders were able to see openly the attitudes of the outsiders, that is, the governors, who were distant local politicians. They apparently had strong views over the naming of the school. They asked the staff to put forward their suggestions, which they did. They wanted a combination of the names of the two schools, thus keeping alive their reputations and continuity with the past, or a historic or geographic name. However, the governors of the new school were to take a more active role in the internal affairs of the school. After due consideration, they overruled the wishes of the committee members of staff, and decided to give the school a new name, the name of a former prominent Labor Party Socialist, Borecross. Why did they choose this name? Was it for a political reason? The whole idea was to break with the past and give the school a new image, in some respects a good idea, if it did mean "a new start." But, there didn't appear to be anything new in the start at all. In fact, what appeared to be happening was that the best of the old traditions were being abandoned without a replacement. The baby was being thrown out with the bath water.

It was inconsistent of the governors to ask the staff as a body to suggest a name for the school but not to debate the house system, which was critical for the school's daily practices and far more significant and important in its educational implications. They were attempting to be democratic in a minor matter, but a school is either a democracy or it isn't. The rules should not be manipulated to suit those in power.

A small but nonetheless significant and interesting point of cultural importance was the change in the newspaper situation. The grammar school staff had always read the *Times*, paid for by subscription to the common room. With the amalgamated common room the subject of newspapers was not mentioned and the *Times* was no longer purchased. Why was this? Why didn't the head teacher intervene and say he wanted standards maintained and raised? This was something within his power. There was also a general decline in the standard of conversation. One of the impressive things about the Boreham common room was that a conversational historian usually sat at a central table in the staff room around which a Habermasian ideal speech situation was partially enacted. Serious, intellectual talk was not the common experience it had once been because there were so many teachers and wide differences of opinion. The most academic staff did level themselves down to suit the standard norm of the common room as a whole. After all, they had no leader. Even ex-Crosslinks house masters lamented the lack of leadership they had been expecting from the ex-grammar school element. I interpret this situation as yet another mistake that was made. In fact, it is hard to think of anything that deserved critical praise.

A colleague, present during the amalgamation and afterwards, recorded his recollections, which are compatible with the perspective I have presented.

I have known Mr. Armitage since we both joined the staff of what has become known as Borecross School, in September 1971. I left the school in 1974 to take up a research post in mathematics education at Chelsea College, but I have maintained regular contact with Mr. Armitage since.

I have great respect for Mr. Armitage as a teacher, both for his concern he has always shown for the welfare of his pupils, and for his concern for the welfare of Borecross School as a whole. We joined the school at the time of its amalgamation. Seen as the creation of a new school, the following years were in many ways very exciting; seen as the merger of two very different schools, this was also a period of stress, with tensions felt individually and by two sets of staff about appointments and about the way the school was to be run. My feeling at the time was that the staff as a whole was thrust into a situation which we knew little about solving, but with which we were expected to cope by commonsense and intuition. As a result, the decisions that were made, though well-intentioned, seemed concerned primarily with restoring some kind of surface stability and with effecting the least painful compromises. I don't know whether, in practice, anything better could have been achieved, but it seemed clear that many of the educational implications of these decisions had not been thoroughly examined. Mr. Armitage pointed this out, with criticisms that were well-judged and well-informed. As far as I remember, his criticisms were not generally well received—which is not surprising, since he was particularly asking those with the greatest responsibility to examine the value of the roles to which they had been appointed and to move beyond self-interest and common sense. These criticisms certainly threatened the surface calm that the staff had tried to create; however, they were made calmly and without malice, with the sincere aim of improving the education that the school provided, and it seems likely, at least in the long run, that we benefit from being asked to face problems openly.

David Gardner B.Sc. M.Ed.
Research Officer, University of Nottingham.

This analysis supports the events of the amalgamation as I have narrated them. That is, debate and discussion of educational problems were absent because the head teacher was silent and therefore didn't lead where leadership was essential. In practice, this meant the educational politics of the school was conducted in silence and a political ideology of silence was imposed. If there had been a political democracy and a political culture, there would have been a "democratic machinery" for promoting educational development and practicing democratic and educational values. Without an active political culture, there was no way of criticizing the underlying ideology of the school and, as a result, there could be no development and improvement since problems could not be addressed.

The authorities of Borecross School and the City Education Authority had an opportunity to begin a new school which would benefit the people who went there. The evidence of these pages shows that they did nothing to suggest that they knew what they were about or had the leadership qualities to implement a new system. There was a lack of the fresh thinking and new practices. There was a lack of critical thinking. The implication here is that the authorities failed to set standards which others would be expected to meet. Education without standards is a contradiction in terms. It is the meeting of higher standards of rationality with which a critical education science is concerned.

IDEOLOGICAL CONFLICT WITH THE CHAIRMAN OF GOVERNORS

Shortly after the amalgamation the chairman of governors of Borecross School, Alfred Wellberry, called a meeting during the evening for all the teaching staff, in order to discuss the introduction of mixed-ability teaching. The proposal originated with him, not the head teacher or the teaching staff, so it was a political initiative with deep political implications by a politician. In retrospect, it connected with Dennis Moore's comment about conflict on the governing body. Since he was the chariman of governors, he probably had a significant political influence on the governing body and he was an important political and cultural personality.

The teachers had previously been asked their views about the naming of the school but their advice had been ignored. The consultation process did not appear to be consistently democratic and rational, or aimed at reconciling differences. Since the governors met in secret, it could not be said they consulted the teachers, who had no direct meetings with them. This led to compartmentalization and barriers to real communication, necessarily resulting in distorted communication. There had been no rethinking of the processes of school government at the amalgamation: There was a rational case for calling the school Borecross but, in the circumstances, the main reason could well have been political and political with totalitarian, cultural implications. The name Borecross is an example of "split reference" since it could be interpreted to mean that the individual Borecross was a role model of a successful person who had risen from the working class to a prominent position in politics during the Second World War or that his name symbolized a working-class, Socialist ideology of a Marxist-Leninist interpretation. The raising of the mixed-ability issue supported this theory (Thompson 1984, 182).

The issue of mixed-ability teaching was deeply political and ideological and, arguably, it was for political, not educational reasons that Alfred Wellberry wanted it introduced regardless of educational consequences. Wellberry never actually said anything at the meeting except that he himself wasn't going to speak and would play "devil's advocate," which he actually didn't do since he had nothing to say, but he was passionately committed to mixed-ability teaching, so it seemed. "Rationality presumes communication," Habermas wrote. But silence is a powerful communicator and a form of political behavior (Eagleton 1976, 34–35). There could not be a rational debate of issues if the person who wanted mixed-ability teaching didn't put the arguments forward, for there was nothing to argue against. This was politically undemocratic conduct since democratic politics is conducted by rational debate. The chairman of governors may have abused his position as chairman by using it to push forward a personal agenda, since the initiative was not put forward by the governing body as a whole. The staff gave many educational arguments against mixed-ability teaching so that it was clear that no one was really interested in introducing it. At the end I made a significant remark which was directed at Alfred Wellberry. I referred to him as "an egalitarian" because this seemed to me at the time to describe his political and educational point of view accurately. He seemed to see Borecross School as an instrument for making everybody equal by "social engineering" and he wanted equality of result.

The teaching staff were so outraged by his attitude that they passed a motion that they would not meet him again. I took no part in it. There was plenty to criticize here. Mixed-ability teaching was more of an educational and political ideology than a practical proposition. Since everything about the school was traditional, from single-sex education to teaching methods and school organization, there were many other problems to be considered before mixed-ability teaching with its radical overtones. Most of all, perhaps, what was required was the institution of democratic processes of discussion.

However, the effects of this meeting carried political consequences. I was invited to a private meeting with Alfred Wellberry, the chairman of governors. The chairman suggested that I had the wrong attitude to comprehensive education which, for him, apparently meant mixed-ability teaching, and I should resign, a judgment he made on the basis of one remark. I argued reasonably for a few minutes because debate is the proper way to conduct a democratic educational system. It was not a luxury but an essential. That in itself was enough to upset him, and when he was argued with he ended the meeting and walked out. Following that, a promotion I had been granted was withheld for three months and was only passed after intervention by another governor, Mrs. Gold.

I infer the chairman's conduct from the theory of politics and freedom I shall outline in a later chapter. He had acted to prevent politics and freedom. He would not accept criticism or opposition and was prepared to punish an offender as an example to others. That was the objective meaning of the act, since it was designed so that he could control the political and educational ideology of the school.

The intention of the chairman's action was ideological since he wanted to impose, undemocratically, an educational ideology based on mixed-ability teaching. This was ideology serving power in an "asymmetrical" relationship. In asking for my resignation, he was saying that the educational ideology of the school was fixed by himself and there would be no tolerance of questioning or opposition. The justification for his position was from the position of Socialist dogma. Moreover, his attitude of self-evident correctness excluded the social values of a democratic society (Peters, 1966). Alfred Wellberry misunderstood the nature of politics. The art of politics is to reconcile differences, not eliminate them. The job of the chairman of governors is a political task, that is, the reconciling of the differing group interests. This was a London school and London is a diverse city, yet he didn't seem to understand that. The chairman should not have been using his position to control others and put forward his own agenda. He should have stepped down rather than do that. He was incompetent as a chairman and as a politician; he should have been seeking compromise and recognition of others as other than himself. Otherwise, he was acting as an ideologue and a totalitarian ideologue; in a comprehensive school there should be room for competing educational ideologies.

The chairman's action demonstrated the operation of ideology in a number of ways. He was claiming that his ideology of education was legitimate, rational and universal. He was demanding that everyone be united in the same ideology and he was unwilling to countenance any opposition by "expurgation of the other." In addition, he was reifying his ideas as unalterable (Thompson 1990, 60).

In retrospect, the significance of opposing the chairman of governors was that I was not willing to enter what Scheff calls "Domination by Joint Accomplishment," which was the accepted norm in this school (Scheff 1990, 186). In the classroom, I had been working on developing a two-way, negotiatory, rational style of teaching and that was the type of relationship that was also needed with the school authorities (Hargreaves 1972). Democratic authority has rational limits.

Alfred Wellberry treated me in an authoritarian manner and demanded an authoritarian relationship. He exceeded his democratic authority. Yet, the teacher–learner situation requires a non-authoritarian relationship because teaching depends on good communication and sound relationship. That is so because every speech act has an "illocutionary" force in which a relationship can be accepted or rejected, as examined in Habermas's theory of communicative competence in Chapter 2.

Equality is one "fundamental principle" of a theory, from the perspective of an educational philosophy. Peters argues that it is a necessary but not a sufficient condition for a theory (Peters 1966, 143). There are other principles such as freedom, the consideration of interests and respect for persons. It is inappropriate to define comprehensive education in egalitarian terms. Educational considerations need to take into account factors outside their control such as the cultural background of the pupils (Cooper 1980, 87–97).

I first became acquainted with Michael Lewis, the clerk to the governors, at this meeting.

Alfred Wellberry defined his political relationship with educators in terms of political dominance. He had in effect articulated the "public transcript" of the school. I had resisted that relationship and felt "the lived experience of power." I was unwilling to accept an unethical position of voicelessness and subordination. I had been charismatically insubordinate and produced "political electricity" (Scott 1990, 206). The teaching staff had supported me implicitly. Relationship is inevitable with other people because of the nature of emotion which is "deeply social." Ball argues that the school is significantly concerned with domination. If that remains the case, then the possibility of quality education is foreclosed. What the logic of this situation means is that educators have to expect relationships of mutuality and accept their "importance" (118). Scott quotes Kant: "The external power that deprives man of the freedom to communicate his thoughts deprives him at the same time of his freedom to think" (118). Since thinking is a function of education, political freedom is also necessary. That is the significance of what Alfred Wellberry denied.

THE POLITICS OF THE HOUSE AND YEAR SYSTEM

I decided to try to change the house system by political action, since no one else had brought the problem into the public sphere (Ball 1987, 22). Action research starts with a problem. It was an act of free commitment and leadership to a cause that necessitated taking a critical stance on an issue based on a practical judgment and a "practical intent." It was against the dominant culture of the school, which was one of formal organization and ideological neutrality. If I hadn't challenged the intellectual basis of the house system, I very much doubt whether the issue would have been debated let alone the system changed. Ideological silence would have ruled. I spent five to six years of steady political effort to see the change to a year system completed, because people in authority wanted a house system even though it was an illogical system. There was an unspoken and powerful rule that conflict and opposition were not allowed, hence the methods of opposition were not acceptable. However, in democratic politics in contrast to authoritarian politics, conflict and opposition are an inevitable part of the process (Ball 1987, 17–26).

The amalgamation took place in September 1972. On March 25, 1974, I distributed a paper prior to a meeting of the entire teaching staff setting out the differences between the house and the year system. I intended both to put the issue in the public domain and to test the opinion of all the teachers. Part of it is shown in Figure 1.1 because it shows the differences between the two systems and will prepare the reader for the dialogue which follows with Simon Creech.

The main difference to note is that the year system is simple in terms of relationship and communication between all the teachers, whereas the house system is unnecessarily complicated and difficult to work cooperatively and administratively. The issue was how important is communication to the organization and effective functioning of a school. I shall present in chapter two Habermas's theory of communication which demonstrates the complexity of interpersonal understanding and therefore the need to facilitate it to make communication possible.

After I presented this paper, I discovered that the common room as a whole understood the force of the arguments; the majority supported a change and was confirmed in the view that when a democratic body is addressed as a whole, the best decisions are made (Ball 1987, 213). The teaching staff passed a motion to set up a committee to review the house system. There was a minority of significant opposition consisting mostly of the senior house teachers, so politically it wasn't possible to change the system without delay, which is what should have happened. One problem of many

Figure 1.1
The Year/Form System

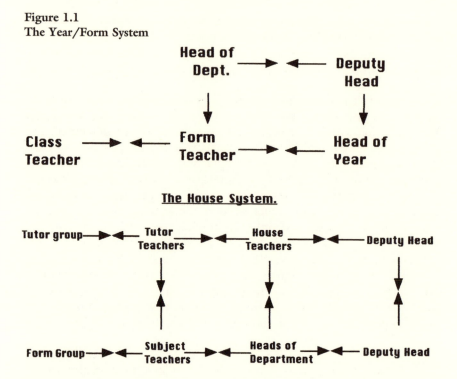

The House System.

would have been solved and time freed up for other problems (Carr and Kemmis 1986, 108–109).

The house teachers delayed action by setting up a committee which was an intentional political tactic by them to prevent any change. If the head teacher and the deputy head of academic studies had spoken and acted, it would have been possible. But, they didn't speak and didn't get involved. Their tactic was silence and tacit approval. I interpreted the purpose of their silence as a failure to admit that they had been mistaken in setting up a house system and their silence meant that they decided to cover up their mistake rather than admit it openly. If they had admitted the mistake at that point, they would not have lost their authority and could have put the school organization on a sound, intellectual basis.

The head didn't lead when it was the right moment and he ought to have done so, since he was the political leader of the school (Ball 1987, 80–87). He was blocking the machinery of politics as talk and the reconciling of differences. In attempting to change the house system, the political ideology of the school was also being challenged. Change and development are not possible without democratic debate of important issues since ideas are not analyzed and criticized. Since the leadership was politically inflexible and rigid, this was a reason for the school's failure to develop.

The next political action came from a minority group within the common room. They excluded me, as the main advocate of a year system, from the committee on the grounds that I wasn't objective. This was as a losing, tactical error since it indicated that the house system defenders were afraid of debating the issues and were concerned to protect their own positions of power. I had proposed the change and persuaded the common room to set up the committee. I had researched the topic for some hours and argued the case. So the real reason could not have been my lack of objectivity since my analysis of the two systems was sound. Rather, it was a self-serving political attempt to subvert the democratic process. "A committee is a cul-de-sac down which ideas are lured and then quietly strangled" (anonymous, quoted in Ball 1987, 243). I believe that was an accurate interpretation. By not including me on the committee, it meant that the leadership of the opposition was prevented from conducting the case in a rational way, by argument. There was no other forum. The argument about lack of objectivity was self-serving but even so, it is a better argument to say that even the unobjective should have their say hence any opposition should be represented.

That a political process and struggle was in motion I have understood with hindsight. The house teachers took their stance on the house system. Those who wanted to prevent debate in public made a political mistake and behaved undemocratically, since they forced the political conclusion that since the advocate of change wouldn't be allowed to argue the case on the committee, it would be necessary to pursue rational change by other means. I also realized that the common room was not a democratic forum for debate since debate was not really wanted on serious issues. This information affected subsequent decisions. The political system was probably autocratic and should have been changed.

The culture of Crosslinks School had been dictatorial rather than democratic, so why should they trust to open government? The head teacher should have intervened and tried to get the decision reversed and greater democracy instituted. But, he stood aloof from political activity. He wasn't present at staff meetings, which was an outdated practice. He could ignore the opinion of the staff in favor of the vested interests of the hierarchy. Change would have endangered the appointments that had been made to positions of responsibility and which involved risk. It was informative and significant that the head teacher neither spoke nor acted, using his power by silence. However, knowledge is power provided it is put to practical use, and keeping me off the committee did not prevent me from pursuing my aim. Preventing debate plays into the hands of the opposition politically. The house teachers delayed change but they didn't stop it. What the above actions did show was that the politics of the school was a problem and a barrier to its progress and a cause of failure.

IDEOLOGICAL CRITIQUE VERSUS PARTISANSHIP AND SILENCE

I decided that rather than accept defeat, I would try an alternative approach, since I couldn't put the case for the year system through the common room committee. I aimed to get the deputy head responsible for the house system to understand why the house system was unworkable, and persuade him to take action. In 1973, I presented a detailed and critically reasoned, written paper on the house system and received a response from Simon Creech, the deputy head teacher responsible for pastoral care and the house system. He thanked me for the "courteous presentation of my case, said I would have to convince the headmaster and district inspector and that he would never be convinced."

There are two points here for speech act, cultural analysis. Language is practice. What a person says is what he does (Bruner 1990). First, Creech considered that the head teacher and the district inspector were responsible for the decision regarding the system. Second, his expression "never be convinced" implied that he was such an ideological partisan in favor of the house system that no amount of communicative reasoning would lead to a change of mind. "Never" means at no time whatsoever. This is an instance where an understanding of a theory of communication could have produced insight into the extent of the communicative process. This partisan and rigid attitude meant that he was unwilling to consider an alternative perspective and this attitude was the ultimate cause of conflict within the school as a whole. The opposition was reacting to this. It is precisely for this kind of situation that a school has a head teacher. His political and leadership task is to reconcile differences, employ reason and ensure that one side of the school doesn't dominate the other. The fact that the head teacher wasn't willing to confront the issue meant that the school did not have effective leadership. Therefore, the leadership was leading in the wrong direction which could only result in a loss of confidence. The decline in examination results, for which the evidence is presented in Chapter 3, was in part a consequence of the house system. Cultural relationships do explain the workings of organizations over time.

There is also the further point that analytical reason as the basis of an academic education was not recognized by this house teacher and deputy head and this is evidence that the academic basis of a grammar school education had been abandoned; not only the teachers but also the pupils must have been aware that the system of organization was not rational or successful.

Simon Creech claimed the "Crosslinks side of the school had to build its reputation to work and people and the house system played a great part in this. The house masters and myself have been here so long that we are household words in this area. The house system in this school demands a loyalty that a year system never could. Of course ex-Boreham boys haven't been here long enough to feel part of it and quite honestly I don't think they ever will (I may be wrong though)."

Simon Creech here presented a highly partisan and ideological view of the system he was responsible for. He used a number of strategies in order to operate ideologically (Thompson 1990, 108). He used "narrativisation" to legitimize the house masters as "household words," and to provide a "rationalization" for the house system and imply its "universalization" as a successful system. He used "standardization" and the "symbolization of unity" by claiming that the house system demands "loyalty." He used "differentiation" and the "expurgation of the other" when he said that the other side of the amalgamation could possibly never be part of the Crosslinks system. He placed the value of "loyalty" to the Crosslinks house system as the supreme value. Therefore, anyone who criticized the house system was disloyal.

The supreme values in education arguably are understanding, rationality and critical reasoning (Peters 1966). These values are not ideological. They are characterized by objectivity, unity, publicity, impersonality, the connection between reason and intelligence and "the transcendence of the here and now" (Peters 1972, 151–158, 209–212).

Sissela Bok on the "pathology of partisanship" summed up the problem succinctly:

In time of war or other intense conflict, partisanship can foster a pathology all its own. When this happens, partisanship goes beyond the emphasis on loyalty and cohesion needed for the well-being of any community and leads people to become obsessive and heedless of their group's long-range self-interest, even its survival. Communities, like living organisms, can succumb to stress, internal weakness, or contagion. These factors heighten the risks that the pathology of self-destructive partisanship will take over. Only with the help of strong leadership and institutional safeguards can communities prevent or withstand such deterioration. (Bok 1989b, 6)

Hence, the issue of the house system was an ideological one and I believe that "strong leadership and institutional safeguards" were absent at the Borecross school.

In reply to a list of written points I had made, Simon made the following replies:

1. *Armitage*: The house is peripheral to the core of the school's activity, the main reason for the school's existence—*work*. "The heart of the school is the classroom. It is through the difficulties and satisfactions of working together that the most genuine and lasting relationships are built up, and the house in a day school simply has not got that basis." (Pedley 1963)

Creech: Relationships are much more lasting on a house basis than a form basis. I have tried both.

Armitage: The point I made is central. You haven't answered it and have merely asserted your opinion unsupported by reasons. There is no intellectual base to your view.

2. *Armitage*: "The house has no physical reality" (Pedley 1963). You can't see it or touch it. In a public boarding school the house is organized round an actual dormitory, common rooms, house dining rooms, cloakrooms and changing rooms. At Borecross there are none of these facilities and the lack of them underlies the artificial, imitative nature of the house system.

Creech: A pity we are not built for the house system, but when staff can withdraw their support at lunch time, perhaps it's just as well.

Armitage: Simon, you have conceded a basic point. The second half of your statement has nothing to do with the first half and is totally irrelevant.

3. *Armitage*: There is no basis for a relationship between the house tutor and the members of his tutor group unless he happens to teach them.

Creech: A good schoolmaster very soon makes good relationships, be it tutor group or form.

Armitage: Simon, you have not considered the problem I posed. Your answer is irrelevant.

4. *Armitage*: The house system is harder to operate in a school that is divided among more than one building.

Creech: A year system is easier for administrative work but we are not in school to take the easy line for ourselves.

Armitage: You have conceded an important point. Are we in school to make life difficult for ourselves? If we could solve this problem, it would leave us time and energy to concentrate on many other problems.

5. *Armitage*: The house system destroys the natural choice of tutor for a group of day school children, i.e., the form master.

Creech: Covering books, etc., can be done just as easily by a tutor group master. Middle band classes of 30 demand much more attention than top band classes; these and bottom bands require most of the pastoral care. I have taken a class of 30 4c year boys where every one, but one, was on probation. If this work had been split up among house masters it would have been much better for the boys. All difficult boys are bunched together in classes where they are difficult to control. Any indiscipline in this school is in teaching units. At least boys start the day right.

Armitage: Again, you haven't really addressed my point. You have conceded it when you admit that "any indiscipline in this school is in teaching units," which is why a form master is needed.

6. *Armitage*: The existence of a house system increases the tendency of a comprehensive school to be run on a hierarchical basis.

A further reason for the rise of the year system is the general movement toward student participation in the running of schools. This has led to a desire of schools to enable pupils to participate within their own group. Participation for all pupils is harder in a house system, which automatically gives leadership to the older pupils or prefects only. The year system by contrast fosters leadership from among and not from above. A horizontal form of organization assists the development of a grassroots democracy.

Creech: Tutor group representatives can put forward any ideas from tutor groups. All ages are represented.

Armitage: In my judgment, my point is stronger and better than yours.

7. *Armitage*: "Principles must relate to empirical fact." (Pedley 1963)

Creech:—

Armitage: They don't in the house system.

8. *Armitage*: Tutorial groups are too big. Frequent staff changes, common to all types of school, wreck the idea of a long-standing relationship steadily built up.

Creech: Some of our tutor group masters have been here for years—ask them!

9. *Armitage*: Every boy in the school should have his own desk in his classroom, a place where he can keep his books safely, a little piece of his own territory. Under the present house system books are kept at home (and incidentally left there when required for use in school), no desks are provided and every boy is something of a nomad. This helps to create a restless atmosphere in the school—hardly conducive to concentration and the production of good work. This is a natural need.

Creech: Not a bad idea for a boy to take his books home. In many cases these are the only books in the home. Could give him a feel for books for the future when he sets up home. A much more restless attitude could be produced if the boys found books defaced or missing. Every boy in the school has a desk even if he doesn't use it much; every boy has his tutor group space.

Armitage: What is the point of having a desk if it isn't used? Boys often complain that their books are heavy and it's inconvenient to carry them around all day. It's regularly used as an excuse for not having them at a lesson when they are needed. Frankly, Simon, I think you're inventing reasons just to keep your case going.

10. *Armitage*: Under the present house system every member of staff is responsible for any part of the school he happens to be in, but he is not responsible for anywhere in particular.

Creech: If only staff would be this responsible we should have a marvelous set-up. Let all staff widen their domain from one particular domain to the whole school.

Armitage: Take care of the small things and the big things look after themselves.

11. *Armitage*: Under the present house system members of staff do not have their own classrooms. As a result, in a typical case, they change classrooms at the end of every second period. This involves the wasting of precious time and energy, time which could profitably be used in the preparation of lessons and writing work on the blackboard before the class arrives. Under present conditions the class often arrives before the teacher and this is self-evidently an unsatisfactory state of affairs.

Creech: I agree it is much better for tutor group masters to teach as much as possible in their tutor group bases, then we should not have some classrooms in such a mess. I have never yet seen a master (or mistress) out of the common room to get to his room before the boys get there from the playground (4 times a day).

Armitage: Haven't you conceded the very practical point that some classrooms are in a mess because of the house system?

12. *Armitage*: The tutor group system creates problems of communication and does not help to solve them.

If members of staff are moving round the school from classroom to classroom how can they be easily contacted without reference to timetables, which are not easily accessible and which many boys are not able to read? With tutor groups it is difficult for members of staff to contact boys.

Creech: I agree it is more difficult than year groups but I find it quite easy.

Armitage: Perhaps you find it easier personally since as a deputy headmaster you teach few lessons and have the time to wander around the school. A classroom teacher doesn't.

13. *Armitage*: The role of a house tutor is less rewarding than the role of a form master. The tutor group is too incohesive, the age and ability ranges too broad to unite, so that many of the things you can do with a form are not possible with a tutor group. There is no common level of understanding so you can't talk to them as a body. Talks by individuals, private lessons for backward readers are hardly practical in the conditions. Private discussions with individual members are not practical when a conversation can easily be overheard.

Creech: I personally disagree, having had much experience of both. Private discussions are always difficult. Talks and reading are comparatively easy.

14. *Armitage*: The house system tends to encourage a competitive spirit, with the idea that "our house" must be the "best house." Some people take the view that this attitude is immature and unfruitful of real educational and social development.

Creech: Idealism??

15. *Armitage*: The good work done by the house masters at present would be continued under a year and form system.

Creech:—

16. *Armitage*: Discipline can be more easily organized on a horizontal basis since various types of deviant behavior tend to be peculiar to specific age groups. A year master could become a specialist in say the fourth-year itch. He could tackle some problems collectively in year assemblies.

Creech: Difficult discipline cases are generally shared by house masters. With a year system you would soon develop masters for years—very specialist work again, whereas a house master is able to deal with all age ranges.

17. *Armitage*: In a house system a boy may have an unsatisfactory relationship with his house tutor and/or his house master. There is nothing he can do to change it. In a year system each boy in the school would have a different form and year master every year.

Creech: Not true—a boy may change house or tutor group but, of course, this is not encouraged.

18. *Armitage*: Under a house system fourth-and-fifth year boys, generally speaking, spend their breaks standing in the hall. If the fourth- and-fifth-year boys had classrooms to go to, they could spend their breaks more profitably and enjoyably there. Many of them resent the loss of this privilege.

Creech: I realize the Boreham fourth- and fifth-year boys were able to use their rooms. The privilege they have of using the hall works well and, as it is personally supervised by me, there has been little or no damage. Boreham and Crosslinks boys have mixed in a bit. Do have a look at the room AI—upper 6th room. This would happen all over the school with your scheme.

19. *Armitage*: The claim that more pastoral care is possible with a house system has no basis in fact.

Creech: The strength of the school is the pastoral care of the house system.

20. *Armitage*: The inappropriateness of the house system undermines the discipline of the school and the stability of the boys.

Creech: I disagree.

21. *Armitage*: Under the house system the organization of the school is basically untidy.

Creech: We are not in school to be tidy.

22. *Armitage*: A substantial number of the staff, and perhaps even a significant majority, are opposed to the house system.

Creech: Before they make any judgment they should visit a school without a house system. I think that most ex-Boreham staff are opposed to the house system because taking a tutor group of mixed ability and a mixed age range is much more demanding than taking a grammar school class of bright, well-mannered, literate and cooperative boys with almost 100 percent parent backing.

23. *Armitage*: The argument that the house system is maintained for political reasons is not justifiable in an educational establishment which is supposed to provide a service for the boys.

Creech: The head teacher and deputy could have changed the system had they so wished. If most of the staff are opposed to the house system why couldn't they have raised one small murmur. I did not hear one single peep—even from you. I have had several messages from ex-Boreham parents who have said they like the house system we have in operation, but none protesting about it. I have worked both house and year, form—house every time.

24. *Armitage*: The amalgamation of the two schools will not become a reality unless the problem of the house system is aired publically and settled rationally.

Creech:—

25. *Armitage*: The teachers parents would wish to see when visiting the school are the form and subject teachers—without the experience of teaching a boy a house tutor or house master is not in a position to comment with any degree of intimate knowledge.

Creech:—

26. *Armitage*: The house system implies that the pastoral side of the school is more central to the school's aims than is practically desirable or even possible.

Conclusion to This Discussion

Armitage: In making a judgment about the house system and the year system, it is advisable to look at each system as a whole. Which is the more logically interconnected and rational? It is abundantly clear from this debate that the year system is logical and workable. The house system is illogical and impractical.

In your reply, Simon, you give the impression that the pastoral system is only for a certain type of boy. Isn't this discrimination in favor of the difficult discipline cases? Should a whole school be based on this idea? You also seem to put a question mark against idealism. I assume you see the house system as dealing with the practicalities of every day life such as food, sleep, clothes and health. I think your house system should combine a little bit of pragmatism, idealism, rationalism and existentialism. Idealism generates the motivation that things can be better than they are if people would aim higher (end of discussion).

This Habermasian practical discourse with Simon Creech was scientific, critical and practical from a historical perspective (Fay 1987, 36–41). It exemplified critical thinking as a "principle of procedure" and "constitutive of means as educational means" (Carr and Kemmis 1986, 78). If ideology was effective as the meaningful solution to educational problems, Creech had an ideology. But, in Habermasian terms, improving education is a "practical task," dependent on the evolution of political communication, not an ideological one.

From a Habermasian perspective as explained in Chapter 2, the above discourse was illustrative (Habermas 1979). First, communicative competence was used to solve the theory-practice problem, the problem of foundations and to test power by an "ethics of suspicion." Here was an attempt to redeem claims to truth and "generalizable" interests in an ideal speech situation. It was assumed that speech acts had a rational basis and that language and power are connected. The case for the house system was based on distorted communication which hid an ideology. When the validity claims of the house system were criticized, they could not have been based on knowledge. The steps in the logic of discourse were followed. At the final stage of "political will formation" Simon Creech politically supported the house system. His conclusion could not be substantiated by argument. The demand for accountability was not met, though the demand for "reciprocity" was. The "generalizable interest" required a change to the year system since it was rationally based. The interests of the house teachers were not generalizable. The house system also failed the test of legitimacy since it was not worthy of recognition and the political order was similarly unworthy of recognition.

I sent a transcript of this dialogue to the head teacher as the next politically meaningful step in a political process to have the situation changed. It was an informal, open, micro-political act that ran counter to the rules of formal organization, which are rigid and designed to control the organization from the top.

The head, Brian Fellows, declined a discussion, as would be expected in a formal system where the leadership style is authoritarian (Ball 1987, 109–124). He sent a brief note which said that he didn't think a change to the year system would bring about the benefits implied in the system. It read as follows: "Thank you for your study. I remain convinced it is wiser to leave well alone, and I feel that many of the advantages you see in the 'year system' are not likely to be realized in practice in our situation. Brian Fellows, head teacher, Borecross School."

The head declined to analyze the issues openly in a recognized, political manner. Here was meaningful evidence that the problem of the school was that the leadership would not recognize let alone discuss a problem. That was his job. It was a political mistake because the system was unjustified and therefore the head took up a weak position politically in relation to the opposition, handed over the political initiative and therefore lost control of the situation; but in an authoritarian system heads don't argue with subordinates. Their relationship is formal and vertical but also unreal. If there had been no democratic opposition, he could have afforded not to act, but in a system of democratic politics, talk is the medium of politics and therefore not to talk was not to act or participate. Since I was acting, the head was leaving the battlefield empty for me to take without a conflict. The problem of inactive leadership is that it doesn't get results and leads to political failure. What the political situation at Borecross School needed to be rational was a "decentralizing political practice" instead of its centralizing political practice. The school was old-fashioned in its practices in a society and culture which was rapidly changing with its declining situation in the world, and it was the centralized political practice which inhibited and frustrated change. The head teacher had the power to prevent change by ignoring problems and maintaining silence. Silence is as important for what it does not say. As Eagleton (1976) writes, "a work is tied to ideology not so much by what it says as by what it does not say. It is the significant *silences* of a text, in its gaps and absences, that the presence of ideology can be most positively felt" (34–35).

Silence by leaders protects their ideology from open critical appraisal. Since a large number of the pupils were also inhabiting a "culture of silence," which is why their education could never get much off the ground, the school was frozen at the top and the bottom. Only a "decentered political practice" could promote communication, since then new ideas could be introduced and considered. Decentered action was considered unacceptable by the authorities who defended their authority when necessary with deceit, denial, secrecy and anger.

Why did Simon Creech favor the house system? Why was he implacably opposed to the year system? His reasoning was that it had been a Crosslinks tradition with which he had been closely identified, hence his position was ideological and irrational. It exemplified "ideological factors controlling intentions." He had not seriously questioned its basis in theory or practice. Since he had not thought the matter through and considered the alternative, he was in effect responsible for a system of which he had an inadequate understanding. Therefore, irresponsibility was at the heart of the school system. A leading theorist of the comprehensive system argued against the house system, yet no notice was taken of his writings. What does it mean when an educational system has no backing or authority from educational theory?

The head teacher was responsible for the house system. He chose it. Why did he institute it? Is the answer that he didn't understand the problem? Then why was he the head teacher if he wasn't taking responsibility? The City Education Authority Inspector, Dennis Moore, said at the disciplinary trial the head teacher was not really responsible for the school system, but here was something over which he had control and therefore he could be held responsible (day 2, page 6).

How did the house system effect the decline in academic and work standards as measured by examination results? Was it negligent to continue with the house system for eight years when its rational justification was implausible? From the educational point of view and that of public accountability, the case that it was is strong, even very strong. Because of the partisanship of the leadership, the school was effectively crippled by its ideology. What is more the meaningful problem of partisanship went right through the system, as the evidence will show.

THEORETICAL FRAMEWORK OF A CRITICAL EDUCATION SCIENCE

A question of this research is: How do you understand the educational process and how do you improve the process in situation by solving problems? This section explains a theoretical framework for practice in process. There are three paradigms of the relationship between educational theory and educational practice. Two of them cannot withstand critical understanding because the theory and practice are at odds, therefore they don't work. The third, which I practiced in this school situation, conceives the relationship correctly and can enhance the educational process; it claims a theory of a critical education science as action research (Carr and Kemmis 1986).

The theory of a critical education science is as follows. It is a "process of enlightenment," both intellectual and emotional, discovered in the problems, experiences and situations of teachers who are victims of social processes which they participate in and maintain but over which they have no control (157). An example of this point in our narrative was the refusal of authority to accept communication and discussion as legitimate when it contravened the position of authority, a point which becomes even clearer as the story develops, and denies educators the ability to control and participate in their own situation. A critical education science seeks to "link" teachers "with depersonalized and alienating processes and to contrast this with the choices they could make as agents" (157). An example from our text is that I chose to participate and debate with authority so that I could not be ignored and I persisted in that choice resisting alienation from my own voice and everyday experience. The theory "seeks to analyze their dissatisfactions and sufferings and to examine the contradictions which their educational situation brings about in order to intervene and transform them." I was dissatisfied with the house system for many practical reasons, as I have analyzed, and I attempted to "transform" it. (156) "It is directed at specific groups." I was a member of the teaching staff. The theory reveals contradictions between, for example, "enlightenment and alienation," between "solidarity and division" and between "empowerment and authoritarianism" (158). These contradictions are evident. There is a contradiction between ideological force and freedom of choice and speech, a contradiction between the division between authority and staff and the potential solidarity of the school as a whole if we could only communicate adequately. There was a contradiction between being dominated by a silent authority and choosing to act and have some power of thought and opinion.

A critical education science aims at "enlightened self-knowledge" and "effective political action" (Carr and Kemmis 1986, 157). I used a theory of the education of the emotions and creativity for the sake of self-knowledge, and I took political action which was "effective." The method is "dialogue." I used extensive dialogue with Simon Creech and was always open to such. The theory has the "effect" "to heighten" a person's self-awareness of their potentialities as an "active" agent of history (157). Political action rather than passivity did enhance my self-esteem and sense of significance and importance and the potentialities of the situation. The theory arises from problems of everyday life and attempts to solve them (157). I discovered many problems in daily life as I have narrated them. "It is a theory of change and links researchers with practitioners so that the duality of their work is transcended." I was concerned to change an institution and became a research teacher. "It uncovers false ideas to replace them with implicit truths." The problem of the house and year systems was a matter of logical truth and falsity. It is a "concrete engagement in the task of educational transformation." The reactions of the authorities were violent enough to suggest that their teaching ideology was threatened. Its emphasis is on practice, transformation and "revolutionary practice." A change to the year system was revolutionary (156, 157). Hence, the situation I have described had all the ingredients of a critical education science.

I will briefly explain the basis of this theory. Carr and Kemmis have developed a *Critical Education Science* for education in practical situations which is enacted and operated by action research. The purpose of their analysis is to solve the problem of how to close the theory and practice gap.

In *Becoming Critical*, the analysis starts from the position that there are three conscious approaches to educational theory, namely, the technical, the practical and the strategic (Carr and Kemmis 1986, 35–41).

Carr and Kemmis consider the technical, positivist approach and the practical, interpretivist approach to education and criticize them to show why they are inadequate (51–99).

The strategic approach, derived from Habermas's critical social science, overcomes the flaws of the technical and the practical. It views educational activities as "historically related." It views educational activity as "social activity." It regards education as "intrinsically powerful." It views educational acts as "problematic" (Carr and Kemmis, 39). The strategic view considers that educators constitute a *"Critical Community of Enquirers."* It is an approach which "leaves great scope for research" (40). It also provides a theoretical framework in which teachers can become "critical" (40).

A feature of strategic consciousness is teachers' knowledge. They are the only people in a position to critically examine their decisions. That knowledge is rooted in custom, habit and assumption. So the starting point of critical reflection is to examine teachers' knowledge. It is problematic with the ideal of "justified true belief." The knowledge must be able to relate theory to practice and is rooted in the actual situation of learning (Carr and Kemmis 41–44).

Educational aims have a "peculiar" nature, Carr and Kemmis argue. Educational aims are intrinsic values (77).

In the key chapter, Carr and Kemmis suggest a redefinition of the theory practice problem of education (103–127). One criterion of educational research is that it is something which people do. Its overall purpose is to bring about change which is a practical task. Hence, "Educational problems are *never* theoretical" (109). While theoretical problems can be solved by new knowledge, practical problems can only be resolved by a course of action (108). Educational problems are always practical problems. Problems are solved by "acting upon a practical judgment" (109). So the testing ground for educational research is whether it can solve practical problems (106, 112).

Educational theory is not "applied theory" and cannot be produced outside the practical contexts in which it occurs. Educational theory "refers to the whole enterprise of critically appraising the adequacy of the concepts, beliefs, assumptions and values incorporated in prevailing theories of educational practice" (115). The "transition" in practice is from irrationality to rationality and from ignorance and habit to knowledge and reflection. "Theory transforms practice by informing and transforming the ways in which practice is experienced and understood" (116).

Carr and Kemmis distinguish the application of scientific disciplines to education from the "scientific investigation of the problems that arise out of educational practice" (124).

The essence of the new Popperian and Kuhnian philosophy of science is criticism that seeks to remove all prejudices and assumptions about know-lege. It is not directed at the elimination of error. Scientific theories can only be "falsified." They are rational if they can withstand criticism (120). Progress in science is akin to "evolutionary struggle." "Objectivity" means shared, intersubjective agreement. Science supports democratic ideals since science needs open, critical enquiry to make progress (122).

Educational theory aims at "the discovery of theory from data systematically obtained from research" that is grounded, substantive theory (125). The "relevant concepts, hypotheses and problems must be inductively developed from the 'raw data' provided by a study of the substantive area" (125). Scientific educational research is subject to notions of "cogency, rigor and critical reflection." A new epistemological framework for educational research is required, which Carr and Kemmis argue that Habermas's critical social science may supply.

Carr and Kemmis state their principal conclusion as follows:

The purpose of educational research is to ensure that the observations, interpretations and judgments of educational practitioners can become more coherent and rational and thereby acquire a greater degree of scientific objectivity. (106, 112)

This definition emphasizes the need for interpretation, practicality, rationality and scientific objectivity in educational research.

Carr and Kemmis argue for a form of critical education science research which is not *about* education but *for* education (155). It is concerned with (1) transforming educational practices, understandings and situations and (2) is directed at educational change; (3) it moves beyond explanation and understanding to future-oriented, transformational action; (4) it does so by involving concerned parties in the task of a critical analysis of their situations, understandings and practices in order to transform them; (5) it is "participatory" and "collaborative," takes place in schools and requires that teachers become researchers.

Carr and Kemmis argue that the criteria of an education science are met by action research and suggest the following categories for meeting their basic criteria for an education science:

1. "A Dialectical View of Rationality."
2. "The Systematic Interpretation of Teachers' Categories."
3. "Ideology-Critique."
4. "From the Organization of Enlightenment to the Organization of Action."
5. "The Unity of Theory and Practice: Criticism and Praxis in Self-Reflective Communities." (129–191)

Carr and Kemmis have defined action research as follows:

Action research is a form of self-reflective enquiry undertaken by participants in social situations in order to improve the rationality and justice of their own practices, their understanding of these practices, and the situations in which these practices are carried out. (162)

The important point to note is that action research starts from the study of practice, theorizes what thinking and understanding informs practices and critically analyzes a practice or practices to change them to more rational practices.

I will briefly describe what is involved in these above criteria in relation to this action research case study. First, the " 'objects' of action research" are educational practices and educational situations such as the practice and theory of the house system, the actions of the chairman of governors, the head's conduct and the common room staff politics (Carr and Kemmis 1986, 180). Second, the actions of all participants take place in a social situation such as my proposal to the staff room to change the system. The process of action research is a "historical" one taking place in and through time. This is evident in the episodes of the amalgamation I described and their practical significance. Action research involves a social process of language action in a social situation. The purpose of the active approach is to "transform the present into the future." Changing the house organization to a year organization is one example, but political assertion from a position of subordination is another. The action researcher needs to conduct a dialectic between subjective and objective conditions, between the individual and society and between theory and practice. This I did in terms of the overt actions of the authorities and the perception of their significance to subordinates. The dialectic between the individual and social constraints was one of domination of decision-taking. There was a gap between theory and practice because theory was ignored. Action research requires commitment to a practical judgment and its hoped-for consequences. Challenging the house system in opposition to entrenched authority was an example that they could be defeated. Action research becomes a project and a program of reform as did the house system and all its related problems. The action I took was based on a retrospective judgment in relation to the prospects for the future. Finally, action research requires a "political struggle" to implement change because it demands changes in others in the same situation and they may not want to change.

The thesis claim contained in Carr and Kemmis's second category of action research is that teachers must develop their own understandings of their practices, which they can do by their understanding of educational research. Educational research, as defined by Lawrence Stenhouse (1975), is research which is public and systematic and which makes a rational claim and needs to be used and criticized for its relevance to a situation. There is a connection between personal knowledge, practice and praxis. My praxis action on the house system was based on research and hence had the authority of research findings.

There is not much to be said concerning the category of ideological critique. It is concerned to uncover "collective understandings." The house system was ideologically based, as I uncovered, and so was the advocacy of mixed-ability teaching.

The fifth category of the relationship between organizing enlightenment and and action is that between understanding the situation and changing it. For this it is necessary to distinguish practices from educational institutions. Practitioners are involved in a research process and "theorizing their own practice." It requires collaborative involvement and participation. This means that a social order in which "rational communication," "just and democratic decision-taking" and "fulfilling work" are normative. It requires "human practices, understanding and institutions malleable enough, to change with changing social and historical conditions." It requires understanding in a "social, cultural, political and economic context."

Carr and Kemmis's final category of the unity of theory and practice in criticism and praxis is based on the understanding that a critical education science in which practitioners are essential to the process must combine "the achievement of theory with the achievements of practice." For powerful criticism must be combined with a "concretely-relevant discourse." It is my claim that the theories expounded in this thesis are concretely relevant.

The importance of this section has been to argue that political practice is a part of educational practice and it is important that the power of educators is recognized as real.

CONCLUSION

I have related the events of the amalgamation. I shall now combine them into a narrative whole to discern a pattern of meanings. Narrative organization is sensitive to time, context and human action. The main mechanism of organizing the events is the plot. I aim to construct the plot in order to turn "scattered events into a meaningful whole." Narrative organization is the method of this study. It is a skill of "emplotment."

How had the story of the new school unfolded? In the first section of this chapter, I narrated and analyzed the meaningful actions of the governors and the head. The governors chose a policy of continuity rather than change and risk, as evidenced by their appointments. There was no articulated policy hence there was a "policy hiatus." The school had no aims, and education needs to be aimed at doing something (White 1982, 6). The silent, undeveloped policy of "melting difference" was a policy of communicative, political domination by limiting participation and the recognition of problems. It was a policy of "brutal" simplification of complexity (Sennett 1980, 165). It was designed to cover over a "nasty political battle" behind closed doors, which this research revealed. The new system took on the old house system and the old leaders without any retraining. There was no meaningful relationship of communication between leaders and led. Bright tie day and a putting match were diversionary tactics to give an air of happiness. There were significant attacks on quality as evidenced by the loss of good teachers without recognition and the loss of the *Times* newspaper. In the second section, the position of the chairman of governors seemed to be authoritarian and a relationship of domination and resistance instituted. It was a significant act that he asked for my resignation and a sign of political malpractice from the leadership of the governing body. In the third section, the politics of the house system revealed the messy political realities of a power struggle and the significance of the wrong way to manage political differences by excluding debate. In section four, the rigid partisan problem became apparent. The significance of the debate with Simon Creech was that he lost the argument on logical grounds but for him the house system was an emotional, historical and ideological matter. It was also the basis of his power in the school, which he didn't want to give up. The crowning point of the story was the refusal of the head teacher to debate the house system, which is a political malpractice since it forecloses discussion. He could have overruled Simon Creech. He probably had realized his mistaken choice of the house system by then but couldn't contemplate a change after the amalgamation, and especially not one pointed out by a subordinate. He chose the path of obstinacy and anti-intellectualism. Here was causal, teleological responsibility at work. He thought perhaps that I would accept his authority without question. However, the school policy had become anti-intellectual and although I think there are many other values than intellectual ones, the British intellectual tradition is not one to be thrown out lightly, and it was what the grammar school stood for at heart. Finally, in section five I outlined a new approach to educational theory and practice which I endorse. I acted on my practical judgment. I assessed the prospects of the school based on a retrospective understanding of the situation. I exercised a "critical praxis." The debate with Simon Creech was democratic practice in action. The action ended when the head refused to communicate about the house system and effectively defined the system as one of authoritarian domination and the denial of conflict. This is the narrative picture that has emerged and is the background to the story that will develop as I seek a narrative explanation to subsequent developments.

The machinery of government and politics at the amalgamation was inadequate for the problems of the school. A critical education science was needed. A public sphere of democratic participation was also needed so that rational decisions could be made for the sake of educational aims and achievements. This would mean recognizing the significance of micro-political relationships and the barrier of ideological political practices to educational change. This chapter has illuminated the problem of ideological, political resistance to democratic participation and change and the need for rational, unauthoritarian political practices.

Chapter 2

Narrative Action and Theoretical Explanation

I narrated the micro-political sequence of events at Borecross School in Chapter 1 and critically evaluated the problem of a political and educational ideology which prevented a process of cultural and political development. I develop the story in this chapter by explaining how I attempted to produce change and the impassable communication problems that resulted. I seek to explain by theoretical analysis how and why this problematic situation had come about, why it was endemic to the institution and how it could be solved. I introduce a "toolbox" of theories relevant to the situation for theoretical perspectives on problems of practice. I work within the framework of a critical education science and narrative organization. Finally, I evaluate the political situation that had developed with theories as "orienting perspective."

There are a few theoretical points about the use of narrative to "exhibit" what kind of knowledge it produces. Narrative "lends meaning and understanding to human action" by focusing on human action in situation. It is committed to an "existential sense of human choice" because it focuses on the person's existence and his or her freedom to choose. Narrative communicates the choices people make in a situation. Existentialism distinguishes creative action from behavior, the former responds to the new and the latter to routine and tradition. The narrative form brings out a tension between the universal and the particular. Narrative challenges the reader to "think freshly." It constructs a sense of the self and the "mindset of institutions" and deals with the real life of an institution. A narrative shows how events are generated. "Good narrative identifies social and political facts" and reveals the ethics of an institution (Minow 1996, 24–36).

I was a protagonist in the story. I was particularly influenced in my practices by the theories contained in Crick's *In Defence of Politics* (1962), Carl Rogers's *On Becoming a Person* (1961) and David Hargreaves's *Interpersonal Relations and Education* (1972). My present role is that of a historian, distanced by writing, "appropriation" and "self-understanding" in order to understand these events from a critical perspective for the sake of historical knowledge, "epistemic gain" and communication.

POLITICAL ACTION FOR CHANGE

There developed a contentious power struggle from the political and educational issue of the house and year system. The house teachers believed with an emotional passion in the idea of the house system and were prepared to defend it as much as possible. It was their culture. This is their right in a democratic system. But, in doing so they are acting in a political capacity. Equally, in wanting to change to a year system, as a member of the teaching staff, I had the right to advocate the differing idea of the year system. Cultural politics arose from this conflict of ideas. Politics is a "contested," not an "invested" activity, hence a power struggle is normal. Educational ideas are politically controversial since they affect behavior and culture.

I judged that the resistance to change was irrational and motivated by vested interest and ideological rigidity since the house teachers felt their power and authority threatened. Teachers were basically treated as place holders in the system without political significance. The authorities were not prepared to acknowledge mistakes or to share power by democratic participation so they were partly responsible for the subsequent, protracted conflict of power. Nor were they ready for nor did they expect any opposition. The scientific theory of organizations which the authorities were using was an inadequate model. Also, they had no policy for working on the educational problems of the school. Their approach was mainly practical and untheoretical, whereas I was interested in using educational theory and developing a policy for the new school situation. The differences were fundamental and not trivial.

In March 1976, I decided that the City Education Authority should be informed about the problems of the school, which were not being seriously addressed. The action was justified since "practical problems are solved by a course of action" (Carr 1986, 108). It was also a working out of the relationship between "teachers' knowledge and strategic consciousness" (41–44). Since teachers' knowledge is also rooted in the actual situation of learning, that should include the organizational framework. This was nearly three years after the founding of the Borecross School in September 1973, which was a reasonable period of time to judge the school's progress under its leadership. I wrote a letter concerning the leadership of the head teacher, following correct procedures.

The following is the open complaint I wrote:

March 13, 1976

Complaint Against the Headmaster of Borecross School Because of the Inefficient Organization and Functioning of This School

Dear Dr. Brownley,
The purpose of my letter, after careful consideration, is to make a complaint against the headmaster of Borecross School, for the reasons which I list below.

The Organization—The House System

The system of organization was never thought out properly on rational lines at the amalgamation, and attempts to discuss rationally an alternative, and better system have been rejected. On the enclosed sheet attached I give twenty-one reasons why the present house system does not work satisfactorily (Appendix 1). This document ought to have been answered fully by the headmaster but it hasn't; furthermore, no adequate reasons have been given for having a house system in the first place. To sum up, the school is fundamentally disorganized.

Discipline—School Rules

There are no explicit rules at all at Borecross School and the reasoning behind this state of affairs has not been explained, or even the philosophy relating to it. In my opinion, the cause is almost pure whim.

Democracy and Internal Government

You will be familiar with the Education Authority's Report on the Internal Government of Schools which recommended "real democratic involvement" by "recognition of the views of others, reasoned argument" and so on. This document has never been discussed let alone been put into action, resulting in a breakdown in meaningful communication.

Remoteness from the School

The headmaster has become a remote, uninvolved figure in the school who doesn't teach, is seldom seen around the school, has delegated almost all responsibility without taking the trouble to see whether people are carrying out their responsibilities properly or even adequately.

He has isolated himself because he is inclined to prevent staff airing difficulties in an open fashion, without fear or favor. Consequently, there are a lot of important things said in private which he ought to be aware of but isn't. If he were in a minor position it wouldn't matter, but in his crucial role it clearly does.

Drop in Academic Standards

There has been a steady decline in academic standards, as indicated by examination results. It has almost become taboo to mention the word "academic" let alone take some action to improve the situation. The split between the academic and pastoral sides of the school is almost a gulf.

Failure to Control the Chairman of Governors

The chairman of governors has publicly described the governors as having an "infinity of powers." On a number of occasions he has acted in an undemocratic and unconstitutional manner. A number of bad decisions, directly affecting the school, have been made, decisions which a responsible headmaster would have prevented.

Size of School, Bureaucracy and Government by Mystification

The school has a problem related to its large size. Also, we seem to have government by bureaucracy with much paper being circulated, but no effective action resulting. There are no explicit policies on discipline, pastoral care, aims of the school and hardly anything on philosophy. The working of the school seems to be characterized by mystery and confusion.

Truancy, Absenteeism

The stagnating state of the school is reflected in the high rate of truancy and absenteeism. It is easy to sympathize with the boys who stay away. At end-of-term assemblies about half the school attends; yet the situation is ignored.

Leadership and Decision-Taking

The headmaster appears to lead from behind and rarely seems to have a stance or definite point of view of his own. His unconfident, hesitant and uncertain manner is echoed throughout the staff and student body. A school cannot prosper without leadership and direction.

To conclude, I hope the authority will take this letter seriously and regard it in a realistic and unsentimental light.

Yours faithfully,
P. B. Armitage

Appendix: The House System

The present serious and deep-rooted weaknesses of the house system, in my view, are as follows:

1. It is an artificial system because there are no house rooms of any kind and therefore a sense of *homelessness* in the school is created. This is ironical since possibly the *first* priority of a pastoral system should be to create a sense of belonging to a piece of space or territory and then to a group of peers and a group leader.

2. The house system helps to fragment the school into pastoral and academic sides which tend to work against rather than with each other.

3. A tutor master cannot know the boys in a tutor group as he doesn't teach most of them and does not work with them (and may not teach any of them). In a large school this is a very serious and important objection to the house system, surely. It means that the individual boy does not get individual attention.

4. The success of the academic side of the school is tested by examinations. There is no way of measuring the success or otherwise of the pastoral system. Therefore, as parents and employers look for exam success, work should be the center of the school's activities. The house system fragments the academic side and puts pastoral activities at the heart of the school's activities. Pastoral activities can easily be an escape from work in the classroom.

5. The natural coordination of classes for subject teachers is a form master, not a

remote house master (remote from the ways of a particular form), nor a tutor master who is seldom if ever used anyway.

6. In my experience tutor masters seldom know very much about their boys until they receive reports from subject teachers at the end of the second term of the school year, and then what they know is secondhand information. Tutor masters are required to advise third-year boys on choice of subjects in the fourth year. What guidance can they offer in their position? The implications of this are considerable.

7. Class discipline, standards of work, pastoral problems could much more easily be dealt with if subject teachers could get together, compare notes, identify problem pupils and develop some kind of coordinated action. At the moment each teacher minds his own classroom in more or less isolation, receiving little support from colleagues teaching the same class. For probationary teachers, let alone experienced teachers, this is an inefficient way of working, especially bearing in mind over-sized classes and the limited powers of teachers today, compared with the past and the attitudes of young people in today's society.

8. It is impossible to find anybody in this school under the present system.

9. With the present pastoral policy of no school rules, the relative lawlessness of the corridors and playgrounds is transferred to the classroom where rules of maths, neatness, class discipline, etc. are essential for any kind of learning and progress.

10. A tutor group of third-, fourth-, and fifth-year boys, for example, bearing in mind the different ages at which young people mature, and their different needs, etc., is a bad way of grouping boys for *pastoral* or academic progress, and yet it is part of the pastoral system.

11. Pastoral responsibility is a task of the school which should be disseminated to each individual teacher. It cannot be, unless individual teachers are in a realistic position to carry out their roles.

12. The house system creates complicated lines of communication between staff and staff, and staff and boys. A simpler communication system is obviously better than a complicated system, and yet we work or try to work a complicated system.

13. It is unrealistic to suppose that we can treat the individual as an individual in a school of this size and complexity. Much better is to approach the individual through the group (Social Psychology says that most individual problems are problems of relations within groups). Therefore, the way we group boys is very important. The house system requires us to group them in unsuitable ways, i.e., tutor groups.

14. "The major advantage of the comprehensive school is variety; the major difficulty is fragmentation" (Michael Marland).

Borecross School is already fragmented into north and south blocks (two separate schools?) and an administration block. With all the choice of courses in the fourth year onward, and all the groups which it involves, four houses, tutor groups and classes, it is difficult, I would say impossible, to feel any sense of school identity as a whole with the headmaster at the center. The present house system at Borecross increases the process of fragmentation.

15. House masters inevitably have different policies and attitudes as regards discipline, etc. This means that the boys in the same class, reported to different house masters, could receive different treatment. This is obviously wrong.

16. The present house system makes the administration of the school more difficult, as the headmaster has said. With the sheer volume of paper work and pressure

on a teacher's time, surely we should have the simplest method of administration possible. Surely, we should.

17. The most serious argument in favor of a house system is that it breaks up the "sink" forms for at least a part of the day and provides an alternative grouping. But is this not a problem of the streaming/banding system and therefore not relevant to this argument. Also, what price are we paying for this apparent benefit in view of all the other points that have been made against the house system?

18. The present house system puts too much work and responsibility on house masters.

19. It is easy for a boy under the present system to register and then truant from school. We have tried to get around that problem by getting subject teachers to check their registers every class. This creates additional work for teachers who have limited energies and it is obviously quite impossible to check up on absentees to each class with house masters, etc. There is too much work involved for little, if any, return.

20. The house system is a disorganizing influence in the school rather than an organizing one, which is what it ought to be.

21. Belonging to a subject department and a house involves conflicting loyalties and sometimes conflicting obligations for particular teachers. Under another system the two roles, pastoral and academic, could more easily be combined.

In my view, the analysis added up to an overwhelming case against the house system of this school. The common room must surely vote to have the entire system reviewed as a first step to changing the system. (end of appendix)

The political action of writing a letter to the authority was a rational, democratic approach to educational problems. It was sent with the appendix to the chief education officer of the City Education Authority with a copy to the head teacher. It was an open act of opposition to the policies and practices of the leadership. But, that is the situation that the authorities had created due to their own inactions, negative responsibility and failure of accountability.

It was now the turn of the authorities to respond. A day or so later, at break time, a crowd of teaching colleagues were gathered around a notice posted publicly in the teachers' room, reading the above letter, on one of the rare occasions that I saw excitement on the faces of teachers at that school. I myself could scarcely believe that the head teacher would act and play into his opponent's hands in this way, since it broke the secrecy surrounding the government of the school (Bok 1989a). It was a political tactic to inflict public humiliation on me, the writer. However, it backfired.

The letter, significantly, was removed within a short time and it was later admitted to me that a mistake had been made. However, since the contents had been made public, the political consequences of the act were irreversible, since all the teachers had been informed and compelled to take an attitude to the letter's ideas. It was a political mistake to publicize the letter since it was an attempt to destroy my position politically. However, the action paradoxically strengthened my moral and political position and authority since it rebounded and caused the head teacher to lose his reputation in front of his teaching staff, because, in my judgment, staff opinion secretly supported the contents of the letter and maintained silence out of irrational loyalty.

The act of publishing this letter was probably motivated by a "crisis of authority" since the opinions of a head teacher had been criticized. It was evidence that the school was an authoritarian organization in practice if not in theory. The point of view expressed in the letter was rational; hence it required a good answer and a political answer by the democratic method of talk. Since there was not a rational answer since the criticisms were justified, the response was an irrational anger. This kind of response came to be characteristic. An emotion is a moral and aesthetic response to a situation (Harré 1979, 202).

The head teacher's leadership role is political. What had happened is that his political role had been put to the test. His best alternative was to discuss the matter and try to resolve the conflict over the house system. Instead, he chose to suppress opposition in an authoritarian manner. As Ball (1987) writes, "The authoritarian head seems to have an almost pathological abhorrence of confrontation" (110).

The force of the letter was to bring matters out into the open in a democratic, public way (104). It was the method of adversarial politics by talk. That was not the way politics was being conducted in that school and here was further evidence of why the school was failing. The authorities were practicing the palace politics of secrecy and authoritarianism (109–119). If the letter of complaint had been irrational, then it could have been responded to by the force of a "better argument" or serious discussion could have taken place to make changes and improvements. It was an ideal moment for a Habermasian "ideal speech situation" to have been instituted and for theory and practice to be united.

The head teacher, in the presence of his two deputy head teachers, called me to his office a day or so later. He was angry and it would have been impossible to talk to him calmly since he had been politically defeated and had humiliated himself. He peremptorily went through each point I had made in the letter and gave a short answer. It was quite inadequate to the task, in my view. What was required was a serious written analysis equal to my own enquiries. Anything less was inadequate to the educational problems and standards of education. Since I thought he was too angry to discuss anything and believed he didn't have adequate answers, I corrected him on one factual error and said nothing more. I had won the argument. Silence had been the head teacher's response to the Creech dialogue in Chapter 1. I had better political skills than the head teacher and, in the circumstances, a strategic silence was the best way of managing the situation politically. There was no point in argument. Like the house system argument, there was no substantial argument on the other side. I came away from the meeting knowing that I had won with a better argument and had remained controlled under political attack.

The head teacher announced his retirement shortly after this meeting. It was a tacit admission of political defeat and confirms this analysis. He could have retrieved the situation by treating the opposition seriously, but he couldn't bring himself to attempt it. He wanted to leave and hand the responsibility to someone else.

The publication of the letter was a political blunder on his part as well as unethical because it resulted in his own political self-exposure. He didn't receive the support he perhaps expected from the common room. He had been cocooned from reality and when the reality was pointed out to him, he realized it. He was an honest and decent person whom I personally liked but he was out of his depth in a post-1960s comprehensive school. His appointment had been an error by the governors who were also out of their depth in all probability. Everyone was out of their depth but at least the opposition was trying to accept responsibility and change the situation for the better.

Ball's theory of the micro-political organization of schools makes this situation understandable (Ball 1987). The role of the head is political but he doesn't have total control to do what he likes. He has to perform. There are broadly four kinds of persons in schools: the officials, the activists, the attentives and the apathetics (Ball 1987, 21–23). The head is an official but also a leader and a politician. He cannot simply rely on his unquestioned authority to manage the organization, partly because politics is driven by talk. Politics cannot be reduced to formal meetings, formal talk and formal agendas. The formal melts into the informal and the interpersonal. Policy is decided in private conversations, in informal relations, in alliances and friendships which cut across formal arrangements. Formal arrangements cannot shut out the emotional tone of a school staff. There are vertical relationships in schools. There are also horizontal relationships. It is the micro-politics which determines the school. This head had failed at political leadership and so deserved the result that he had created (Ball 1987).

THE POLITICS OF COMMUNICATION

The political situation was temporarily resolved since the head teacher had retired and removed himself from the situation. However, to prevent any further unintended consequences, he should not have ignored the political situation that had developed. But he did by no action. I had no discussion with him. He managed the school by political inaction. The mistakes and secrecy continued. In addition, the situation was politically mismanaged by the City Education Authority. I received the following letter from Mr. Stephens, the assistant education officer:

May 2, 1976

Dear Mr. Armitage,

Further to the Education Officer's letter to you of March 25, I am now in a position to reply in detail to your letters of March 13 and 14.

I must make it clear at the outset that I have every confidence in Mr. Fellows as a headmaster and in his ability to lead Borecross School. There appears to be full democracy at the school since I understand that no request for a full meeting of the staff common room is ever refused, and no restriction is placed on topics which can be discussed. Obviously, here is the ideal medium through which any differing views which you may hold can be aired. Indeed, I am told that even before you raised your points about the house system the staff committee had set up a sub-committee to review the situation. I am sure you will agree on reflection that a headmaster who allows such a level of discussion cannot really be remote from the school.

Turning to the other points in your letter of March 13, it seems to me unnecessary to have a formal set of school rules, provided, of course, as in the case at Borecross, it is made very clear to pupils and all concerned that they are expected to behave reasonably and will be punished if they do not. While it is true that academic standards, as determined by examination results, may have fallen a little in 1975 from the peak of 1974, this is hardly surprising since the school has, in common with many others, been the victim of staff shortages and consequent part-time working.

Of course, the very size of a school such as Borecross could lead to problems in communication, but I think these are largely overcome in your school by the excellent "Instruction to Staff" booklet and the "Staff Week." I think it was perhaps unfortunate that it was not clear whether your letter dated March 13 (which on the headmaster's copy was dated March 10) had been posted or not. It was because some senior staff believed you had not posted the letter that they advised you against doing so. Because of the letter's implied criticism of other members of staff, I think the Headmaster was quite right to let the chairman of the common room have a copy. As is normal, a meeting of the common room was held following a request from 60 teachers.

During the course of that meeting, as you know, a motion was passed by the staff reaffirming its belief that the only acceptable method of bringing about changes is through discussion within the school. I am glad to learn that you supported this motion and am sure that in future you will use this democratic method to try to bring about any desired changes.

Yours sincerely,
A. D. Stephens
Assistant Education Officer

What does Mr. Stephens's letter mean? He was required to make an important judgment which he seemed to have done by supporting the head teacher as an authority figure regardless of the merits of the case. He simply closed ranks and failed to deal with the problems. This was a mistake, since the history behind the complaint was not confronted as it should have been. His analysis, such as it was, was inadequate. It is to his credit that he did make some sort of written reply. He said basically that the letter of complaint was unjustified. He had every confidence in the head teacher.

His letter was unbelievable, in my view, and did not stand up to critical analysis. The head retired or resigned following the complaint. Why? He didn't explain that fact. His expression of confidence had no basis in fact because the school had no written policy or philosophy. The head had adopted and maintained the house system against rational considerations and hadn't answered the criticisms of the complaint openly in writing so his reply could be analyzed.

Second, if there was "full democracy," Mr. Stephens ought to have invited me for a debate with him and preferably the chief education officer. Since he didn't and the education officer refused a discussion, it meant they weren't willing to discuss specifics and enter an argument which they could lose. That was the real test of democracy by discussion. Democracy is characterized by a relationship of equal access and equal participation in a public sphere. It depends upon "reciprocal ratification" of social relationships (Scheff 1990, 7). It has a foundation in the morality of relationships. Without such a test, they could not and did not fully investigate the facts and arguments of the case.

In addition, Mr. Stephens is factually incorrect to say that a committee was set up to review the house system *before* I raised the matter. On the contrary, it was set up *because* I raised the matter. Several independent witnesses to the subsequent tribunal confirmed this. Mr. Jim Shaw wrote, "What I can only call his moral courage has been very considerable. Many a time he has defended alone, or in a minority, an educational viewpoint in the common room. Indeed, he pioneered the issue of a year system—which we have now adopted—at a time when the house system seemed unalterably entrenched." Alan Brown wrote, "Mr. Armitage has been prominent in discussions on the development of the school. . . . Although he failed to convince the majority of his colleagues of the advantages of a year system over a house system when he first brought the matter up for discussion, and he found little support for his criticisms of consultative procedures, it is interesting to note that this academic year the school has changed to a year system, and has made major revisions in its consultative procedures." Mr. A. C. Humphries wrote, "he initiated, to my knowledge on two occasions, discussion of different pastoral systems amongst the staff."

Hence, Mr. Stephens hadn't grasped and had perhaps conveniently denied a crucial fact. If he had recognized the fact, his view of the case should have been different. It was in Mr. Stephens's interests to believe that I had not initiated and pursued the issue of the house system which was a test of the head teacher's (and the district inspector's) competence to make good decisions, since it enabled him in the name of the authority to ignore and misconstrue the situation that had developed. But, since Mr. Stephens had got this fact wrong, then his analysis of the situation was invalid. Hence, he did not manage the situation in a competent manner. He was therefore in part responsible for the situation as it subsequently developed. For, if he had made a different, practical analysis, he would have arrived at a different conclusion. He would have to have said the complaint was justified and the authority should take responsibility for the situation. He would then have needed to investigate the situation properly. This would have included a meeting with me. The reason why this situation had occurred was that a new system of education had been introduced without adequate preparation or planning. As David Hargreaves (1982), who became a City Education Authority's chief inspector, wrote, "The cavalier way in which comprehensive reorganization was hastily implemented" (208). This statement is significant because it carries the authority of a chief inspector and a leading researcher into the comprehensive school. Hence, it had validity and authority.

Mr. Stephens's analysis can be criticized in other respects. He wrote that "he was told" about the staff committee on the house system. However, he was not told correctly. He didn't know and he didn't check his sources. Hence, he was prepared to believe uncritically what it suited him to believe. As a result, he did not investigate the matter competently.

Why had the head teacher and the City Education Authority instituted such an unworkable system in the first place? No City Education Authority official defended the system when its flaws were pointed out to them. Where was their responsibility? Mr. Stephens, in the name of the chief education officer, had nothing to say about that.

The head teacher announced his retirement within a week of the letter. Given the circumstances and the close connection in time between the sending of the letter and the announcement of his retirement, it was only reasonable to believe that the two events were connected and there was no reason to believe that they were not. If they weren't, the head teacher would have delayed the announcement for several months and need not have retired in any case. The political consequence of the announcement was that there was no point in pursuing the matter further. The letter of complaint had been resolved. However, there was an air of secrecy surrounding the whole affair. It was simply covered up. The system had no interest in right and wrong, a situation predictable under systems theory.

Mr. Stephens thought an "Introduction to Staff" booklet covered communications. Whatever may be said about such a booklet in theory, it does not follow that people communicate in practice. I have shown with evidence that the amount of communication was quite inadequate. The evidence of this case history shows that in practice communication was extremely limited and then it was mostly conducted by the opposition rather than the authorities. In practice, unless there are two parties to a discussion, there is only restricted communication.

Mr. Stephens excused the head teacher's conduct in having the letter of complaint posted on the notice board by supporting him because of the letter's implied criticism of other members of staff. But, why did the head withdraw it and admit a mistake? Mr. Stephens did not explain the contradiction.

The school did not need any rules, according to Mr. Stephens, the assistant education officer of the City Education Authority, that is, provided the students behaved reasonably and were punished if they did not. This raises two questions. What are the arguments for saying basic rules were unnecessary? What is the logical connection between rules, reason and punishment, if any? Mr. Stephens supposes that there are no connections and that young people can follow reason without rules.

I argue that rules are importantly necessary in a school on rational grounds, with reference to educational theory with the observation that Mr. Stephens did not justify his statement.

R. S. Peters, in *Psychology and Ethical Development* (1974), argues that the empirical findings from psychology support the logical approach to the development of a rational morality. Man is a "rule-following," purposive animal. To learn in a human way is to learn rules of behavior and rules for performing tasks. His moral position is that of a rationalist. So if man is "rule-following," then what is the objection to rules?

How can children learn to adopt a rational morality? There is the empirical evidence derived from the child development studies of Piaget and Kohlberg of three main and six minor stages of moral development. They are "invariant" stages which all persons must pass through if they are to reach the higher stages and develop into rational beings. The main stages are, (1) egocentric, (2) rule-following, and (3) autonomy (Peters 1974, 367–375). Stage two of rule-following is divided into the good boy morality and the law and order stage. At this stage people learn the rules of their peer group and adult society by internalizing social rules. Progressive educators tend to ignore this stage in the name of freedom. But, Peters argues, if they do, they are ignoring the logic of child development. Hence, for Mr. Stephens to say that rules are unnecessary is probably wrong. On the contrary, 12- to 17-year-olds need rules if they are to control their wishes, wants, needs and passions and use reason in behavior. It is the job of a school to impart moral behavior and a main avenue is through rules.

Mr. Stephens also misses the logical connection between rules and reason, because at the egocentric stage of development children obey rules out of a fear of punishment. They have not learned to understand the reasoning behind rules. Rules are necessary to protect them from harming themselves or others, since if they break a rule of crossing the road without looking, they could be killed.

In an article, "What Is the Point of Rules?", Roger Straughan (1982) provides clarification. He argues the point of rules is not simply that they must be obeyed, but rules are a "bridging device" between a motive for action and a norm for action based on a logical reason. If there is a school rule for safety on the stairs, such as no running, it is because there is a reason. The reason is impersonal and applies to everyone. That is, if people observe the rule, it is easier to move around smoothly and safely (Straughan 1982, 66–68).

But, we can go further. Every teacher must impose rules in a classroom if there is to be order and learning. Learning is a skilled performance that entails following rules under the guidance of a teacher. So why should there be rules inside the classroom and not outside the classroom? That is illogical since teaching is a rule-governed activity.

Roger Straughan also argues that young people learn rules from a trusted adult and they gradually learn to see the point of the rule when they understand the reasoning behind it. It is through rules that they learn reasoning (67).

Professor Peters states, with good grounds, that "sensible children, who are capable of reasoning later on, emerge from homes in which there is a warm attitude of acceptance towards children, together with a firm and consistent insistence on rules without much in the way of punishment" (Peters 1974, 370). The research evidence supports this contention. Mr. Stephens assumes that people can reason without rules and also assumes that punishment is effective in changing behavior. But punishment, by its painful consequences, actually distracts the young person from paying attention for fear of punishment if he gets things wrong (370). Children have to be encouraged to explore the environment. Rules provide structure and form, not content. They need alot of experience to see the connection between rules, principles and cases to which the rule applies. Hence, I conclude that Mr. Stephens's point about rules was not based on logic or evidence. In a Habermasian discourse, he would probably have been obliged to change his mind.

As regards Mr. Stephens's last point about the subsequent meeting of the staff room to discuss my letter, the purpose of the motion put to the common room was to say that the common room was not associated with its contents. I adopted the tactic by supporting the motion because they were not. Hence, there was no argument and no opposition on the issue. The aim of the meeting was to defeat my position politically and it failed. Mr. Stephens seems to have selected a phrase from the hastily considered motion to suit his case. Besides, it was not up to the staff room to prescribe methods for bringing about change. This was a restrictive practice and unreasonable, especially given the history of the school since the amalgamation.

The meeting was called by members of staff opposed to my advocacy of a change to a year system, since it was a sacred Crosslinks institution. It was conducted in a highly emotional, irrational atmosphere and I faced a lynch mob. It was anything but a democratic forum of debate. The head teacher had tried to get the staff on his side and against me. The other implication is that Mr. Stephens is trying to order me to act to suit his authoritarian interests. There is nothing undemocratic about approaching the City Education Authority.

Mr. Stephens's letter did not address all the specific points that were made in the letter of complaint so he did not manage the situation competently. His contention that the decline in examination results was due to staff shortages is simplistic since other factors such as inadequate leadership, the lack of rules, and other factors which have been analyzed must have played a part. Hence, Mr. Stephens did not demonstrate an understanding of the situation.

The failure of Mr. Stephens to manage the situation politically had longterm consequences. One long-term consequence was that when the year system was finally instituted in 1979, the house teachers who became the year teachers appointed every teacher to the new system as a form teacher, except me. When I asked for discussion, discussion was denied.

I wrote to Dr. Alan Brownley, the education officer of the City Education Authority requesting a meeting to discuss the situation, and received the following reply:

May 28, 1976

Dear Mr. Armitage,

I have noted the contents of your letter received on May 11 in which you express dissatisfaction with the terms in which Mr. Stephens replied to your criticisms of your headmaster.

I would like to make it clear that the opinions which were expressed in those letters have my support and that our assessment of the school is based on evidence from a variety of sources. I understand that, since you wrote, you have had a long interview with your district inspector, and I hope that he has been able to satisfy you over many points which you have raised, so I shall not deal with them in any detail in my reply.

I would only say that it seems clear to me that you have had opportunities in the past, and now have further opportunities, to persuade your colleagues on the staff of the rightness of your own views on matters of school organization. If you are successful in doing so, I am sure that the headmaster would take due note of the feelings of the staff.

I note that there has been in the past discussion between the staff and the governors of the school on school aims, and it is of course open to members of the staff to make representations to the governing body, providing the headmaster is informed that they intend to do so, but, on considering those representations, the governors would naturally wish to know to what extent they have the support of the staff within the school.

Dear Mr. Armitage,

Thank you for your letter of June 14.

I regret that I cannot add to previous correspondence with you as I feel that the subjects you raise have already been adequately covered. Nothing will be gained by further discussion.

I think much could have been "gained by further discussion" with Dr. Brownley in order to communicate adequately on the Habermasian model. "Rationality presumes communication." I did not meet him or Mr. Stephens since they didn't consider it in their interests. I interpret their action as "power underpinned by distorted communication" and evidence of the lack of communication within the City Education Authority. Their interests were not served by communication whereas the interests of democratic participation were. I was not "satisfied" by a meeting with the district inspector since he refused to discuss matters he considered "unprofessional," which amounted to a blanket of secrecy. Hence, I did not have a "long" meeting with the district inspector. Second, Dr. Brownley is factually incorrect to say that a meeting to discuss mixed-ability teaching was a meeting about school aims. There had been no discussion about the aims of the school. The school had no aims. David Hargreaves wrote:

Our loss of focus on the whole picture was not entirely caused by the many social changes to which I have referred: a principal cause was the lack of any agreed set of aims or purposes for the new comprehensive school. For many teachers and most parents there has simply been no explicit and clear rationale for the comprehensive school. And when aims and purposes are clouded, we lose our way. (Hargreaves 1982, 78)

Hence, my position was supported by the City Education Authority's chief inspector.

THE POLITICAL SITUATION

I have dwelt on the responses of the authority by Mr. Stephens and Dr. Brownley at some length because of the intellectual vacuum at the heart of the new system and the characteristic of "muddle through with a stiff upper lip." Let us return to the analysis of the school situation and process. The official response to my critical letter was received on May 3, 1976, nearly two months after the letter of March 13. Dennis Moore, the district inspector of the City Education Authority, invited me to meet him to discuss the complaint in a political context. I repeated the substance of the case made in the original letter and in my view succeeded in persuading him of its justification. However, he walked out of the meeting without discussion when it seemed to me he was losing the argument and "robbed" my actions of any political or emotional meaning. As he said in evidence at the tribunal, he wouldn't discuss the real issues since it was "unprofessional."

On day 1, page 71, Dennis Moore says that "there was certainly no way in which I was going to discuss the merits of a headmaster with a junior member of staff. I would have regarded that as most unprofessional myself. I would not do it. Therefore, if you remember, we did not."

On day 1, page 70, I asked Mr. Moore, "Do you think you made certain assumptions when you came to that meeting about the propriety of my making a complaint against my headmaster." Mr. Moore replied:

1. I made certain assumptions about the way in which a complaint should be made.

2. I made certain assumptions about the relationship which a junior member of staff should have with his headmaster.

I also asked him, "Did you think I was a little upstart really, to put it very bluntly, stepping out of line?" Mr. Moore replied, "Presumptuous, I thought."

It was clear that rational argument and democratic debate were not the conditions of relationship between teachers of differing status from Dennis Moore's evidence. The implication of his remark about the relationship between a head teacher and a teacher was that it was a submissive relationship, that is, it was an authoritarian relationship and not democratic and morally reciprocal. This is why he couldn't handle the complaint against the headmaster. For him it was a moral matter. Juniors shouldn't complain against seniors.

It was unprofessional to discuss the organization of the school, discipline and school rules, democracy and school government and other professional issues, in Dennis Moore's view. He protected the head teacher and the authority from answering questions and the authority including himself from taking any action. This was where his professional duty and responsibility lay, since there are three criteria of professional. A profession relies on a body of knowledge and theory; second, a profession's first duty is to its clients and third a profession is entitled to make autonomous judgments and decisions (Carr 1986, 8). If these had been Dennis Moore's criteria of a profession, he would have entered into a full discussion of the issues facing the school and the new comprehensive system of education as a matter of professional obligation and pride. The meaningful conclusion to be drawn is that when tested in practice, the concept of professional had no meaning. It also meant that Moore regarded communication as unimportant, whereas I regard it as the system which makes the system work and function to integrate society.

The issue of professionalism could have been the subject of a Habermasian ideal speech situation. It is an "abstraction" like formal organization. The purpose of standards of professionalism is to improve the goals and quality of education in a practical way. Here is what happens when abstractions are misused:

But abstractions are also dangerous in policy, as in life. They become more important than the goals they are meant to facilitate. They replace rational examination of costs and benefits and the chance of success. They become weapons in arguments with rivals and opponents rather than guidelines for action that need to be constantly reexamined. (Jim Hoagland, *Washington Post*, December 4, 1997)

Dennis Moore positioned himself to avoid all communication and used his formal position to defend an educational matter which had been shown to be unjustified. I had positioned myself correctly because I was on the right side of the house and year system issue. Hence, Moore lost his authority in the face of a junior in the hierarchy. He could not justify his position. A political position is also a moral position. To position oneself incorrectly is to lose face. Moore never admitted his mistake and this entire narrative is driven by his positioning. He may have expected that I would simply forgive and forget, but if he did he failed to realize that I had interests to protect, I was an embodied person with emotions, and I did have some rights of participation. Or better still, I had communicative power and I was practicing a micro-political form of organization which was closer to reality than formal organization. The social theories that I introduce in this chapter explain the situation. Communication has an emotional component and establishes a relationship.

Dennis Moore also had a misconception of the nature of politics. True politics is not domination but freedom. As a free person, I had the right to proper consideration of the issues I had raised.

I conclude from this situation that we had come to a practical problem and cul-de-sac. How did we reach a situation of deadlock? I turn to theoretical understandings for answers. There was a problem of communication, of politics, of power and conflict and of the nature of organization and human relationships.

A THEORY OF THE HUMAN BOND

What we have witnessed in this school situation is a breakdown in practical communication between me and the authorities and between the micro and macro levels of the organization. The relationship between theory and practice in a critical education science is united so communication is essential to the theory and is partly why a practical approach to education produces the problem of the theory and practice gap. So I consider various theories of communication in order to understand the practical problem. I start with Scheff's micro-theory of "human nature and the social bond." Scheff's theory is a critical theory because he argues that the human bond in modern Western culture has been suppressed and is the cause of so much social breakdown. He argues that the most basic human motivation is the social bond. The human bond is a system of communication and a system of

emotional deference, shame and pride. What is at stake in all human interaction is a system of shame and pride. Each party in a communication evaluates at some level the state of the relationship and the amount of respect
accorded to it by each party. For the relationship to develop there needs to
be "reciprocal ratification" of the legitimacy of the interaction. The pride/
shame system underlies all human interaction. In any conversation there are
two levels of understanding: (1) the topic of conversation and (2) the implicit order of the relationship. Essential to the relationship are the social
bonds of pride and shame in which parties to the interaction measure the
state of the bond (Scheff 1990, chs.1 and 5).

Applied to the educational situation I have narrated, the human bond was
lacking because of the different statuses of the participants in the system.
The officials at the macro end of the continuum wouldn't enter a relationship with me at the micro level. They assumed a system's macro-perspective
of society. I assumed a micro- and macro-perspective and attempted to
communicate from the micro to the macro. However, in a system of domination this kind of relationship is disallowed.

But, if Sheff's theory is correct that the maintenance of the human bond
is essential to the social order, then the practices which destroy it are de-
structive and equally, the practices which enhance the social bond are important.

A THEORY OF DOMINATION AND RESISTANCE

The situation that had arisen had the character of a conflict between authoritarian domination and resistance. The process I have described was
modeling relationships of domination and submission, because if that was
the norm between myself and Dennis Moore, then it should also be the
relationship between the teacher and student in the classroom. But, I argue
this is where the educational process had become distorted and the problem
was to change the relationship between the political authorities and the
educator in the classroom. James C. Scott has theorized such relationships
under domination in *Domination and the Arts of Resistance* (1990). He
argued that in the political sphere there is the public transcript of authority
and the hidden transcript of subordination, which are connected. In this
chapter Mr. Stephens was the public authority and I was the subordinate
challenging authority. The public authority has to legitimize its power by
communication. But in relations of domination and control, the subordinates may not answer openly without retaliation. They therefore resort to a
hidden transcript out of the fear of authority. This transcript depends upon
a mutuality of relationship between subordinates but it is hidden from authority in the same way that authority disguises its hidden intentions and
any cause to question its legitimacy. The relationship between authority and
subordinate in a system of domination is that of the "frustration of recip-

rocal action." If someone questions the public transcript, this is a "charismatic act" and it provokes "political electricity." And this is the point: I was questioning authority openly and they conducted themselves by disguising the real situation and relationship. So although the system was supposed to be open and democratic, in the reality of practice it was not, and this in itself was a discovery. A small point of interest is that the teacher in Chapter 1 who was refused promotion in the new school resorted to the political disguise of "grumbling" and he in part motivated me to act openly, since grumbling is psychologically unhealthy and I consider my mental health important. The situation of domination and subordination creates false consciousness, because people disguise their real feelings even from themselves for fear they may act on them and challenge the authority of the status political quo (Scott 1990).

A THEORY OF COMMUNICATION AND NEGOTIATION

Habermas's theory of communication arose from a critical analysis of the psychoanalytical relationship between a patient and a therapist. The patient was emotionally sick and disabled because internal communication had broken down and was "distorted." The task of the therapist was to help the patient to relive and reconstruct the narrative of his or her life in order to understand blockages in communication which inhibited understanding, so the patient could grow beyond them and live a state of internal communication. From this Habermas argued that if there is a state of distorted communication, then there must be an ideal state of communication which could be theorized. This he did (McCarthy 1978, 193–213).

Habermas's theory of communication is part of a theory of society. He claims that communication is the foundation of a rational society because social interaction, not action as Parsons thought, is the basic unit of social analysis and the mechanism of social integration. If he is correct, then communication in educational situations is indispensable because rationality is an aim of education. His theory is based on the "reconstructive sciences."

Habermas's main organizing idea is communicative competence. To communicate competently means to succeed in communicating a statement in a manner acceptable to the receiver so that the communication is understood. It contains a propositional and a pragmatic element, that is, a statement and a manner of making a statement (Habermas 1979, 41–44).

The analysis begins with the pragmatics of a speech act. The four presuppositions which a speaker and the hearer presuppose when they understand each other are:

a. *Uttering* something understandably.
b. Giving [the hearer] *something* to understand.

c. Making *himself* thereby understandable; and

d. Coming to an understanding *with another person*. (2)

A competent speech act is rational and is aimed at achieving "understanding, mutual accord and consensus." However, if it were questioned as to its rationality and legitimacy, the presuppositions of comprehensibility, truth, truthfulness and rightness could be "redeemed" in a discussion (3).

The speech act has established three "relations to reality." Thus, a competent speech communication embodies three rules:

1. A rule to establish a relation to outer reality (so that the learner can share the knowledge of the speaker).

2. A rule to express his intentions in such a way that the linguistic expression represents what is intended "so that the learner can trust the speaker."

3. A rule to perform the speech act in such a way that it conforms to recognized norms or to accepted self-images (so that the hearer can be in accord with the speaker in shared value orientations). (29)

The three "relations to reality" are *connected* to the validity presuppositions of speech; that is, "truth" to outer reality, "truthfulness" to interactive reality, and "rightness" to inner reality and the "norms of self-images" between people.

What is an act of speech—as speech act? When a person says something such as "everyone sit down" he both makes a statement about a reality in the objective world and performs an action on his own behalf which he wants to see enacted. The second component of performing an action is implicit rather than explicit. John Austin (Habermas 1979) called this second component the "illocutionary force" of a speech act, since it was not spoken (34). Its function is "communicative." The power of illocutionary force is to "generate" a relationship within an utterance. There is an element of risk in a speech act since the hearers can accept or reject the request on offer. Thus, an important element in a speech act is its "acceptability." Will the relationship implied be taken up?

Speech act analysis is concerned with explicit speech acts. The standard case of a speech act is that it has two components: a propositional component and an illocutionary component (Habermas 1979, 36). The propositional component has the representative function of relating to the objective world and is composed of constative grammatical forms. The illocutionary component is the interactive component concerned with establishing normative relations. The expressive component is implicit and is expressed in representative grammatical forms.

Searle's principle of expressibility states that any utterance can be analyzed from its simple form to extended, complex form which will yield all the implicit components of that utterance including its hidden expressive content (Habermas 1979, 34–41).

What are the implications of the characteristic "double structure" of speech which is a feature of language? (41). First, the propositional structure can be fixed while the illocutionary force can be varied according to the wishes of the speaker. That is, the illocutionary component can be uncoupled from the propositional component. This implies that when two speakers engage in conversation, they always communicate on two levels at the same time, the propositional level of content and the intersubjective level of the relationship. It further means that speech acts always have a self-referential component; they are the speech act of a particular person in a particular context. There is an objective level of making statements and a subjective level of performance and "it is not possible simultaneously to perform and to objectify an illocutionary act." Language is inherently "reflective" that is chosen by the speaker. Therefore, Habermas (1979) concluded that speech act theory must incorporate a rational understanding of this double structure of speech (41–44).

Habermas concluded that the universal-pragmatic meaning consists of two components, since the two meanings can be separated into a representational, propositional meaning and an invitation to take up a relationship which gives meaning to the utterance on the communicative, intersubjective level (44).

A propositional speech act has cognitive content. The act of cognition claimed in a speech act is implicitly a claim to truth and therefore a propositional claim is tied to the validity basis of speech as previously outlined. Similarly, an illocutionary act makes a claim to rightness or appropriateness which is also a validity basis of a speech act (50).

What are the conditions of understanding and acceptability? Searle (Habermas 1979) has argued that a speaker must seriously mean what he says when he makes a speech act, that he must be seriously "engaged" in offering an interpersonal relationship. The rational foundation of illocutionary force finally comes down to the correlation between the rules of speech acts and the underlying validity claims which support them. A validity claim is a claim which is rationally justifiable, since human beings, by virtue of their linguistic ability, are responsible and have access to truth and thus can and do act rationally (59–68).

Habermas (1979) summarizes his conclusions on the rational foundations of illocutionary force as follows:

a. A speech act succeeds, that is, it brings about the interpersonal relation that S intends with it, if it is comprehensible and acceptable, and accepted by the hearer.

b. The acceptability of a speech act depends upon (among other things) the fulfillment of two pragmatic presuppositions: the existence of speech-act-typical restricted contexts (preparatory rule); and a recognizable engagement of the speaker to enter into certain speech-act-typical obligations (essential rule, sincerity rule).

c. The illocutionary force of a speech act consists in its capacity to move a hearer to act under the premise that the engagement signaled by the speaker is seriously meant: in the case of institutionally bound speech acts, the speaker can borrow this force from the binding force of existing norms; in the case of institutionally unbound speech acts, the speaker can induce this force by the recognition of validity claims.

d. Speaker and hearer can reciprocally motivate one another to recognize validity claims because the content of the speaker's engagement is determined by a specific reference to a thematically stressed validity claim, whereby the speaker, in a cognitively testable way, assumes with a truth claim to provide grounds, with a rightness claim, obligations to provide justification, and with a truthfulness claim, obligations to prove trustworthy. (65)

Habermas's theory demonstrates the importance of not only the content of what is said but *how* or the manner in which it is said in practice. The term "pragmatic" means "dealing with matters in the way that seems best under the actual conditions, rather than following a general principle; practical." The illocutionary force of an utterance determines the nature of the relationship taken up with another person. It is the practical aspect of his theory which shows the difficulty and need for communication in education, not only between teacher and student but teacher and teacher.

The Logic of Theoretical Discourse: Truth (McCarthy 1978, 291)

A speech act ("using a linguistic utterance in a linguistic context") raises a validity claim where the purpose is interpersonal understanding. The participants discuss and examine the truth of the claim. Participants are obliged in the situation to submit themselves to the "unforced force of the better argument" (292) in the interests of a "rational consensus" (292) since rationality is the binding force of all speech acts. They subject themselves to "the conditioned for the unconditioned" (292) since all who enter a dialogue are obliged by the rules of speech acts to speak rationally.

The Process of Argument: Levels of Discussion and Reflection (McCarthy 1978, 305–306)

There must be adequate discussion in order to achieve a grounded, rationally motivated consensus, characterizable by the formal logical properties of an argument. Rational presuppositions made in an argumentative discourse consist of levels of argumentative discourse, which follows from discussing a validity claim. The following table summarizes this discussion process.

	Theoretical Discourse
Conclusions	statements
Controversial validity claim	truth
Demanded from opponent	explanations
Data	causes (of events); motives (of behavior)
Warrant	empirical uniformities, hypothetical laws, and so on
Backing	observations, results of surveys, factual accounts, and so on (Held 1980, 342)

What are the "conditions" in which this process can happen? Habermas argues that participants must "radicalize" the argument to deeper levels of reflection. The following table summarizes this process.

Steps in Radicalization	*Theoretical Discourse*
Acts	statements
Grounding	theoretical explanations
Substantive	metatheoretical
Language-criticism	transformation of language and conceptual systems
Self-reflection	critique of knowledge (Held 1980, 343)

"Constraint" or fear of communication must be absent in the argument for there to be a rationally motivated consensus, so then it can proceed from one level to the next. A precondition of the "pragmatic of communication" is that everyone must be able to enter the argument. This is a "general symmetry requirement." The truth of statements is "linked" in the end "to the intention of the good and true life" (McCarthy 1978, 306).

The "ideal speech situation" presupposes that "truth belongs categorically to the world of thoughts and not to that of perceptions." Consequently, it is an appeal to participants in discourse to be guided by the "force of the better argument" (310).

On the Logic of Practical Discourse—Morality (McCarthy 1978, 310–333)

What are the presuppositions of the "pragmatic logic" of an ideal, practical discourse? First, Habermas argued that a rationally motivated consensus is possible by means of the "unforced force of the better argument" in an "expanded conception of rationality" which is an expression of a "rational will," a rational understanding and rationally motivated. The validity claims raised as discussion points arise in a practical discourse, from the regulative, interactive use of language (commanding, ordering, refusing, prescribing, permitting, recommending, advising, warning, appraising, evaluating) which in pragmatic speech acts are validity claims of rightness and appropriateness and occur in relation to the social world of norms and values, needs and interests. They take place in a different "region of reality"—the social realm. The structure and conditions of practical discourse have a logic of morality. The moral statements of participants become the subject of discussion and criticism in a logic of morality, which rightness/appropriateness claims raise inherently.

The following table shows an analysis of a practical discourse.

	Practical Discourse
Conclusions	precepts/evaluations
Controversial validity claim	correctness/propriety
Demanded from opponent	justifications
Data	grounds
Warrant	behavioral/evaluative norms or principles
Backing	interpretation of needs (values), inferences, secondary implications, etc. (Held 1980, 342)

Steps in Radicalization

The radicalization of the argument for practical discourse proceeds from regulative speech acts to their grounding in theoretical justifications. The second step is "substantive language-criticism" which takes the form of meta-ethical and metapolitical discourse leading finally to a practical "rational critical will" appropriate to the pragmatic context of speech acts. The following table summarizes this process.

Steps in Radicalization	*Practical Discourse*
Acts	commands/prohibitions
Grounding	theoretical justifications

Substantive language	meta-ethical /metapolitical
Criticism	transformation of language, conceptual systems
Self-reflection	formation of rational, critical will (Held 1980, 343)

The most controversial and therefore the most difficult problem of a practical discourse is the problem of consensus concerning social norms and social values, social needs and social interests.

The aim of practical discourse is to come to a rationally motivated agreement about problematic rightness claims, an agreement that is not the product of internal or external constraint on discussion but solely of the weight of evidence and argument (McCarthy 1978, 312).

Social norms are criticizable and therefore in practical discourse their existence is threatened and they are put into a state of suspension. Irrationally motivated norms are the subject of public debate and discussion. Hence, the practical psychological difficulties are formidable. These include such things as discussion, competition, fear of losing face, fear of conflict, fear of internal change, anger and frustration. Habermas argued, however, that individual needs can be rationalized and that generalizable needs are possible when "inner nature" is linked to interaction in language. Language acts as a "transformer" which converts inner subjective wishes through a process of language rationalization into needs which can be communicated and can be shared. The social universe is "intersubjective," not a relationship of isolated subjectivities (315).

The two forms of discourse, theoretical and practical, come together at the fundamental level of self-reflection, since what is required is a critique of knowledge in which norms and values, needs and interests are evaluated in connection with the present state of our "knowledge and power." Rational people can reach a consensus within the structure and conditions of theoretical and practical discourse subject to the conditions of argumentation, even though it is difficult.

THEORIZING THE EMOTIONS

Habermas's analysis of communication aimed at overcoming distorted communication in a system of instrumental rationality rather than reason. There was no place for emotion in the theory. Recent critical research has advocated a "linguistically sensitive account of emotion" and has demonstrated that the emotions can be incorporated into Habermas's theory of speech acts, since the three validity claims have an emotional dimension; that is, the "facts of a situation" warrant the emotion expressed. The agent who expresses the emotion really is sincere. The moral-social relation to the situation warrants the reaction. This an important addition to Habermas's theory (Crossley 1998, 20).

I shall briefly outline a critical view of the emotions as outside the scope of sociological understanding, because a narrative view of understanding (which is a concern of this study) cannot avoid the existence of emotions in social relationships. I owe this brief critical analysis to articles by Simon J. Williams and Gillian Bendelow, Arlie Russell Hochschild, Nick Crossley and Margot Lyon, contained in *Emotions in Social Life* (Bendelow and Williams 1998).

Emotions have had an "ethereal existence" in sociology because Western rationality has excluded them as unobjective forms of knowing and they have been feminized by a masculine philosophy and historical culture (xv). Emotions are "social things." They are responses to situations (19). They are embodied and come "from" a body rather than being about a body. An emotion like anger or envy has a language to describe it. Emotions are distinct from sensation because the known world can only be expressed in language which includes the language of emotion. Emotion in existentialist thought, which is critical of rationalist thought, regards emotions as "intentional," "purposeful" and "meaningful." They are part of culture and have a "socio-relational" aspect. Emotions are "engaged," "deeply social" and "relational." They can be "managed." Emotions connect with social agency.

People are connected to each other and persons interact as bodies, not merely intellects. The body is part of social analysis as the "means by which we experience and actively apprehend the world." When someone is bodily angry, that anger can be subject to an account. Therefore, without a concept of emotion, cultural analysis is insufficient. The emotional realm is a "public realm." Emotions are positioned in a social world and expressed in a context. They unfold through time. Emotions are communicated in communication. They can be things we put a value on. Once emotions are accepted into sociology, the divisions between the private and the public, the micro and the macro, break down. The social structure itself is both "medium and outcome" of "Emotionally Embodied Practices" (xviii). They are part of the "expanded understanding of the place of the body in society." The emotions make for an intimate relation between the self and culture. Embodied agency is "institution-making." An emotion is "sensuous conduct." The "style" of a person constitutes the emotional aspect. Context is crucial to emotion.

The arts such as music and literature are concerned with the development of feeling and emotion. They thrive in informality for the emotions are the most active part of a human being. To leave out the emotions in education, as formal education tends to, is a basic mistake. An emotion is complex; having an emotion involves selection, a situation and judgments of value. They are embodied and engaged. An emotion can be an object of sensitive study, which is why it can be developed. Music and literature are capable of enhancing emotional freedom by introducing new and fresh emotions and extending the range and scope of emotional experience. Literature is an agent of emotional freedom. A particular emotion has a future. The scientific attitude encourages a withholding of emotion. To study and understand the emotions of others is to enter a field of "emotional possibilities." Emotion is also important to morality since feelings are balanced with principles which can be rigid. The arts have to be appropriated intelligently if they are to be educative since feelings can become stereotyped and repetitive. It is important to keep the importance of the emotions in mind in relation to scientific forms of organization which ignore them as unimportant (Hepburn 1972, 484–500; Peters 1972, 466–483; Dunlop 1984).

A THEORY OF INTERNAL COMMUNICATION

I regard "social theory as practice" (Taylor 1985, 91–115). I regard the theory I explain below as a critical theory of human relationships. Habermas's theory of communication can be improved by an understanding of the nature of human relationships at the emotional level. Critical social theory is also concerned with a "critical confrontation" with other theories (Calhoun 1995, 36). The theory is important for my claim that political relationships are essential for educational development and for the perspective it puts on relationships in situation.

Rogers (1961) views relationships from a psychotherapeutic perspective. He regards the whole task of psychotherapy as a "failure of communication" (330). In an "emotionally maladjusted person," self-communication has broken down. As a result, communication with others has also broken down. Rogers claims that the nature of human relationships, though he worked out his theory in a psychotherapeutic situation, are applicable to all human relationships including parents, teachers and administrators in organizations (37). I agree with his claim and it is important to my thesis that political relationships are not a different kind of relationship with different rules.

Rogers criticizes an approach to human relationship "through the intellect" as a "failure" (33). He regards the acceptance of another on the emotional level as important and that means the acceptance of another's feelings. He regards experience as the "highest authority." He finds "order in experience." Internal life is a process of flow and change (27).

Rogers regards a helping relationship as one of trust and dependability which starts from being helpful to oneself, communicating the true self, expressing a positive attitude to others, being separate from the other, permitting the other his or her separateness, and entering the others' feelings and personal meanings in order to understand the other as a process of becoming (50–55).

In the process of becoming there are three tasks. Task one involves getting behind the mask (108). Task two is willingness to experience feelings (111). Task three is the discovery of the self in experience (113). The person who "emerges" from these tasks is open to experience, has trust in his or her own body and evaluates situations from an internal locus and is willing to be a process (115–123).

Rogers delineates eight stages in the process of becoming a person. Stage one is the experience of fixity and remoteness from experience and an unwillingness to communicate the self (132). At stage two there is a "slight loosening and flowing of symbolic expression" (133). In stage three there is a freer flowing of expression (133). In stage four, this process is continued more freely (137). At stage five, feelings are more fully experienced, there is knowledge that a feeling has an object to which it is attached, there is a willingness to own "feelings" and wanting to be, there is less remoteness, a tendency to identify feelings exactly and to face contradictions in experience (139). In the sixth stage the "self as an object disappears" (147). In the seventh, the "self becomes increasingly the subjective and reflexive awareness of experiencing" (151). To sum up, Rogers describes a process of change, of educational change at the emotional level.

The process of self-development at the emotional level is characterized by Rogers as a movement "away from facades," "away from oughts," "away from meeting expectations," "away from pleasing others," "toward self-direction," toward being process and being complexity, toward openness to experience, acceptance of others and trust of self (167–173).

I claim that Rogers's view of interpersonal relationships, feelings and communication provides an important perspective on an educational aim and of all relationships in educational institutions. His theory is of growth and creativity.

A THEORY OF SCHOOL ORGANIZATION

How are schools actually organized for communication between persons as participants? There are two contending models of theoretical understanding that is the formal scientific, bureaucratic and a new contrastive model, the informal and micro-political. Social and political practices depend on which theory has influenced the "self-understandng" of the individual. If two individuals each have conflicting theories then their practice is necessarily in conflict. I have in mind the basic point that:

Whatever picture of social life the scientists present is the outcome of selective observation and interpretation, because his theory determines not only how the "data" are explained but also what are to count as data in the first place. (Ball 1987, 26)

It is impossible to move from the senses to theory. Any theory selects a perspective and it is important to understand what it is, otherwise it becomes dominant and ideological in culture and society.

What is the design of formal, scientific, positivist organization? This is an important question because knowledge takes the shape of a design and to understand knowledge in a connected way, it is necessary to understand the complete design. The rational purpose of scientific organization is to organize the members to pursue the goals and objectives of the organization. It is structured to pursue these goals by hierarchy and specialization. A useful working model is a car assembly factory or a government bureaucracy. A theory can be explained and evaluated by the theory's underlying assumptions.

The design of an organization is a "structure adapted to a purpose" (Perkins 1986). The purpose of a scientific organization is to organize its members for a specific purpose or purposes in the best way. The following provides a good summary of the structure of scientific organization:

1. Organizational tasks are distributed among the various positions as official duties. Implied is a clear-cut division of labor among positions which makes possible a high degree of specialization. Specialization in turn promotes expertness among the personnel by narrowing the range of duties of jobs and by enabling the organization to hire employees on the basis of their technical qualifications.

2. The positions or offices are organized into a hierarchical authority structure. In the usual case, this hierarchy takes on the shape of a pyramid wherein each official is responsible to the superior above him in the pyramid for his subordinates' decisions and actions as well as his own, and wherein each official has authority over the officials under him. The scope of authority of supervisors over subordinates is clearly circumscribed.

3. A formally established system of rules and regulations governs official decisions and actions. The regulations ensure the uniformity of operations and, together with the authority structure, make possible the coordination of various activities.

4. There is a specialized administrative staff.

5. Officials are expected to assume an impersonal orientation in their contacts with clients and with other officials.

6. Employment by the organization constitutes a career for officials. (Blau 1974, 30)

Scientific organization is characterized by specialization, hierarchical authority, rules, specialized administration, impersonality and career structure.

In *The Micro-Politics of the School* (1987), Stephen J. Ball has critically analyzed the formal scientific method of organization and undermined its presuppositions. He is a critical theorist of organization.

Ball has conceptualized an alternative. He considers the position of actors in defining their own situation in relation to others from a micro-perspective and the reality of persons rather than from the abstract, disembodied top-down approach. This is an empirical and data-led approach (Ball 1987, 7) which relies on teachers' knowledge (2–6).

The micro-political theory takes account of informal as well as formal organization and constitutes a more adequate framework for understanding a school, Ball claims, because schools are "places organized around talk" (237).

Conflict is recognized as normal in the micro-political model, in contrast with the organizational model's tendency to pathologize conflict, since groups and individuals have differing interests. These interests are communicated in a political process which takes place in staff meetings, committees and "behind-the-scenes" individual negotiation. Organizational science's view is a "fiction." Schools are organized on the basis of "loose-coupling."

Society is based on conflict rather than consensus (18). Organizations grow through conflict and it is essential to their health because it can "revitalize an otherwise stagnant system." The functionalist system's model of organizations excludes an understanding of change and conflict (17–26). So it has failed to provide a model for school organization.

Ball theorizes the informal aspects of the life of organizations, because schools are not formal organizations but are characterized by informal, micro-political processes. The micro-political model is based on the way teachers experience schools as a lived reality and the way and manner in which interpersonal relations interact with the "constraints" of the organizational. It is concerned with the "shaping" of relationships on the work site.

Organizational science has been prescriptive rather than descriptive and explanatory and theory-led rather than data-led, and therefore has failed to offer a "sensible" analysis of schools as organizations. Teachers' knowledge of organizations is necessary in order to understand how schools change and how they are limited by organizational constraints. Scientific organizational theory became ideologies in practice reflecting the interests of administrators who could exert political control. The organizational-management type of theory has become the one way to run a school, which is why schools are oppressive and undemocratic.

As a result of this acceptance a whole variety of non-compatible concepts are set aside and condemned. Such theories marginalize empirical studies of school practice and dismiss the "folk-knowledge" of teachers as irrelevant. (Ball 1987, 2–6)

Schools are "arenas of ideological dispute" because of the "peculiar content of policy-making and decision-making" there (13). They are "anarchic" organizations (12). Educational concepts are concerned with philosophical issues such as justice, freedom, knowledge, rationality, understanding and human nature, which can't be ignored since they affect attitudes and practices. Educational ideas and decisions are "value-laden" (Peters 1966). They are problematic.

There are differences in emphasis between the micro-political and the "orthodox" approach. However, the micro-political set of concepts are "antithetical" to the top-down systems approach. They "take account of the conflict in preference orderings, objectives, interests and ideologies among organizational participants which result in contest or struggle for the control of the organization" (18). Their differences are contrasted in the following chart (8).

Micro-Political Perspective	*Organizational Science*
(explicit adherence)	(explicit or implicit adherence)
Power	Authority
Goal diversity	Goal coherence
Ideological disputation	Ideological neutrality
Conflict	Consensus
Interests	Motivation
Political activity	Decision-making
Control	Consent

Organizational theory has suffered from inadequate "conceptual development." The micro-political model recognizes the reality of "ideological disputation" since political change gives rise to ideological "disputation" as change affects the interests of groups, benefiting some and harming others. For example, the question of mixed-ability teaching is deeply ideological since the proponents of mixed-ability adopt an "idealist perspective" and the opponents adopt an "academic perspective." The middle ground is taken by the "disciplinarians" (35). Organizational science's concept of ideological neutrality is a fiction. Educators are ideologically committed by the very nature of their work and their situation.

The role of the head is a political one in the micro-political theory of organizations. The content of education is ideas and issues. The head is the formal leader and "licensed authority" with legal backing. He is the "critical reality definer" and the "focus" of micro-politics. His performance is watched closely by teachers. He has to be street-wise and put on a performance (80–120), because although the head has the advantaged position as a leader, "circumstances can be great equalizers" and his positions are open to challenge and opposition (85). Hence, it is necessary to understand the politics of leadership.

The head's political performance is a "style." S/he communicates beliefs and values to the school as a performer. S/he is "preeminently" a leader and has a political task. Schools as organizations are not "abstract, formal bureaucracies" but "arenas of ideological dispute" dependent on leadership.

Therefore, talk is of central importance since power emerges from the struggle to persuade people to adopt the policy of the school and make it effective in practice. Head teachers are "strategic performers" with the intention of controlling and dominating the organization under the present system in Britain, in which a head is given the powers of a despot.

Ball has adopted a specific concept of power. It does "not involve reference to position or capacity as such but to performance, achievement and struggle" (25). Power is taken to be an "outcome." The head has to realize headship by acting with others cooperatively. It is inevitable that there will be opposition; such is the nature of education. But his job is to work with conflict and opposition and work out a practical compromise.

The micro-politics of the school is "focused" on the politics of the head's leadership position since he has "licensed authority" and "his school is the expression of his authority" (King 1968, 88). "The role of the head is central and critical to any understanding of the micro-politics of the school" (Ball 1987, 80–83).

The four leadership styles below are "forms of resolution of the basic political dilemma facing a head teacher." The head's political task is centered around the concepts of control and opposition. He has to maintain control of the organization and integrate its activities through the commitments of the teachers. The styles of a head are different means to the same ends which is the maintenance of political stability. The authoritarian approach is "static and conservative," while the adversarial approach is "dynamic and radical." The styles of a head consist of three ideal types (interpersonal, managerial and political), while the political is divided into two types (adversarial and authoritarian) (87).

The political process is recognized as "a major element of school life" in the case of the political style. But, this "recognition" can either be accepted or rejected. In the case of the adversarial style it is openly accepted and is legitimate, but in the authoritarian style it is "illegitimate" and "remains covert" (87–119).

The head who rejects his political role has opened himself to challenge and defeat for he falls back on his formal authority and hopes that no one will question it. He is like the teacher in the classroom who will not allow a student to question his authority or judgment. The concept of "positioning" is relevant to social systems. Social systems have some characteristics which are "position-practice relations." That means that formal relations in reality can never take precedence over informal relations of interaction involving the identity of persons in face-to-face relations. Positioning is context sensitive. This is important because it shows that real social relationships cannot be bypassed.

The following analysis (Ball 1987, 124) shows the "forms of participation and types of talk in school decision-taking":

	Forms of Participation	Response to Opposition	Strategies of Control
Authoritarian	Prevents public access to voice.	Stifles.	Insulation, concealment, secrecy.
Managerial	Formal committees, meetings and working parties.	Channel and delay.	Structuring, planning, control of agendas, time and context.
Interpersonal	Informal chats and personal consultation and lobbying.	Fragment and compromise.	Private performance of persuasion.
Adversarial	Public meetings and open debate.	Confront.	Public performance of persuasion.

The authoritarian mode is committed to the status quo. It adopts "selective recruitment" to defend itself and "acquiescence is a major quality sought in candidates" for promotion. It is bureaucratic, dominative, dehumanizing, alienative and anti-political.

The mirco-political is the appropriate model for schools during changing times but what is happening in British schools is the organizational model is increasingly being adopted. As a result the role of the head is invested with "acute political discrepancies." Ball argued:

Headship is, on the one hand, the focus of "innovations" like management practice and management teams, related to which is the increased divergence of "them and us" type relationships exposed by cuts in educational funding and changes in teachers' conditions of work. The management-line relationship is at heart disciplinary and punitive. On the other hand, heads find themselves confronted by pressures for high-speed organizational and curricular change, which demands high levels of creativity and personal initiative, and it is highly questionable whether traditional, hierarchical management relationships are best suited to respond to such pressures. Indeed work by Corwin indicates that such circumstances call "for a diffuse decision-taking structure with corresponding autonomy for individuals and groups" (Ball 1987, 226); activities need to be relatively unstructured and power decentralized. All the indications are that organizationally schools are moving in the opposite direction. (Ball 1987, 165)

Another problem for schools is the mutual adjustment between the organization and the individual:

1. There is a lack of congruency between the needs of healthy individuals and the demands of formal organization . . .

2. The results of this disturbance are frustration, failure, short time-perspective, and conflict . . .

3. The nature of the formal principles cause the subordinate . . . to experience competition, rivalry, insubordinate hostility and to develop a focus toward the parts rather than the whole. (Corwin, quoted in Ball 1987, 189–190)

The micro-political concept of opposition arises from "contending definitions of the situation which compete for the attention and the acceptance of the populace" (Ball 1987, 144). Opposition is visible and an attempt to "change things, to challenge formal power, to overturn the status quo, to subvert the accepted channels of decision-taking" (134). It is not "simply a matter of personal disaffection and disgruntlement but can be a commitment to challenge and attempt to change policies, in whole or part, of the dominant coalition" (148).

There are three "scenarios" of opposition based on the leadership style of the head. When the head maintains the status quo, opposition will be "progressive." When the head is a gradualist, the opposition will be indulgent. When the head is innovative, the opposition will be "defensive" (144–146).

Schools confront a conflict between two antithetical modes of organization, the scientific and the micro-political. The former, the formal model, results in the domination of communication and the lifeworld of the individual; the latter takes account of the possible growth and emancipation of teachers and is a benign form of organization.

The micro-politics of the school arises from the consideration that conflict is the basis of school life. Also, the position of the head is basically concerned with domination. It is with the interaction between conflict and domination that the micro-politics of the school is concerned (278).

Ball's study communicates contradictory messages. In the one case, micro-political processes prevent and inhibit change. In the other, the micro-political process demonstrates the amount of uncertainty and potentiality for change which exists.

Ball's understanding of micro-political organization gives a critical view of organizational science and its practices. This is why it is emancipatory. It shows how domination works over the heads of actors and how it can be neutralized. His analysis is an example of the usefulness of a critical theory about practices.

THEORIES AND A CONCRETE EVALUATION SITUATION

The events of the amalgamation caused me to intervene to change the situation. I had tried to change the house system by democratic, political means and this resulted in a political struggle between differing interests. I wrote a confidential letter of complaint to change the situation. The head teacher made the letter public knowledge, couldn't answer the criticisms and retired and thus avoided responsibility. Mr. Stephens rejected the criticisms I had written and either answered them inadequately or didn't address the problems at all. Significantly, I never met him personally and his office was ten or so miles away. I didn't meet or have a discussion with Dr. Brownley. Dennis Moore refused all discussion as "unprofessional." Thus, the events of the amalgamation signified an absence of real authority and responsibility. There seemed to be nobody taking responsibility from a position of leadership for political leadership is conducted by talk and discussion. What I have diagnosed was a political and educational vacuum at the heart of the school.

I examined theoretical claims and understandings to critically explain this situation, including a theory of the human bond, resistance to domination, communication, communication and the emotions, internal communication and relationship and school organization, to support my argument that educational institutions need to take a critical attitude to human relationships and to understand the poor performance of the school process. All the theories have in common the importance of communication in human relationships. The human bond is basic because it is what all humans care about and if it is broken problems arise which hinder and prevent education. The episodes of the case history demonstrated that the bond between educators and the authorities was based on formality, domination and resistance, and that is a grave impediment to the educational process since if people can't communicate how can they educate, a proposition supported by philosophical analysis.

The most important point about the nature of a critical education science is that it is critical and criticism is a form of knowledge. The officials in this study had an uncritical attitude to school rules and professionalism, according to the evidence, and hence were working in a practical paradigm of education in which there is a gap between theory and practice, a gap which is closed by a critical praxis in situation.

The norms of a formal scientific, bureaucratic organization explain Dennis Moore's attitude to professionalism and politics (Ball 1987, 8). In a hierarchic organization, members of the hierarchy support each other and impose their power by authority. They are not required to communicate or justify their actions or policies. I operated under the micro-political model in which the use of power and political activity is legitimate.

The distinction between the formal (professional) and the informal (interpersonal) is not a rigid distinction (246). It breaks down. I met Dennis Moore as an official but also as a person. The head teacher was both an official and a person. Moore stated at the subsequent tribunal of enquiry that I would have been a good teacher if I had gone back to the classroom and not interested myself in anything beyond that, and had left administration and decision-taking to the administrators. That is, he advised a politics of non-participation and irresponsibility. He also criticized my actions in adopting an adversarial style of politics. This meant that he considered opposition as against the rules, which also meant that the system was based on people asking no questions. So problems could not be addressed.

This chapter has demonstrated the political failure of the formal bureaucratic organization, which is a failure of political awareness. Schools are not simply formal organizations. Officials are political leaders in the interests of education. Political activity was not the accepted method in a formal organization; hence all of the official participants did not act politically, which would have necessitated discussion with relevant parties and the attempt to work a negotiated solution. As individuals, Brian Fellows, Dennis Moore, Mr. Stephens and Alan Brownley were bound by bureaucratic rules which rendered them powerless to act. They were all confined to a structure. But, micro-politics is concerned with interaction and change.

The case history has a part/whole perspective. Thomas J. Scheff's concept of part/whole ladder illuminates. Scheff argues that both micro- and macro-analysis are necessary to understand human affairs. To this must be added practice. "Analysis and interpretation are part of human intelligence, but they are incomplete without the trial of performance, of practice in the complex world of everyday life." He continues, "intelligence at its most effective involves part/whole relationships. In an open system, any part implies a larger whole, which is in turn part of a still larger whole, up the ladder" (Scheff 1990, 189–195). Applied to discourse, this idea suggests a movement back and forth between small concrete parts and ever-larger abstract wholes. Dr. Brownley was at the top of the ladder and the author was in the middle. He had the opportunity for "dialogical rationality" and for "reciprocity" which he declined. He thought the discussion had been "covered." I thought there hadn't been any discussion since I didn't meet him. Hence, there was no ladder in reality. He had pulled it away so that authoritarian domination was the norm. This was why the system could not be more effective. The system was disembodied and emotions were outlawed. The authorities had the power, but failed in the Habermasian performance and practice. The failure was political practice.

Chapter 3

A Micro-Political Process

We ought to *act* under the presupposition of the unifying power of communicative reason.

—Habermas 1985, 195

How do you understand the educational and political process of a school and how could you change it for the better? This is the question that motivates this study. I narrate and interpret the meaning of the developing micro-political process for the struggle for the definition of education in the new school and discuss how a false concept of politics had been introduced, a concept of politics as instrumental and authoritarian rather than politics as the freedom of free citizens. I describe the changed situation with a new head teacher and the resulting stagnation. I then describe a political intervention with the school governors, the partial success at communication and then the return to the status quo by internal authority. I then describe a further attempt to overcome a stagnant situation and how this ended in a complete breakdown in relationship and communication within a system of domination. I evaluate the situation politically. Finally, I explain a view of culture for its explanation of how to understand a school organization as a culture and how to see it as a process in change.

A NEW HEAD TEACHER

The meaning of the evidence so far points to a micro-political failure of language and cultural meaning since the bureaucratic, scientific, formal organization and government of the school were inadequate to address the educational tasks and problems which had arisen in the new situation. The head of the City Education Authority had been given an opportunity to talk and to act but there was still no school policy or attempt to define aims or values. Active interpersonal engagement is not required in a formal, authoritarian organization and this was a formal system of education. Yet, it is human action which produces educational change (Simon 1994, 14).

Alan Tottenham was appointed to the headship of Borecross in September 1976. He was an ex-teacher of long standing, at the Crosslinks school, who had been head of mathematics, then director of studies at Borecross School for one year before leaving to become the head teacher of another school for three years. His appointment was therefore politically significant in a historical sense because it meant that the governors had decided politically to go with the Crosslinks tradition and the status quo, with continuity and stability. They would have appointed someone with no historical association with the school, a complete outsider, if they had wanted innovation and change, which is what the situation required since a new system of education had been instituted. The appointment carried micro-political implications because the deputy head of the pastoral system and the four senior house teachers were all Crosslinks appointments and so were three successive directors of studies. Now they controlled the head teacher's position. That is, the problem of the school was becoming the political dominance of an oligarchic group of teachers of similar background and thought.

The influence of the grammar school teachers and their strongly academic, intellectual culture had been largely reduced, since they had left or were leaving and really didn't want much to do with the new system, and probably the system did not want much to do with them. This was a tragedy since the strength of the English educational system had been its intellectual and academic style, and once dismantled would take years to redevelop. The head of a grammar school was selected on the basis of high academic achievement at a leading university, a subject specialist and his colleagues were interested in teaching a subject in which they had a passionate interest. In other countries, they would have been university educators and able to pursue research.

The political significance of Alan Tottenham's appointment meant that the ideology of the Crosslinks system would be even more difficult to change. What really happened de facto was that the standards of the Crosslinks school became the standards of Borecross School; that is, the historical, intellectual and moral tradition of the grammar school was abandoned for a different, undefined and qualitatively lower standard. The decisions had been made formally by the governors behind closed doors where their conversations and relationships were secret.

A second political significance of Alan Tottenham's appointment was that the governors supported and prolonged the status quo and the Crosslinks system. A system is a scientific abstraction and not an individual, real person with a body and with feelings. Tottenham was a scientist by education, likely to favor a formal scientific system of organization rather than an informal, arts style of organization in which interpersonal relationships were allowed to flourish. The issue of arts versus science runs through this case history because I am a graduate in English Literature and have an arts perspective on education, since I see art and literature and the humanities subjects as the right way to understand human nature. So the difference in perspectives between Tottenham and myself were deep-rooted. A perspective on life through the eyes of a mathematician is different from the perspective of someone with a literary background. These differences cannot just be ignored and "melted" as Dennis Moore stated was the policy. They make a weighty difference to the meaning of practice.

Alan Tottenham had benefited greatly from the new comprehensive system since he rose from the head of mathematics to director of studies for one year and then head teacher of a smaller school before being appointed to the headship of Borecross. He was in a strong position politically since the educational point of view he represented was in the ascendancy. As the director of studies, he had the opportunity to question the house system and its effect on the organization of the school, but he did not raise the matter. In formal organizations, you never question the system because the system is right, self-perpetuating and self-justifying (McCarthy 1978, 230–232).

I viewed his appointment over time as an educational and political mistake. Tottenham was an unqualified teacher at a time when professional qualifications in education were, in my judgment, necessary for such a position of influence and power. Here was a leader in a top position in education with no apparent professional education. So from where did he derive his authority? Professional qualifications were as necessary and useful as subject qualifications because without a knowledge of the educational literature and the ability to analyze educational concepts and situations, it would not be possible to understand the social and cultural complexities of a large school. The purpose of institutions like the London University Institute of Education is to study education. Why have them for educating teachers and then ignore them? This was the actual meaning of the situation. It was perhaps especially necessary in the case of Alan Tottenham because he had a member of his staff who took educational theory seriously. When the amalgamation took place, for example, I submitted myself to reeducation to adapt to the new system. I followed a certificate of education with an in-service B.Ed. which took three years of part-time study, and I also completed a diploma in the philosophy of education. Hence, I had three professional qualifications. This meant that if a head is to maintain his authority, he must be able to justify his actions and attitudes and be able to argue his position logically, otherwise he will be found out and lose confidence (Albrow 1997, 74–88).

At any rate, Alan Tottenham's appointment raised the issue whether knowledge of educational theory is useful and connected with educational practice. That problem was considered in Chapters 1 and 2. There is a widespread belief in British culture that educational theory is useless. The belief is mistaken and the governors associated themselves by implication with that belief; if it is wrong the appointment was a serious error with educational consequences.

The appointment was a continuation of the old Crosslinks/Boreham merger politically. A background in teaching at the Crosslinks school was not an adequate preparation for the headship of a large school, especially without any training. His appointment meant that the school was so rooted in the past that it was afraid of any real social and educational change.

Alan Tottenham inherited a political situation but he was an unpolitical person since his relations with others were formal and vertical. The job of a head teacher is political leadership (Ball 1987, 80–87). This is carried out by talk. I had no intention of giving up the political position I had earned by careful work and political skill. I believe in politics as an important art. It is the way that individual persons shape their relations with others. I wanted to see a democratic, political culture in the school and intended to work for it because I judged it to be in the general interests of everyone. Tottenham should have informed himself about the political realities of the school. But, it seems that he didn't and as far as the governors were concerned it didn't matter that he didn't. This was the meaning of the situation.

The overt style and performance of the head teacher was that of a stereotyped bureaucrat in public (84). The first public act he performed as head teacher stated his position symbolically. I witnessed him on the first day of school with a bunch of keys acting as a caretaker opening classroom doors punctually at school opening time. Here he defined his style. Since he became an anonymous, neutral figure who revealed hardly anything about himself, he projected his personality to the school by silence and body language. "Organizations use ideological neutrality to escape the force of traditions" (Habermas 1981, 308). He seemed to want to abolish prize-giving so that he wouldn't have to make any speeches and be required to project a personality in front of the public, which was another indication that he saw his role in bureaucratic terms. Another significant action was the holding of fire practices adding up to three within a short space of time, which indicated his cultural priorities. Since a head teacher is a public figure, it is these symbolic acts which are communicated to the teachers and pupils. He is implicitly communicating what he respects and implicitly what he doesn't respect (Harré 1979, 27). Most significant perhaps was the absence of any statement on the philosophy of the school and hence the absence of leadership.

It is important to stop and consider the situation. The governors had appointed as head a person who didn't talk yet the head is in a position of micro-political leadership. A good head has a policy. A head doesn't own a school. A school is a site of ideological conflict and a head has to interact and carry his teachers with him. He has to give direction to the school. The only way he can do it is by talk. Politics is sui generis. Relationships are carried on by means of talk. Teaching is done through talk. Silence and neutrality are an abnegation of the head teacher's role. Consider the theory of the neutral teacher:

For a social worker is essentially non-judgemental, and must try to be so. At first sight this might seem to be the condition to which the teacher should also aspire. The concept of the Neutral Teacher was one that had a certain vogue in 1960s and 1970s, and there was considerable debate among educational philosophers about what his neutrality should consist in and how he should preserve it. But a teacher cannot, in fact, be expected to adopt and maintain an Olympian stand, observing calmly the goings on in his class-room. Even if, as we have seen, he has to try to teach his pupils to look all round a particular question, on the political front, without prejudging for them any answers, yet in the field of instant morality he must be resolute, strong, and, if necessary, interventionist. There is no case at all for a *morally* neutral teacher; he must be seen by his pupils, whatever their age, to be on the side of fairness, honesty, and kindness. He cannot be non-judgemental because he is in the seat of judgement for most of his working life, especially when his pupils are young, hardly out of the nursery. (Warnock 1988, 119)

At the time of Alan Tottenham's appointment, I maintained a continuous micro-political effort to get the house system changed. The house system was a Crosslinks creation and the governors had appointed a head teacher who had long established ties with the Crosslinks school and the teachers there. Alan Tottenham took a publically neutral and secretive stand toward the house system in the years that followed. He was thus following the organizational sciences' model of ideological neutrality (Ball 1987, 8). An appointed leader cannot be morally neutral about something which affects the culture of the school intimately and for which he has direct and overall responsibility. Otherwise he is not fulfilling his role as a leader and the school has no direction (80–87). The position of a head teacher is that of a political leader. A leader has to talk and take sides on an issue; otherwise he is not leading but following and waiting for someone else to lead. The reason for his silence could have been misplaced loyalty to the Crosslinks school. From a political point of view, the head should have made up his mind in public in order to establish his authority and not leave a political vacuum at the top. If he didn't, he would be abdicating his leadership role and inviting others to lead. This was what happened in practice. The debate over the house system was in part a political issue between the Crosslinks and Boreham concepts of education and between an instrumental and educative concept. Both Mr. Moore and Mr. Stephens, two City Education Authority inspectors, denied that the work which the opposition did on changing the house system was their work. Hence, they supported the head teacher's position politically but irrationally and uncritically.

· The situation which had developed can be understood within the method of scientific organization. Scientific organization does not recognize conflicts of viewpoint and the need for political activity. An organization is a rigid, timeless structure in which authority, goal coherence, ideological neutrality, consensus and consent are the important ideas (Ball 1987, 8). Thus, conflict is pathological and promotion through the system goes to those loyal to the principles of organizational science. However, the model is flawed and is dysfunctional. Even the head teacher is bound by its rules. The alternative micro-political model which I adhered to is simply more real to persons and to informality and to the reality of talk. Hence, the conflict which follows is understandable in the context of the conflict between ideas of organization.

In 1974, the City Education Authority issued a document on the internal government of schools. It was a radical, innovative document for political change and improvement. This document is the justification and authorization for the democratic stance I take throughout this case history.

The following is an extract from the final paper of the document entitled "Suggestions for the Consideration of Teachers":

14 Arrangements for the involvement of heads and staffs in the internal government of their schools should be looked at afresh in the light of this report with a view to strengthening and improving them. A clearly defined structure of consultation is required in all schools which is understood and used. This is not to minimize the value of informal consultation, which should continue. The objective should be the full involvement of the staff along with the head in the ordering of the affairs of the school.

15 The responsibility for decision-making should be clearly defined, all staff knowing exactly what is delegated and to whom. Appropriate powers of implementation must also be delegated.

16 Where responsibility for areas of decision-making is delegated to individual members of staff (e.g., heads of department), before any decisions are made there should be consultation with staff likely to be affected.

17 Every effort should be made to ensure an adequate programme of in-service training suitable for teachers and heads at all levels of responsibility. Courses should go beyond the technical managerial problems of school administration to consider the total role structure and interpersonal relations within the school and the relation of both to the identification and pursuit of aims and objectives.

18 Heads and staffs of schools should give high priority in managing their resources to making time for an adequate system of consultation. Consideration should be given to what adjustment of existing commitments is possible to allow for greater involvement.

19 As part of their arrangements for consultation, schools should pay particular attention to the question of communications. In this respect schools will require

additional resources in order to increase secretarial assistance and the provision of adequate facilities for duplicating and record-keeping.

This City Education Authority initiative was not discussed let alone implemented by the school authorities. They had good reasons since they maintained their authority through secrecy and silence and talk would have exposed their thinking and competencies to public view. The Borecross authorities lacked the political skills to implement the document. Paragraph 17 recommended in-service training but the head teacher was untrained. Paragraph 14 recommended informal consultation and full involvement of the staff yet in practice this was denied.

GOVERNORS' MEETING I

In *Exit, Voice and Loyalty* (1970), Hirschmann has argued that members of organizations have three political options. They can leave if they don't like the policies. They can be loyal to the aims and philosophy or they can give voice to their objections and try to change "an objectionable state of affairs." He has defined voice as:

any attempt at all to change, rather than to escape from, an objectionable state of affairs, whether through individual or collective petition to the management directly in charge, through appeal to higher authority with the intention of forcing a change in management, or through various types of actions and protests, including those that are meant to mobilize public opinion. (Hirschmann 1970, 30)

If the exit alternative is used, it will "tend to *atrophy the development of the art of voice*" (43).

I chose the voice option. I decided to meet the governors of the school given the situation at Borecross and with the knowledge of the City Education Authority's document on the internal government of schools. Transformative action was needed to implement a comprehensive school in practice. A critical education science is a "practical task," not an ideological one (Bernstein 1985, 31). There were theories of education but the real problem was the gap between theory and practice. It was important to engage the governors since they ultimately controlled the school through appointments, and generally they had been appointments with a conservative political message.

I sought a meeting with the governors two years after the first complaint, which was a substantial trial period to study the style of the new head teacher. Although there was a new head teacher, there had been no fresh initiative, in my view, which would lead a reasonable person to believe that the school was moving in a positive direction. Working through the common room had proved to be unproductive since the real decision-taking took place elsewhere. The conservative, traditionalist teachers were being promoted and anyone who had significantly opposed the system was not being promoted (Ball 1987, 114). Relevant educational qualifications were ignored. The status quo was dominant and guarded its own interests carefully behind the scenes. There would have to be a fundamental shift of attitudes. That could only come through political action.

I was perfectly prepared to work with and through the authorities. I was willing to be patient. There was a significant opposition in the common room but due to the undemocratic, authoritarian nature of the organization, it was silenced.

A formal structure is fixed. Change is dependent on process and that process is driven by interaction. There was a basic conflict in the organization between structure and change. The head didn't want change but the opposition did. Ball presents the problem as follows:

The emphasis on the enactment of power is an emphasis on structure, on the relatively fixed quality of relationships between actors. The emphasis on interaction is an emphasis on process, on "the fluid, continuously emerging qualities of the organization." (Day and Day, quoted in Ball 1987, 215)

The intention of the following documents was to open up communication on the future policy of the school. They were the beginnings of policy documents in a school without a policy. It was an attempt at democratic discussion and participation. I met the governors in April 1978 and put the following documents on the table as a basis of discussion. The first one was a historical evaluation of the school's situation:

April 1978

Outline of Case for Consideration by the Governors.

Introduction.

I would ask the governors to appreciate that what is written below is only an outline of a complex matter running to many pages. I have organized the subject matter under the following headings: history of the present situation, short analysis of the amalgamation, what are the priorities?, debate on the house system, democratic methods of involvement in decision-taking, letter to Dr. Brownley, unfair treatment, and moral education, the pastoral system, authoritarianism, and conclusion.

History of the Present Situation—Short Analysis of the Amalgamation.

The fairest, most plausible objective and justifiable analysis of the amalgamation of Boreham and Crosslinks was as follows. There was a silent but vindictive hate campaign quietly conducted against the grammar school side by people (understandably perhaps) totally and virulently opposed to everything the grammar school stood for.

In this atmosphere it was impossible to start any realistic, rational form of dialogue. With the adoption of the pervasive house system and the installation of all the Crosslinks senior house masters into the heads of houses positions in the so-called new school, it was clear from the start that a submergence, not an amalgamation, was in progress. For reasons of diplomacy and tact, the submergence was never resisted, but that it has had a lasting effect on standards of academic and technical work can hardly be disputed.

The pastoral/house system policy of the school, until now, has been as follows. The house system is "wonderful" for the "lower ability" boy; the so-called "upper ability" boy does not need any help. He has the natural ability and doesn't need to be taught. It is an extreme version of child-centered education which is generally judged to be strong on method and weak on content. The result of this discriminatory policy has been a gradual and continuous decline in standards and attitudes to work, as measured by public examination results. It seems to be thought that everything comes naturally, and that achievement is possible without sustained work and effort.

What Are the Priorities?

A reasonable judgment made by many members of staff is that we are trying to achieve more than our limited resources and competence will permit, and in so doing failing to achieve certain realistic objectives. Quality has been sacrificed to quantity. "The chief advantage of the comprehensive school is its variety, its chief danger is fragmentation" (Michael Marland C.B.E., a leading headmaster of the comprehensive movement).

By putting all the emphasis on pastoral care and setting it up as a total panacea (it is a vague notion whose results are not measurable), is it ever likely to work? First, we have no trained social workers, child psychoanalysts. Second, we do not have the facilities for such work.

If the pastoral side were to confine itself to certain limited functions of support for the academic/work side such as organization of hobbies, sports, discipline and competitions, it could achieve something worthwhile. By attempting to monopolize the educational attitude of the school, it not only stunts its own chance of success, but also undermines the main function of the school.

This general argument is specifically made in a report by Her Majesty's Inspectors, recently published, saying that the pastoral care concept has been over-stretched.

Debate on the House System.

As a result of two debates and the formation of a committee to enquire into the merits of the house and year systems, the recommendation is that we change over to the year system. Naturally, there has been some opposition given the vested interests and the history of the subject, but the common room as a whole has looked at it from an unbiased, rational point of view, in the interests of the good of the future of the school. Even the opponents of change have conceded that the house system is administratively more difficult to operate, and has a poor communications system. Given the size of classes, the increasing psychological pressures on teachers, and the constraint on teachers' time, it can't be right to continue with an unsound system of organization. It also undermines the confidence of the staff in the management of the school.

Democratic Methods of Involvement in Decision-Taking.

The whole trend in comprehensive education is to make schools more democratic, more effective, and more accountable. In this school, a call for open discussion by the head teacher, a detailed document sent out by the City Education Authority (CEA) outlining procedures, and the introduction of staff/governor meetings have all been significant introductions.

This policy was not, however, fully implemented and followed. It was tried; a staff committee was formed and was active for a while, but it soon became clear that it had no status and did not receive the cooperation it was entitled to expect from the head teacher.

It also became clear that the then chairman of governors and the head teacher were prepared to use sanctions such as halting promotion, making damaging comments on references, and so on, in order to inhibit and to intimidate.

Letter to Dr. Brownley.

After four to five years of patient and polite persuasion with no possibility of progress, in a gradually deteriorating situation, and in view of the open discrimination I had suffered, I reluctantly felt forced to write a letter of complaint to Dr. Brownley, the chief education officer. Following an interview with the district inspector, a week later the headmaster retired.

In that letter, and in subsequent correspondence, I set out a list of points such as system of organization, school rules, problems of size and bureaucracy, decision-taking. These were legitimate questions, which had all been raised but ignored on previous occasions.

Unfair Treatment.

At the proposed meeting with the governors, I shall outline, if necessary, the history of the continuous discriminatory treatment I have received as a result of fairly, reasonably, and politely raising these issues. In the light of the government debate on education and public concern generally, this whole matter has a wider dimension than the boundaries of the school.

Moral Education, the Pastoral System and Authoritarianism.

The main function of the pastoral system is to replace authoritarian attitudes, relationships, and punishments by more humane and rational methods. Since the essence of misunderstanding which has taken place seems to me to be the changing relationship between heads and staff within comprehensive schools, parallel with the changing relationship between staff and pupils, parents and children, I have reproduced in outline the contrasting features of the two types of authority, quoted from a leading authority on education.

Moral Authoritarianism.

Authoritarian morality is status-orientated. Authoritarianism is fundamentally insecure against a possible realization of its nature. For should it occur to anyone to question the demands made and the rules insisted upon, structural collapse is imminent, or else resort must be made to open force. Questioning is by implication an assertion of personal autonomy, of one's dignity as an individual, and hence one's fitness to be given good reasons to gain one's confidence, and compliance. This intimate connection between reason, autonomy, equality and dignity has been several times mentioned already.

Such a realization makes the fictive impressiveness of the authoritarian difficult to sustain. Once questioning gets under way the spell is broken and the images are scattered. For it is then seen to be a straight and obvious fallacy to cite his personal demands as reason why I should do anything at all.

To gain my compliance, he must submit to shared public criteria of what is to count as a good reason, such as the formal principles of fairness and the consideration of interests. The presentation of, listening to and the criticism of reasons are, as Popper rightly observes, bound up with the acceptance of the "rational unity of mankind." (Dearden 1968, 170–172)

Rational Authority.

Rational authority insists without intimidating, and attempts to make the value of the rule a sufficient motivation to acting upon it. Because it limits its demands to what is mutually acceptable, on any fair view of all the interests concerned, it may reasonably expect greater cooperation and hence to be much less in need of resorting to punishment, whether corporal or of some other kind.

Whereas moral authoritarianism is always fundamentally insecure because of the possible realization of its nature, rational authority has no such insecurity. It is indeed an invitation to its own criticism. Again, since individual spontaneity and independence are not under the wholesale suspicion characteristic of authoritarianism which stakes its all on obedience and sees natural impulse only as threatening a possible breach, rational authority can refrain from its own exercise in praise and welcome encouragement of any natural inclination toward fairness, considerateness, sympathy, gratitude, generosity or any other of the finer emotions. (174)

Conclusion.

In view of certain comments and private conversations, and after a year's delay for time to reconsider attitudes, I would request that this matter be finally dealt with.

I also gave the governors a copy of the following school evaluation:

BORECROSS SCHOOL CURRICULUM EVALUATION: A Preliminary Analysis.

Role of Evaluation.

Curriculum evaluation is a method of improving schools. Its main purpose is to provide decision-takers with an up-to-date assessment of a school's objectives, performance, strengths and weaknesses, teaching methods and so on in order to assist clear thinking, appropriate curriculum planning and quality control. An evaluation is intended to be illuminating. It is not intended to be right, but to be competent. It can serve as a basis for discussion by all interested parties.

In this evaluation, a number of hypotheses will be advanced. A hypothesis can only be tested by patient enquiry to see whether the facts support the hypothesis. Facts of course are always open to interpretation; social science research techniques aim at objectivity but in the end practical value judgments have to be made. They are more likely to be effective if they are made on the basis of adequate evidence and thought.

Hypotheses.

1. Borecross School is still a traditional school in the worst sense of the term. There is confusion about curriculum aims and objectives, curriculum content, teaching methods, the changing role of the headmaster and changing attitudes between teachers and pupils. It is, on the whole, out of touch with the changing needs of the pupils in times of social change. It is too parochial in its outlook.

2. Practice and theory are largely separated. In general the important relationship between theory and practice is not recognized.

3. The basic ideas of the founding fathers of comprehensive education and of the leading practitioners in the profession are not being seriously implemented. The ideals and aims are not even discussed.

4. The lack of communication between staff, without which future development is unlikely, may be the most serious problem.

5. The school is administered but not managed educationally. There is a lack of curriculum coordination and central purpose. The hidden curriculum is not supporting the stated curriculum.

6. Equality of opportunity often seems to mean everyone is equal, meaning everyone is the same. The distinction between equality of opportunity and equality of achievement is often not understood. Consequently, individual talents and differences are not sufficiently encouraged and the whole community suffers. Conformity to fixed ideas and values is perhaps the most potent cause of lack of achievement in many pupils.

7. Equality of opportunity will not be achieved without freedom and tolerance of different attitudes. Moral education and the education of the emotions (a task which comprehensive schools can approach) are not possible in an intolerant atmosphere.

Evidence.

The research method used for this evaluation is participant—observation over a period of years. It is also based on a knowledge of the literature in curriculum studies, which is concerned with the application of philosophy, sociology and psychology to education.

Is Borecross a Healthy Organization?

The following criteria are used to measure health: goal focus, communication adequacy, optimal power equalization, resource utilization, cohesiveness, morale, innovativeness, autonomy, adaptation and problem-solving adequacy. (Stenhouse 1975, 173)

Goal Focus.

The large numbers of pupils in the school, the split site and split staff rooms, the quantity of subjects of the timetable, the range of attitudes, cultural background and interests of pupils and staff make goal focus a problem. What is not recognized in the school is the nature of the problem and what steps and methods can be taken to try to solve it. Without clear goals, objectives and aims, there is bound to be a lack of purpose among the pupils. The behavior of many pupils (which is poor) suggests a lack of purpose. The overall purpose of the curriculum needs to be communicated in simple terms to the pupils.

Communication Adequacy.

Borecross School is a plural society but it seems to be assumed that unity can only be preserved by controlling the attitudes, thoughts and feelings of individuals to conform to dominant opinion. This breeds an intolerant atmosphere. It also produces a tension and often unhealthy silence at staff meetings, the majority of staff refusing to participate. So worries, problems, difficulties are ignored, swept under the carpet and never solved. For example, an hour at the beginning of the school year is an inadequate amount of time for a staff meeting. The occasional meetings after school which have recently been introduced are a step in the right direction, but the key lies with the head and deputy head whose competence and authority are tested at staff meetings, if staff perceive, rightly or wrongly, that a controversial opinion or argument is likely to undermine or antagonize another of an official higher status, with more official power and authority. Communication on public occasions will only be improved when a relaxed, tolerant atmosphere is produced, when the differences as well as the similarities among the staff will emerge. At present the complexities of education are not discussed adequately and the problems of the school remain publicly undefined and unrecognized.

The consequences of this lack of communication are very serious since without it the development of the school is stunted. In a multi-racial school it breeds misunderstanding, conflict and intolerance. When important decisions have been made (i.e., over corporal punishment, staff promotion and disruptive problems), the irritability and confusion is the result of lack of communication on which human relationships depend.

Optimal Power Evaluation.

In a healthy organization the distribution of influence is relatively equitable. Staff relations would be based on collaboration rather than explicit or implicit coercion. While you would expect some intergroup struggles, intergroup struggles would not be bitter.

The C.E.A. has distributed a guide to the internal government of schools which has now been formally accepted by the staff, but no interest or comment or detailed discussion on how it is to be implemented has been shown by the authorities. The head and deputy heads seem to be passing the authority for important decisions to the staff, while maintaining a non-committal, neutral stance. For example, on the issue of the house/year system the headmaster's thinking and attitude is neutral. Yet, the organization of the school would seem to be a management decision since management is supposed to have the knowledge and skill to make the decision and they have the task of implementing it.

The power seems to be passing to the staff. This seems to be the consequence of the ambivalence over whether we are an authoritarian or democratic institution.

Resource Utilization.

The resource referred to here is teachers. Are they using their talents effectively? Do they feel neither overloaded with work or idle? Are the efforts of individuals and the aims of the school in proper balance?

No thinking and discussion has been given to the problem of changing from a small school (where most teachers have their experience) to a large school. For example, teacher autonomy and isolation in individual classrooms is maintained, when the large-school situation calls for effective cooperation and coordination between teachers to improve performance and coordinate action. Without an overall strategy, a teacher can be doing good work in isolation from his colleagues, and it could be undone elsewhere due to misunderstanding. Most teachers have a heavy and potentially endless work load. The administrative load of the teacher could be reduced and the educational function given more priority and importance, since in the end the school stands on the performance of the classroom teacher.

At present, there seem to be confusion and intolerance between the efforts of individuals and the aims of the school, partly caused by lack of communication.

Morale.

In private, the feelings of most staff are that things are not on the right path and some basic rethinking of attitudes is required. Morale could be much better.

Cohesiveness.

The role of the management seems to be largely administrative. Until an educational role is assured, based on appropriate techniques and strategies for a comprehensive school, the fragmentation and loss of effectiveness of the curriculum will continue.

Innovativeness.

A healthy system would tend to grow, to develop and change rather than be standardized and routine. It would be activity-oriented rather than embedded.

In the end, curriculum development depends on changing attitudes, staff and pupils alike. A barrier to this in education is the separation of research and development, the gap between theorists and practitioners.

Most of the innovations at Borecross are at a superficial level. Without adequate thought, preparation, evaluation and discussion the real changes promised by the introduction of a comprehensive system will be illusory.

Autonomy.

A healthy organization has an independent relationship with the environment. While it should be responsive to outside demands and aim to serve the community, it does not allow its behavior to be determined by them. The relationship might be characterized as mature, reciprocal, considerate but not submissive.

Due to an almost complete lack of communication and understanding, of cumulative effect over the years, the relationship between the governors, the head and the staff is largely coercive. The relationship between staff and pupils is similarly confused since modern educational practice encourages the practice of considerate, reciprocal relationships, but the pupils, some of whom are accustomed to coercive relationships, take advantage of the weakened authority and power of the staff and implement their own coercive methods.

The dominant influence on the governing body seems to be unaware of the true situation in the school, and needs to be considerably more informed and careful before adopting attitudes and making decisions which are unhelpful to the staff and pupils. They ought to encourage openness and strength of personality among staff since a submissive teacher will be ineffective in the classroom and despised by the pupils. The teachers cannot retreat from their responsibilities in the classroom where feedback on their behavior and performance is mercilessly and directly forthcoming (since young people don't know how to be indirect), whereas governors are largely uninformed about the day-to-day consequences of their actions and have a quick method of retreat.

Problem-Solving Adequacy.

Any organization always has problems, strains, difficulties and instances of ineffective coping. The issue is not the presence or absence of problems, but the manner in which the organization copes with them. An effective organization solves its problems with a minimum of energy, they stay solved, and the problem-solving mechanisms are not weakened but maintained and strengthened. There would be active coping with problems, rather than passive withdrawing, compulsive responses, scapegoating or denial.

While some progress has been made toward examining the school's problems, the process has not really started, and the discussion of problems has been too sporadic and disjointed to build up staff interest and momentum. It is too stop–go, stop–go.

Role of the Governors.

The role of the governors has assumed an active form, particularly in relation to staff appointments and in promoting certain attitudes. It sometimes seems that they do not distinguish clearly between their political role as a local councillor and their educational role as a governor. If teachers were to confuse their teaching role with their politics, governors would rightly be annoyed, since indoctrinating is not teaching by rational methods; in any case no school subject can be properly learned by methods of coercion and indoctrination.

The governors need to decide how they can best give a constructive lead to the school. The *Taylor Report* needs to be implemented.

Bureaucracy or Community.

A large school almost inevitably becomes bureaucratic, which tends to mean a rigidly hierarchic organization, one-way communication between the top and bottom of the hierarchy, poor communication between departments, a loss of identity and alienation of individuals, interdepartmental rivalry, and so on. In a school, too much bureaucracy, especially if bureaucratic attitudes become commonplace, cut across the educational function of the school. As the problems of the school increase, as they will if they are not faced, it will be easy for responsibility to be passed to the system and round the system, so that in a sense everybody is to blame, yet nobody is to blame.

A sense of belonging, a sense of identity, a sense of community will only be developed through shared experience and shared achievement. Borecross will, if anything, be adding to, not reducing the delinquency and social problems apparent among young people, if they ignore the community responsibility. Moral and social development depend on a sense of identity with a community; if the teachers largely function as anonymous, impersonal bureaucrats their educational role will be largely destroyed. There is a great danger that the process has already gone too far.

Highest Common Factor/Lowest Common Denominator.

All schools have a tangible and an ideal curriculum. Without an ideal the educational process becomes haphazard, fragmented and lacking in either coherence or direction. Education is about growth and development. Psychologically, you have to build on the strengths of a school, and the pupils and staff in it. It is no good lowering the standard of the top to suit the apparent wishes of the pupils at the bottom.

So far Borecross seems to be leveling itself with the lowest common denominator.

It is, therefore, betraying its ideals and undermining the achievement of its own curriculum aims.

From Mechanistic to Organic.

Comprehensive schools are slowly moving from a mechanistic to an organic structure. The characteristics of each one are shown below. The role of the teacher is changing from a restricted to an extended role.

Mechanistic Structure	Organic Structure
1. Total task is broken down into specialized, differentiated tasks.	1. All special knowledge and experience contribute to the general task.
2. The people pursuing these subtasks have purposes, means and techniques more or less distinct from those of the concern as a whole.	2. The total situation of the concern sets the individual task realistically.
3. At each level of the hierarchy these subtasks are coordinated by immediate superiors who themselves are responsible for a special part of the main task.	3. As work progresses, tasks are adjusted and continually redefined.
4. Rights, obligations and technical methods are precisely defined for each position in the hierarchy.	4. Responsibility may not be shed; problems may not be posted upward, downwards or sideways as someone else's responsibility.

5. These constitute responsibilities of each position.

5. Commitment of members to the concern is general rather than to special parts of it.

6. Control, authority and communication are in a hierarchical structure.

6. Authority, control and communication form a network, not a hierarchy; responsibility is to the concern as a whole, not to an immediate superior.

7. The final reconciliation of tasks, the assessment, and the only overall picture are located at the top of the hierarchy.

7. The boss is no longer omniscient; control, authority and communication may be located temporarily with anyone who has the special expertise on an ad hoc basis.

8. Relationships are vertical (i.e., between superior and subordinate, in the main).

8. Lateral more than vertical communication; communications are consultations rather than commands.

9. There is a tendency for operations and working behavior to be governed by instructions and decisions of superiors.

9. It is information and advice rather than instructions and decisions.

10. Loyalty and obedience to superiors is a condition of membership.

10. Commitment is to task, progress and expansion rather than loyalty and obedience.

11. Prestige attaches to local (internal) knowledge rather than to general (cosmopolitan) knowledge.

11. Importance and prestige are attached to knowledge and expertise valid outside the particular concern.

It should be clear why an organic structure is to be preferred. It is more dynamic, encourages social responsibility and is functionally more effective. It is in the interests of staff, pupils and the local community. It is not rigid.

Evidence of Staff Attitudes.

Academic Standards.

The following discussion paper was produced (by A. B. and T. A.) at the request of the common room last term. It has already been discussed at a heads of departments' meeting, as a result of which a subcommittee was set up which will report to the heads of departments next week, October 12. The paper is distributed with "Staff Week" for information of staff and in the hope that it will encourage our colleagues to represent their own opinions to their heads of departments before next Thursday's meeting. The agenda for the meeting is given in this edition of "Staff Week."

A number of colleagues have privately expressed the opinion that many of our pupils are underachieving, and this opinion seems to be echoed by people in other walks of life about many pupils in many schools.

The "O" and "A" level structure is changing, neither drastically nor rapidly. These exams are the boys' lines of communication with their futures. We do not believe that we are keeping these lines reliably open; and it is more than probable that our methods and organization are actually cutting off some boys' prospects. Underachievement is emasculation!

Look, for a moment, at the cant phrase "child-centered." As a matter of emphasis, there is a point beyond which it is improper to think in terms of adopting a child-centered approach in secondary education. An adult-centered approach is needed—the adults being those whom the children will become.

True! Not all boys are able to take "O" or "A" levels. But we suggest that more could if our approach were different. We have no right to consign a boy to C.S.E. courses if it is not necessary to do so. Necessity equals suitability in this context. C.S.E. too easily becomes an educational placebo.

We have, at Borecross, not much less than our fair share of 111 boys. Clearly, we have not a large number of "middle-class" boys; but we have plenty of bright ones, most of whom need more help than they are getting to establish a self-disciplined habit of work and a productive attitude to school.

Last year, only thirteen boys achieved three or more "A" level passes. This is a frightening fact, in a school of 1,700.

Also frightening, in a school so large which is, more or less, English-speaking, is the state of English studies in the sixth form. Is it not sad that we can no longer maintain a conventional, university-orientated "A" level?

In the science department we are concerned that in the fifth year only 23 boys are studying three sciences, and in the fourth year only 26. There are about 300 in each year, and we should remember that these totals include candidates for both O.L. and C.S.E.—numbers smaller than one form in a three-form entry grammar school. We feel convinced that some boys who have shown promise in the first years fail to realize their potential, and not only in science. Of course the fault may lie within the science department itself, but as similar views seem to be held by colleagues in other departments about their subjects, and as in science we may modestly claim to be moderately successful with those pupils we attract, we think that the root causes permeate the whole school. It is becoming increasingly difficult to make boys do even a small amount of homework, and when that homework is reading, it is almost impossible, even, or we might say, especially with sixth form "A" level students. During the last week in a fourth-year chemistry set, not one boy did some reading required in preparation for a fairly difficult piece of practical work; in a top group maths set only three boys did the examples set, and in 1T only 17 boys out of 30 attended on a day when they had two tests. One day, boys were missing from several lessons because they were required for a house badminton competition, although it was agreed last year that such interference with lessons should be reduced.

The number of boys applying for higher education courses has dropped markedly in the last two years. While acknowledging that passing examinations is not the sole aim of education, nor perhaps the main one, we are failing our pupils if we do not provide them with the appropriate atmosphere and opportunity to realize their intellectual as well as their physical potential. We think that unless we examine now the attitudes we hold toward the academic progress of our pupils, and the atmosphere we provide for them in which to make such progress ("a school which is working is orderly: a school which is orderly can work"), we may find a situation developing which will be difficult to change.

We offer no instant remedies, no simple solutions, for there are none. Any measures we take must be long-term ones, agreed on and supported by the whole staff. We hope these comments will provoke discussion and lead to decisions about such measures.

Recommendations from This Evaluation.

1. A curriculum coordinator with a sound theoretical training in curriculum studies is needed.

2. A policy for staff training and development must be formulated and implemented.

3. Somebody with a responsibility allowance should be appointed to coordinate the various committees on the staff.

4. An overall policy on pastoral care/discipline should be formulated and the functions and responsibilities of the pastoral system clarified and communicated.

5. The thinking and attitudes of the staff must be ascertained and a continuous staff conference maintained.

6. A policy of language across the curriculum (Bullock Report) is the best policy for reducing educational disadvantages. It needs full support from the authorities.

7. Serious consideration should be given to the advantages of a faculty structure.

8. A year system should be introduced.

9. A school policy on study skills should be developed.

10. The school's performance must be regularly evaluated, problems identified and remedies sought.

11. Staff attitudes to the relationship between theory and practice need to change.

12. In-service training needs to be encouraged and recognized.

13. A sense of standards of work and behavior must be transmitted and continually reinforced.

14. Leadership is necessary, otherwise a vacuum is caused.

15. The long-term program needs to be thought out from first (comprehensive) principles (i.e., block-timetabling, common curriculum, mixed-ability teaching, etc.).

16. The timetable should include time for all the various staff committees to meet and carry out their functions.

17. All changes must be carefully thought through, justified, publically discussed and carefully communicated in everyday language to parents.

Some of the Books on which the Foregoing Preliminary Analysis Is Based:

Cave, Ronald G. 1971. *An Introduction to Curriculum Development.* Ward Lock Educational.

Golby, Michael, Greenwald, Jane, and West, Ruth, eds. 1975. *Curriculum Design.* Open University.

Hargreaves, David H. 1975. *Interpersonal Relations and Education.* Routledge and Kegan Paul.

Kogan, Maurice. 1978. *The Politics of Educational Change.* Fontana.

Lawton, Dennis. 1973. *Social Change, Educational Theory and Curriculum Planning.* University of London Press.

Lawton, Dennis. 1975. *Class, Culture and the Curriculum.* Routledge and Kegan Paul.

Nisbet, Stanley. 1957. *Purpose in the Curriculum.* University of London Press.

Richardson, Elizabeth. 1973. *The Teacher, the School and the Task of Management.* Heinemann.

Stenhouse, Lawrence. 1975. *An Introduction to Curriculum Research and Development.* Heinemann.

The above documents constituted a serious attempt to analyze the problems of the school and to promote educational change. I spent five or ten minutes at the most with the governors as there was no discussion of any significance. How did they interpret the above documents? There is no way of knowing. Did they or could they understand them? They faced a political dilemma. They could continue on the same road that had been followed since the amalgamation or they could change course. In effect, they decided to continue. I had carried out a school and curriculum evaluation and there was no comment or discussion. Other members of staff had reported a serious situation of educational underperformance. From the micro-political perspective of organization, this was a political meeting. It was an attempt to discuss an alternative view of education to the one adopted by the school. It is also worthy of note that I articulated the difference between the formal and informal models of organization in terms of the mechanistic and organic models, so they had been informed of the basic problem with the school. The real significance of the meeting was the failure by the governors to open up a conversation and to implement open government. By not engaging in any discussion in detail, they maintained a formal relationship with me and prevented the development of the relationship. What matters is what they didn't do, not what they did do.

The head teacher absented himself from the meeting. This can be interpreted in terms of theories of organization. Why was he absent? A governors' meeting is a forum for discussion and talk, so the head teacher refused talk by failing to attend and refused to discuss the situation of the school. Discussion with the governors was considered illegitimate because formal organization doesn't permit political activity between members of a hierarchy, since it is a way that a head's authority can be challenged. It is also possible that he refused discussion for fear that his competence could be called into question. By not attending and talking, Alan Tottenham abdicated his responsibility as the head. It was a weak political action since its effect was to avoid rather than contend with his political opposition. The reason for not attending, he told me afterwards, but not before, was that he had nothing to do with what happened under the previous head teacher. But, there was much more to the meeting than that. The reasoning was fallacious as has been implied through much of the argument of this narrative, because for a head teacher takes over a historical situation. The history of the school as presented in these pages was relevant to the present and future. The purpose of studying history is to understand the past in order to change the present and the future. Therefore, at best the reasoning behind his decision was merely a mistake, the kind of mistake a mathematician with no background in history might make. But political mistakes carry political consequences. Significantly, he gave me his reason for not attending *after* the meeting rather than before so that I wouldn't have had any warning and would not be able to discuss the matter. I considered his action a deliberate deception and I didn't believe his statement. Also, I did not think his action worthy of a head teacher. Without him the meeting was wasted since he was the chief executive and "critical reality definer." Once again, it had been demonstrated that the problems of the school started with the politics since without democratic discussion, the problems of the school could not be understood.

Alan Tottenham's management style was a mixture of the managerial and the authoritarian rather than the interpersonal and the adversarial (Ball 1987, 124). His relationship with others was entirely formal. He cut off the formal from the interpersonal but the formal and the interpersonal interpenetrate.

It is possible and not uncommon to find the managerial head in the role of desk-bound bureaucrat, administering from behind the closed door of the office. Approaches to the head go through proper channels, "by the book." (Ball 1987, 99)

Here was bureaucracy as a form of domination. The head refused to talk and accept the methods of micro-politics. Here was an example of "styled distance" from a colleague. Here was "the separation of conception from execution."

It appeared that the first meeting with the governors had a limited success. Dennis Moore, the divisional inspector, was present. After a brief discussion, I left with the understanding that the past was to be put behind us and we would make a fresh start.

I met the governors the first time in the belief that generally speaking, if you keep talking people will come to see reason and reality. That is what I had done over the issue of the house system and other issues and it worked over time. It worked in my first meeting with the governors. It was a good meeting in the sense that I was able to communicate, the atmosphere was positive and conciliatory and I left with the understanding that I would have a scale 4 post for language across the curriculum and some tasks in curriculum studies. This would get over the problem of my lack of promotion and would give me the practical experience I needed to complement theoretical studies.

The motion passed at the meeting was: "suggest that the question of the development of your responsibilities be discussed between the Divisional Inspector and the Headmaster."

I was satisfied with this result. However, it was not implemented, in my view. At a meeting with Mr. Moore there was no discussion as the governors had ordered, since as one party involved, my opinion was not sought. It transpired that I would not receive recognition for the job, which rendered it without status and authority and it couldn't be done properly. I was excluded from relevant committees and would have to work through the director of studies and head of English. I considered myself more qualified than the director of studies since I had an in-service degree in curriculum studies and it was later revealed that the director of studies at Borecross only did timetable work; therefore the very title of director of studies was mis-named. I was being put in the wholly ambiguous position of being expected to lead but not officially recognized as a leader. I couldn't see how it could work. What was clear was that certain people were intent on keeping me from a position of authority within the school. Once again it seemed to me that the politics of deception was being practiced. The only way reforms can work is by open communication since the teachers have to want the reforms and their cooperation is essential. Leadership is a consensual activity.

It was of political significance that Dennis Moore had taken over the head's work and he seemed to be protecting the head from functioning in his micro-politcal role as the head teacher.

GOVERNORS' MEETING II

I decided that the first meeting with the governors had failed politically since my point of view and situation had not been sufficiently recognized, and I considered that the head teacher didn't have the qualifications and qualities necessary to make Borecross into a comprehensive school. I also decided that I had to continue the work for real change. It was a political conflict I didn't want, but if a situation needed changing, rational opposition is the right way. The justification for conflict is that it can lead to "mutual adjustment." The history of education shows that educational change results from a conflict of interests (Simon 1994, 16). Therefore, conflict is a good idea.

I decided it was necessary to meet the governors a second time. I ap-proached them through Dr. Cathy Hall, a fairly new governor, whom one of my colleagues had known at university and had recommended.

I had two meetings with two governors, Dr. Hall and Dr. Kinship, who had the authority to decide whether I could meet the governors as a whole a second time. The governors had selected two new governors who did not know the history of the school, hence they were unqualified for the task. They made a political mistake, in my view, and ensured the continuation of further conflict since new and uninformed governors could not resolve the political situation. I had warned the governors in the first meeting that au-thoritarianism and the suppression of rational disagreement doesn't work "once questioning gets under way." The meetings with Hall and Kinship were successful politically since I obtained my objective and was given permission to meet the governors as a body. Hence, any attempt to block a meeting by one or two other governors failed.

I wrote a document in preparation. The meeting was called at very short notice, allowing me four days to consider carefully what I wanted to say and to type it. I didn't have the time or quiet during the week. I happened to meet the secretary to the governors, Michael Lewis, on the road outside the school on the Monday morning and since we chatted whenever we saw each other, I asked him as a favor to type the almost illegible document. On the following Monday, I found that it had been distributed without my knowledge or permission and I first heard of its distribution on July 17, which was the morning of the governors' meeting.

When I met the governors, I was informed by Dennis Moore, that I would be charged with unprofessional conduct and therefore the document could not be discussed. Thus, he imposed silence.

Moore had acted politically to prevent opposition. There appeared to be twelve or so governors there, most of them unfamiliar faces. I left the meeting within a short time.

The governors passed a resolution, part of which said: "d. consider that in his own interests in view of the strain he is under, a medical examination should be arranged for him by the Authority's Medical Adviser." As will be seen in Chapter 4, it seems that the people behind this resolution were Dr. Hall and Dr. Kinship, people whose knowledge of me was superficial and whose knowledge of the school was superficial. The headmaster, Alan Tottenham, had nothing to do with the resolution, nor did anyone such as my head of department, Tim Atherton.

The request for a medical inspection was unfounded and irrational and a political attempt to discredit any opposition to the authorities, as the evidence and narrative demonstrate, and it was the use of medicine for political purposes. From the point of view of a rational and democratic morality, it was an unjustified act, since it thwarted the democratic process by an abuse of power.

I was pleased to see the City Education Authority psychiatrist, though I was under no obligation to do so. He saw immediately, as I entered the room in a smiling, controlled and friendly manner, that I was a mentally sound person and he passed me fit within a minute as I knew he would. It meant, therefore, that the governors passed a resolution intended to discredit the reputation of the opposition and they were proved wrong. Did they ever apologize? No. A competent body of governors would have made sure that their action was justified and defensible. Since it was not, the alternative explanation was that it was ideologically motivated. It was an attempt to "expurgate the other" for a difference of opinion and it enabled them to escape their responsibility to answer the issues that I had intended to raise. If, therefore, they were so wrong about this, it raised questions about their competence as governors, as indeed do many other matters in these pages.

The governors did not apologize for their mistake and act of oppression after I was passed fit, as they should have done; nor did they investigate the matter further. This is not the way competent management would act.

Mr. Graham, the chairman of the tribunal, asked the following questions of Alan Tottenham, my headmaster:

If one reads the circular it appears to be, whatever its content is, a completely logical, rational document. What was the basis of the Governors' decision to make a recommendation that he goes and sees a psychiatrist? (see confidential document chapter 6)

Alan Tottenham answered, "It came as quite a surprise to me, that particular aspect."

It is clear from this statement that the governors passed this resolution without the recommendation of anyone who had worked with me and knew me. In doing so they acted on wrong advice and no evidence. The only possible rational conclusion can be that they acted irrationally. A possible explanation could be that in criticizing the school, I had criticized them implicitly as I had indeed done so. In fact, together with the education authority, I consider they acted irresponsibly in several of their decisions, and they were responsible for the obvious decline of the school over several years. At the very least they neither recognized the situation nor did they act to do something about it.

It is significant that the chairman of the tribunal considered the document "a completely logical, rational document."

In my view, the governors should have had a serious rethink about the school and they should have included in that process a wide-ranging discussion with all the teachers in the school. Then they should have have taken some hard decisions to change the course and direction of the school so that people could acquire confidence in the government. This they didn't do.

ORGANIZATIONAL THEORY

This situation is understandable from a Habermasian theoretical perspective, which I shall examine in Chapter 8. Borecross School was a large organization which operated under the principles of "objectified intelligence" and "system integration," since the recommendation for a medical inspection was a political method for preventing criticism and opposition (Habermas 1987b, 307). The culture was a model bureaucracy characterized by formal hierarchy, specialization, formal rules and centralized authority. Hence, social integration by communicative rationality and communicative

ethics was irrelevant to the system, since democratic discussion was mini-
mized so communication was, to a great extent, meaningless. *"Communicative action forfeits its validity basis in the interior of organizations"* (310).
"Members of organizations act communicatively only *with reservation*"
(310). "They know they can have recourse to formal regulations, not only
in exceptional cases: there is *no necessity* for achieving consensus by communicative means" (310). The institution of a medical inspection stopped
opposition and resorted to "formal regulations" for social control. That was
its meaning.

In a bureaucracy, there is "growing independence from elements of the
lifeworld that have been shoved out into the system environment" (311).
"Social reality is separated off from the identity of the actors involved"
(311). These statements are supported by the evidence in the case history,
since political communication was not welcomed within the system. The
system was only interested in "self-maintenance."

In a bureaucracy, action rationality shifts to systems rationality. "The rationality of bureaucracies cut loose from vocational-ethical attitudes" has
developed an internal dynamic (307). Hence, in the case history, political
action was responded to with deceit, anger and punishment. Ethical relations were irrelevant; hence moral and political education were weakened.

"Organizations gain autonomy through a neutralizing demarcation from
the symbolic structure of the lifeworld" and become indifferent to culture,
society and personality (307). Social reality becomes "an objectified organizational reality cut loose from normative ties" (307). The evidence for these
statements has been presented.

These problematic events are explained by a conflict between two contradictory methods of organization, the organizational, formal, scientific and
the micro-political. Alan Tottenham and Dennis Moore practiced the scientific and I practiced the micro-political. Tottenham practiced the managerial, authoritarian mode of management and I practiced the interpersonal,
adversarial approach (Ball 1987, 104–119). There was a conflict between
two ways of leading a school, the one closed and the other open. The formal
leadership operated a closed system which was based on old, fixed ideas
which were not open to challenge or change. They were concerned to defend the status quo and their own vested interest. They practiced a style
which considered conflict pathological and illegitimate. To them there is
only one view of reality. Authoritarian politics works by preventing "public
access to voice, by stifling opposition" and by "insulation, concealment and
secrecy" (Ball 1987, 124). Alan Tottenham's absence from a meeting of the
governors symbolized the authoritarian and managerial style since he didn't
accept talk. He managed by the authority of the written word. In the scientific style of management, authority is a key concept and power is ignored.
Alan Tottenham assumed that his authority should be unquestioned and he

didn't contemplate the importance of power, the power of talk, words and ideas. Ball analyzes the concepts of power and authority as follows:

System theorists, almost by definition, tend to eschew the concept of power in favour of authority. In doing so they assume legitimacy and consent and again pathologize conflict. Significantly, studies and accounts of headship in schools invariably begin with a pre-emptive definition of role in terms of authority; the articles of governance are frequently quoted. Again, my claim is that the assumption of authority is unhelpful and distorting. (25)

The practices of the micro-political are a direct challege to the managerial and the authoritarian. Its vehicle is talk, interaction and communication. Gossip is a very real factor in organizational life and is the "issue of informal relations" (Ball 1987, 216–221). It is in behind-the-scenes informality that reputations are made, knowledge can be used, associations developed and influence created. The formal, bureaucratic model doesn't recognize or understand the informal and the interpersonal. It is stuck in vertical relations and doesn't realize the reality of horizontal relations. Horizontal relations are interpersonal and are the arena of the emotions, of love and hate, of envy and jealousy (216). The formal attempts to exclude all emotion. I wanted to meet the head on the horizontal level of relations in which everyone could speak. He wouldn't agree. In the sphere of the micro-political, the personal is the political and the political is the personal. The micro-political is an "ongoing dynamic process." Consulting the governors was an attempt to influence them, and is a legitimate action for a member of the organization as a professional. The managerial authoritarian way to manage a school is wrong because it is dehumanizing and depersonalizing. The school was promoting a dehumanizing form of education by formalizing all its relationships into a vertical and hierarchical model. Dennis Moore was so frightened of talk that he ordered a charge of unprofessional conduct. In the micro-political model "networking is an important resource of influence." Governors must be communicated with. The head had no policy for the school. A good head has a policy. Without a policy, where was he leading? An alternative policy for the school was being presented to the governors but they were not allowed to hear it. The possibility of a coup d'état was unthinkable. By not allowing talk about policy, the conception of education was being separated from execution.

In retrospect, speaking informally and personally, I had aquired a great deal of experience as a micro-politician and I was probably the only serious activist in the school. I had successfully initiated change in a school that didn't want change. I had acquired considerable practice at talk and micropolitics. I had obtained power through struggle. Persons who live by the formal model of orgnization conduct all their relations formally and hierarchically. I could not go back to formal relations. I had really become the de facto leader of the school and found myself in the position of a coup d'état. The governors had been given a choice between the head and a rival. That was the real meaning of the situation.

Dennis Moore probably feared that if he let me talk to the governors, an impossible situation would have arisen. He wanted me out of the organization because he was a formal person and wanted a formal organization. He didn't want change. I wanted change. We were in conflict.

The system puts teachers in competition with their colleagues. A career is a struggle for control (Ball 1987, 166–190). Alan Tottenham and I were concerned about our careers. He and Dennis Moore had the vertical power and they used it and the governors supported them. But, they were all mistaken; the formal model of organization is unreal. A person cannot be depersonalized and cut up into formal and informal parts.

An educational institution is set up for the purposes of learning. How can a formal organization promote learning adequately if it doesn't permit change? How do people learn, including teachers, but by talk and language? But the formal model outlaws language and communication. In the formal model there is a separation between the leader and the led since the relationship is vertical. In formalizing his relations, the head is depersonalizing himself and making himself lonely since he can't interact with colleagues as equals. Responsibility for the organization is separated from the people who constitute it, which leads to a reified and dehumanized conception of the school.

It is not enough to criticize formal bureaucracy because it misses the informal and the emotional. It is necessary to conceptualize the nature of the informal and micro-political as Ball has done. Politics is talk and the attempt to get influence for your ideas and point of view. Talk is the lifeblood of education and learning.

In order for there to be change, there needs to be persuasion, to overcome conflict. Critical theory is a "theoretically grounded form of advocacy in a situation of social conflict" (McCarthy 1978, 332).

CULTURE AS PRACTICAL SYMBOLIC ANALYSIS

Habermas claimed that the bureaucratic system of formal, scientific, organizational culture dominated the lifeworld's culture of the symbolic subject and agent and required a culture of democratic, communicative action to redeem the situation. He claimed that the system grew from the lifeworld of culture and language and not the other way around, so that the reasoning of the lifeworld is prior to functionalist reason.

I clarify, first, the cultural perspective on schools since, in this case study of the school, organizational science is in conflict with the school as a culture taken as a whole. Recent work has emphasized the relevance and importance of culture for the understanding of human nature and society (Geertz 1973; Bruner 1990; Thompson 1990).

Culture is both material and symbolic. I focus on the symbolic. The human ability to symbolize and intend meaning through the instrument and operation of language shapes culture. Bruner has argued that the proper study of mankind is the mind and its meanings because there is a connection between saying and doing and the mind is transactional rather than isolated. Psychology therefore is "cultural psychology." (Bruner 1990, 19) Meaning is expressed through the intentional states of the individual agent and it is impossible to understand these without language. By crying, children intend meaning and have intentions toward the world. Before children can talk they learn to have basic intentions. Symbolic gestures are intentional. Pierce argued that there were three components that bridge the gap between the subjective and the objective, the inner and the outer. First, there was the linguistic sign, then there was the thing signified and the third component was the symbolic interpretant which is what connected the subjective and objective components, the sign and the signified (Bruner 1990, 69).

The symbolic interpretant carried the meaning of the word in context. It had gained its meaning in the language system from all the other words in the symbolic system of language. Meaning and language therefore are the central constituents of the human being. Language consitutes reality. Man "is an animal suspended in webs of significance he himself has spun," a meaningful creation. So, the conclusion is, if you want to understand a school, you need to study the culture and symbol systems. The concept of culture originated from agricultural cultivation but referred to cultivating the cultural contents of the mind such as beliefs, attitudes, thoughts, feelings, language and values. Culture makes meaning the central ingredient of mind irreducible to information. It is "constitutive" of mind and individual minds grow in and from the culture which they are born into and inherit, a pre-interpreted domain, a socio-historical world. Culture is "in" the mind (Geertz 1973, 1–32). The self is a "symbolic project," a "narrative of self-identity." Culture is a symbolic construct. Humans create culture and are created by it through cultural products.

An anthropologist studies culture and does ethnography (Geertz 1973, 3–30). The principle of "operationalism" states that to understand an academic discipline, it is necessary to understand what the people who practice it do. Ethnography is defined by the kind of "intellectual effort it is," an effort at "thick description." If a person, for example, "twitches" the eyebrows that is one thing and it has no communicative intent or meaning, a mere physiological reaction. But, if she winks at another person it is a cultural act and has a meaning. By winking the person has acted deliberately and intentionally, to someone special, to communicate, according to certain rules and without anyone else knowing. Hence, to understand a wink is to make an effort at "thick description," to get at the meaning of the wink, to interpret it. A thin description is the meaning of a human action such as the act of winking. What has she done? What is the impact of her act? What is its significance? To analyze a culture is to sort out "the structures of signification." To do ethnography is a form of literary criciticism, "like reading a manuscript" (Geertz 1973, 3–30).

The culture of a school can be understood through "extrinsic," symbolic action. Ethnographic study is "microscopic." The analyst moves from simplicity to complexity, from "small acts" to "large matters" (Geertz 1973, 3–30).

A symbolic act is saying and doing something. It can be an act of speech, an action or a product of culture such as the curriculum or a book. It is essentially meaningful, shared and public. It is shared because language and meaning is shared. Language is a social construct. A symbolic speech act is conducted at a particular time, place and situation. It is tied to rules such as rules of cooperation. There is no secret, privatized self.

In *The Impact of the Concept of Culture on the Concept of Man*, the anthropologist Clifford Geertz observed, "What this means is that culture, rather than being added on, so to speak, to a finished or virtually finished animal, was ingredient, and centrally ingredient, in the production of the animal itself."

Geertz writes,

Most bluntly, it suggests that there is no such thing as a human nature independent of culture. Men without culture would not be the clever savages of Golding's *Lord of the Flies* thrown back upon the cruel wisdom of their animal instincts; "they would be unworkable monstrosities with very few useful instincts, fewer recognizable sentiments, and no intellect: mental basket cases." Further on he [Geertz] writes, "Without men, no culture, certainly; but equally, and more significantly, without culture, no men." Furthermore, "We are, in sum, incomplete or unfinished animals who complete or finish ourselves through culture—and not through culture in general but through highly particular forms of it. (Geertz 1973, 49)

Culture is "constitutive" (Bruner 1990, 11). "Folk psychology" or common sense is the individual's "instrument of culture" and is learned through the culture's stories (33–65), because the organizing principle of a culture is the narrative mode. It is the culture and its history which provides the "prosthetic devices" by which individuals enter the culture and live through its meanings.

The narrative use of language is an essential vehicle of culture due to its inherent characteristics such as its sequentiality. Narrative organizes time and experience. "Language is a time system." A child enters the culture through stories which organize experience. An infant cannot grasp meaning. Children are assisted to make meaning by caretakers in the family. The narrative use of langauge arises from social interaction that is cultural interaction (67–97).

A narrative is "a means for emphasizing human action" or "agentivity." Human meanings and intentions tied to beliefs and desires require a mode of expression and it is narrative that connects the individual to the culture. A narrative is sensitive to what is canonical and what violates canonicality, and hence the narrative form introduces a child to the moral relations of a culture. There must also be a narrative perspective; a narrative cannot be "voiceless" (77). Narrative is built around "established canonical expectations and the mental management of deviations from such expectations" (35). Narrative conveys the orthodox behavior acceptable in a particular culture.

Culture is a "behavioral phenomenon," language and communicative behavior. This is the concept of culture I work with. Cultural analysis aims at the interpretation of "symbolic-expressive behavior."

I conclude here that to understand the Borecross school, you need to approach it through its culture as a whole rather than as a formal organization detached from informal practices. For example, when the head and one of the deputies played a game of putting at the amalgamation, what was happening? What did it mean?

CULTURE AS A SYMBOLIC PROCESS

Renato Rosaldo has proposed the study of culture by process and narrative analysis. Cultural forms have a structure and a process. Cultural analysis has traditionally taken the form of an objective, formal analysis of social structures by a detached, scientific observer imitating the methods of the physical sciences. This kind of analysis took a static, atemporal view since it considered culture as a completed event and ignored the element of time. It was suited to the formal analysis of culture.

Bourdieu has demonstrated that time is a constitutive feature of cultural practices; for example, the time interval in accepting an invitation is a constitutive part of the reality of a social, political relationship. If there were no time, there could be no planning or strategy for the future (Rosaldo 1989, 107).

The method that has been developed for incorporating the time element is the case history method, which is a record of social actions over a time period to see what happens in a culture as it changes. It is suitable for analyzing political change and political conflict. Humans have the power of agency. Human actions happen in time and their actions have consequences which take time to unfold. Events in time record social actions and their consequences. It is particularly adapted to the unfolding of events, ideas and institutions as they interact with each other. Since a time process has a sequence, the narrative form is an "apt vehicle" for process, event analysis (127).

Unlike a static, logical analysis, the narrative form has a number of distinguishing characteristics which are suited to social analysis. It has structure. Events are propelled by actors who act meaningfully for reasons. Events get constructed into a plot and a story with a sequence. Narrative records peoples' intentions. A narrative recognizes emotional force, subjectivity and relationships. It is sensitive to meaning and point of view.

Narrative analysis is the medium of historical understanding. It is context sensitive. The object of a social, narrative analysis is understanding. An objective analysis is insufficient to provide true knowledge of a culture, though it does provide knowledge. It needs to be supplemented by processual analysis and considered from the point of view of change. Change does not follow from a structural analysis. Human society is best understood through the concepts of agency and structure, and not merely structure.

CONCLUSION

My primary task is to retrospectively weave these events into a plot as the historian, plot analyst, and eventually to plot the story to the ending. I am also an educational diagnostician. The first event was the coming of the new head teacher and what it meant in educational and political terms. It meant no change and an implicit policy of continuity and stability. I sought a meeting with the governors and presented an educational analysis. The head teacher absented himself as uninvolved. The governors promised me one thing which after the meeting turned into insignificance. I obtained a second meeting. At this meeing I was recommended for a medical inspection and placed on a charge of unprofessional conduct with the echoes of unprofessionalism mentioned in Chapter 2. I then put the situation in terms of conflicting concepts of organization. Finally, I introduced the understanding of a school as a culture.

From an educational point of view, the events of the plot have added up to the anti-intellectual, authoritarian nature of the school organization and government. Intellectual concepts of education and the person who uttered them (myself) were simply rendered meaningless. This was theory divorced from practice in situation.

The importance of this chapter is the conclusion that a school is a culture which can be understood by narrative and plot analysis of the actions and decisions made by the participants in situation that is from an existentialist perspective.

Chapter 4

Disciplinary Tribunal for Criticizing a Head Teacher

The story moves in this chapter to a courtroom, tribunal situation in front of a lawyer and four members of a jury whose task is to adjudicate the evidence, in which the interested parties tell their side of the story in relation to the events that led to a charge of unprofessional conduct against me for criticizing a head teacher. I outline my defense in the first section. Then, I record the story and evidence of Dennis Moore, who initiated the charge, and why he did so. Next, Dr. Cathy Hall, a Borecross governor, tells her story followed by Dr. Kinship, also a Borecross governor. These are the three main witnesses for the prosecution of misconduct. Two minor witnesses, representing the authority in the same cause, also give evidence. Then the side of the defense is heard by one witness and written testimony. Finally, I construct the plot and story and analyze it from the point of view of the charge of unprofessional conduct. The evidence contributes to the inter-weaving of the events and actions into a meaningful whole. This is a retrospective analysis to discover the true significance in terms of causation. Who and what caused it and why?

THE DEFENSE

The City Education Authority made the following charge at a disciplinary tribunal:

Mr. Armitage "has been involved in a criticism of the previous headmaster" and "had continued to criticize" under the new headmaster, Mr. Tottenham. The document which was written by Mr. Armitage "was considered to be unprofessional in content" (Chapter 9, first section). Finally in the opinion of Mr. G. A. Stephens, assistant education officer, "Mr. Armitage erred in asking the divisional officer to have this document typed and by preparing the document laid himself open to the complaint of unprofessional conduct."

I was informed the Monday morning of the governors' meeting that a document which I had been writing had been distributed without my permission. So once again Mr. Stephens was factually incorrect, since I did not ask the divisional officer to have the document typed. Thus, the tribunal was based on a factual distortion. Like the medical inspection, the institution of a disciplinary tribunal was a political action designed to suppress political opposition and implicitly to prevent educational change. I didn't possess a copy of the document since I had given my original copy to Michael Lewis, the clerk to the governors, for typing.

At the governors' meeting, I was confronted with the news that the document could not be discussed and that I was to be put on a charge of unprofessional conduct. This document was distributed secretively and without authority which meant that it was politics without ethics.

The defense at the tribunal was that the distribution of the document was unauthorized. This was, of course, true, and was confirmed by Dr. Hall and Dennis Moore. I said in evidence that I wrote the document but had doubts about the way I was going to meet the governors. I asked Mr. Lewis in his capacity as a friend, to type the document, not to show it to anyone and return it to me. There was no written instruction. I telephoned him to find out when it was ready. I asked him to type it because the meeting was called at short notice and I hadn't the time to type it myself, an important point since in the ordinary way I would have done so. The governors did not consult concerning how much time was needed to prepare for a meeting.

EVIDENCE AND CONTENT ANALYSIS OF WITNESSES

The purpose of analyzing the evidence is to uncover the thinking which led to the events of the story and how the actions of the witnesses contributed to the development of the plot.

Critique of Dennis Moore's Evidence (Day 1)

The evidence of Dennis Moore, the district inspector, who initiated the charge of "unprofessional conduct," was confusing and inconclusive in a number of ways. First, he says he was *not* concerned with the distribution of the document (day 1, page 67). But he confirms he was told by Mr. Lewis after the governors' meeting that I had told Mr. Lewis to return the document to me for typing and other specific instructions (day 1, page 67). He had then authorized its distribution without knowing whether I wanted it to be distributed. Moore is then vague about how he came across the document. He says he can't remember what happened (day 1, page 68). He even says he hadn't spoken to the divisional officer about it, which is scarcely credible (day 1, page 68). On page 69, Moore says he has "no idea" when he received the document, whether on the Friday or the Monday before the governors' meeting. Since it was distributed on the Friday, he must have seen it on the Friday or before. This is entirely unsatisfactory since the key issue of the tribunal was whether the document was distributed with or without the author's authority. Since Mr. Moore's evidence is at best ambiguous and could be deliberately deceptive, the tribunal should not have considered his evidence valid. Also, since it was distributed on the Friday, the information that it had been distributed was deliberately withheld, since I telephoned Mr. Lewis on Friday afternoon to ask if he had completed the typing so that I could collect it. I had been intentionally deceived about its distribution. Why was the document distributed secretly? Was this professional not to say ethical conduct?

On day 1, page 70, Moore admitted that he instituted the charge of unprofessional conduct. But he contradicted himself when he said the real decision came from the education officer, which meant he didn't want to accept the political responsibility for the charge because the education officer must have acted on his advice. He also says he made "certain assumptions about the way a complaint should be made" and "certain assumptions about the relationship which a junior member of staff should have with his headmaster."

Moore assumed that the relationship between a headmaster and a member of staff was a dominant-submissive, authoritarian relationship and criticizing a head teacher's work is something which isn't allowed in any circumstances.

On day 1, page 71, Dennis Moore said that "there was certainly no way in which I was going to discuss the merits of a headmaster with a junior member of staff. I would have regarded that as most unprofessional myself. I would not do it. Therefore, if you remember, we did not." This meant he had refused to discuss the first complaint examined in Chapter 2, in which case, how could the complaint be judged in a rational manner? It couldn't have been and it wasn't. It would have been possible to have discussed the house system issue and the other issues in a logical manner. The issue was not exclusively the merits of the headmaster but the issues of the school. It was the latter that Dennis Moore refused to discuss. Raymond Moore regarded me as a "junior member of staff" but this was an irrelevant point. What was relevant was the logic of my arguments.

On day 1, page 70, I asked Mr. Moore, "Do you think you made certain assumptions when you came to that meeting about the propriety of my making a complaint against my headmaster?" Mr. Moore replied: (1) "I made certain assumptions about the way in which a complaint should be made." (2) "I made certain assumptions about the relationship which a junior member of staff should have with his headmaster." I also asked him,

"Did you think I was a little upstart really, to put it very bluntly, stepping out of line?" Mr. Moore replied, "Presumptuous, I thought."

On day 1, page 70, I also asked Mr. Moore,

Can I put it to you then that you could have possibly got hold of this document—hypothetically—which you got from the office from Mr. Lewis (and we do not know how you came across it) and supposing you did not have any feelings toward me, adverse or hostile, you could have said, "We'll get this document distributed. I can go to the meeting on Monday and announce to the governors that it is unprofessional conduct and say we are not going to discuss the document; it is going to be a matter for the tribunal." If you thought that way, you could have done that, could you not?

He replied, "I could have, but I did not." His reply contradicts what he said elsewhere which is that he instituted the charge of unprofessional conduct in order to prevent discussion. Is this statement therefore a deliberate deception? Is Mr. Moore asking others to believe that he didn't know what was going on? He is quite clear that he didn't want the governors to discuss the document. This seems to have been uppermost in his mind.

When asked whether he was a party to the resolution that I needed a medical inspection, Mr. Moore said, "I had no vote on that." He said, though, that the governors had "a point" in advising one since Dr. Hall had given a "report" and she had spent a "considerable time" with me. However, Dr. Hall had had two conversations with me and in the circumstances was it not a considerable length of time. She in fact had misread the situation, and the headmaster said in evidence he was surprised by the resolution and had made no contribution to the debate. Since Mr. Moore said they had a "point," he must have made a misjudgment since the CEA psychiatrist said I was "fit for duty" and I am indeed a physically and mentally fit person. It leaves him open to the interpretation that in order to assist himself, he believed in an action intended to harm me. Moreover, I think it reflects the poor quality of discussion on the governing body and the quality of their decision-making. Since part of my intention in speaking to the governors was to open the problems of the school up to debate, not being allowed to was a direct hindrance of rational debate. Furthermore, since the mark of mental ill-health is irrationality, and of good health is rationality, then surely it was rational for the governors to engage me in conversation. Yet, this is what Mr. Moore wouldn't allow them to do and which they were reluctant to do themselves. Therefore, they were indeed encouraging an irrational atmosphere and encouraging the very mode of behavior they were trying to criticize.

On day 2, page 5, Dennis Moore admits that he didn't give two visiting inspectors a copy of an evaluation I had done of the school. If he had wanted to promote democratic openness, he would have done so since it was relevant to their purposes. Why didn't he do so? Because he didn't want participation and openness within the authority although it had been expressly called for?

On day 2, page 6, Moore agreed that my way of interpreting a remark he had made to the effect that "nobody was really responsible for anything that they did" was a possible interpretation. In other words, "we were all in a system for which no individual was responsible," even an inspector or headmaster.

Moore also said on day 2, page 7, that the cause of problems in the school which I ascribed to the headmaster were in his opinion caused by other reasons. What were the other reasons? Here is a real issue because it relates to the question of responsibility in the system. Wasn't the house system the headmaster's responsibility and wasn't this a clear case of responsibility? Why hadn't it been changed? Why hadn't it been properly investigated by the authorities?

Moore gives one reason for the school's problems as "partly at the amalgamation itself—which was a nasty political battle in which both sides were very badly bruised. There was a long period when the important thing was to melt disparity as far as possible."

On day 2, page 8, Moore was asked about the governors' recommendation that I should see a medical advisor. He thought that there had been a "mounting hysteria" "going through the long succession of papers we had had." When Moore was asked, since he had formulated the view that "the person who had written the document was in need of medical advice," why he made "no attempt to advise Peter Armitage of the dangerous position in which he was placing himself," Moore replied, "I do not think Mr. Armitage needed advice." In other words, he didn't see me as mentally sick.

Moore said on day 2, page 9 that, "it seemed to me that it was extremely important at the governor's meeting that the governors should not be allowed to discuss this document." The reasons for this view that Mr. Moore gave were confusing. He said:

1. The headmaster might make a complaint against Mr. Armitage. But that is hardly a logical reason since Mr. Tottenham was free to act as he chose fit.

2. That Mr. Armitage "could have pursued" the document and made "a complaint." That was Mr. Armitage's decision one way or the other. Why should Mr. Moore interfere?

3. Mr. Moore also said, "I felt it was wrong that they should prejudice a decision of a board of Investigation by considering it at this stage."

It is very hard to make any sense out of Moore's remarks. I went through normal procedures to meet the governors. What is wrong in talking to the governors? It seems clear that Moore was determined to stop the governors from discussing the document, perhaps because he believed the contents to be substantially true and he didn't want to allow me the opportunity to put my case.

The next question was that, "Nevertheless, you did indicate to the governors that it was your intention to bring a complaint of unprofessional conduct when you were aware that under the provisions of the staff code they would have to consider the matter in the first instance at a subsequent governors' meeting." Mr. Moore's answer was, "I had to tell them that to save them from discussing it." In other words, his intention was to prevent them at all costs from discussing it and the charge of unprofessional conduct was an excuse.

On day 2, page 10, Moore was asked whether his complaint was brought under section X of the staff code relating to "misconduct." He replied that, "Again, I am sorry to be hair-splitting but I had not made a complaint. I had made a report to the chief inspector about a member of staff whose conduct was concerning me. My understanding of the way we operate is that it is for the chief inspector to advise the education officer as to whether a complaint is to be made. My stage ceased at the report to the chief inspector." Here it seems to me that Moore is passing the responsibility to higher authority who in any case must have made the decision on his advice. Moore expresses a bureaucratic view of the CEA in which it is possible that nobody accepts responsibility. Yet Moore was clearly the cause of this charge of unprofessional conduct.

In the next question on page 10, Mr. West, the questioner, says that he wanted to get to the bottom of the "basis of unprofessional conduct as grounds for complaint" "since it is not something on which there can be a consensus" in the profession. Mr. Moore said there were "many aspects" to the complaint of "unprofessional." (1) Mr. Armitage's "disregard" for the wishes of the education officer as expressed in 1976. That is disobedience. (2) Making difficulties for two headmasters.

It is significant that Moore used the word "wishes" in regard to the education officer. A teacher is under no obligation of total obedience to someone else's wishes just because they are higher in authority, and if their wishes are against reason. Mr. Stephens's concept of democracy was self-serving.

The next question was central. West asked him, "I ask you whether criticizing the head, per se, was evidence of unprofessional conduct?" Mr. Moore replied, "Not per se definitely." "Criticism per se is accepted and proper."

On day 2, page 12, Moore said, "No, it is not persistence per se though I think what I have just said is one of the strands. The manner in which the case has been pursued seems to me to be important." In Moore's view, this comes down to:

1. The inclusion of quite spiteful attacks on the personality and integrity" . . . "of the head" and "other senior members of staff." He said, "In my book that is not the way of conducting a persistent argument.

2. There is more than a degree of "intellectual dishonesty" which he claimed amounts to "selective quotes" and the "intermingling of personal interest with professional concern for the management of the school."

3. Moore said Armitage's "method of argument, it seems to me, is essentially a negative one." "He is short of solutions."

4. He then makes two contradictory statements that (a). I see things as "the head's fault" or "the fault of senior members of staff," and "he sees everything in terms of systems, not realizing that often it is the people who have to implement the proposals who are, in fact, the key factors."

Asked what amounts to "misconduct," Mr. Moore replied, "I think it is the totality of the matter."

Referring to Mr. Moore's statement that I had used a "degree of intellectual dishonesty," Mr. West of the tribunal asked, "Would you say that after a person who arranges their argument with a selection from documents in a way which you thought was intellectually below standard because there is no suggestion, perhaps, of deliberate misleading here, would you say that was, per se evidence of misconduct?" Moore replied, "Yes I would."

Moore then said he could easily pick out "areas"—"where" Armitage's "argument is intellectually suspect." But he was told, "This tribunal is not concerned with whether Mr. Armitage's arguments are intellectually suspect or not, but whether it amounts to misconduct."

When asked finally what it was in the document that amounted to "misconduct" Mr. Moore said he had nothing to add but that it was "the combination of things."

After Mr. West had questioned Mr. Moore on day 2, it was the turn of Mr. Benford. He asked his question in rather a loaded way when he said "one can assume Mr. Armitage deliberately intended to circulate the document in that way." Moore said it was his assumption but the questions "ought to be addressed to an administrator who handled it." The administrator and division head, Mr. Flood, didn't attend the tribunal as a witness.

Mr. Moore next confesses to be "extremely perplexed" as to why I had written this document for the governors' meeting. He seemed to have had no understanding of cause and effect relationships as had been presented in these pages.

What comes through most clearly from Dennis Moore's evidence is that he was not a democrat in his approach to human relationships within organizations. He believed in the total power of head teachers and the subordination of subordinates. He, therefore, regarded complaints as against the rules. That was why he took the action he did. He also took it because he might have thought that I would prevail in any argument with the governors, which I probably would have done. In this his assessment was correct. Mr. Moore's action was designed to prevent democratic discussion and rational behavior. It was a politics of suppression and domination.

The second witness was Dr. Cathy Hall. She began with a statement.

Dr. Cathy Hall's Statement.

To: Mr. White
TS13, County Hall
February 12, 1980
Peter B. Armitage
Statement for Disciplinary Tribunal of Enquiry

I joined the governing body of Borecross School in September 1977 and was present at the governors' meeting on January 26, 1978 when the governors received a five-page document from Mr. Armitage of the English Department. On March 13, 1978 I attended the special governors' meeting which was called so that Mr. Armitage could present to the governors his complaint that he had been treated unfairly and suffered discriminatory treatment. I was also present at the governors' meeting in November 1978 when Mr. Armitage's request for a second meeting with the governors to discuss his unfair treatment and attempts to obstruct his career was refused by the governing body.

In April 1979, Mr. Brown, head of science and a teacher governor, telephoned me at home. Mr. Brown said he was acting for Mr. Armitage who had asked for a private meeting with me to discuss his case. I was willing to meet with Mr. Armitage on certain conditions; first, that the chairman and headmaster be informed of the request; second, that I be accompanied by another governor and third, that Mr. Armitage be accompanied by a friend. I later telephoned the chairman, Mr. Pickett, and told him of Mr. Armitage's request and said I proposed to ask Dr. Kinship, a newly appointed governor, to accompany me to the meeting. The chairman approved this suggestion and I wrote to Mr. Armitage agreeing to his request and stating the terms of the meeting (10.4.79). Mr. Armitage agreed to Dr. Kinship being present and I wrote again (23.4.79) to suggest possible dates for the meeting.

On May 14, 1979, Dr. Kinship and I met Mr. Armitage in the conference room at Borecross School and were joined later by Mr. Atherton, head of English. Mr. Armitage sent us an eight-page document on curriculum evaluation prior to the meeting, which he thought would be a basis for discussion. We began the meeting by telling Mr. Armitage that we proposed to limit the discussion to matters arising after March 13, 1978, when he had put his case to the governors, and second, we would only concern ourselves with those matters affecting him personally. Mr. Armitage agreed to these conditions and there followed an hour of firm but friendly discussion. Mr. Armitage felt that he had been discriminated against because of his campaign to reorganize the school. He felt that he should be a head of department and via the Heads of Department Committee he would be able to implement major policy changes in the school to make it fully comprehensive and to relieve the "top-heavy bureaucracy." With Dr. Kinship's support I tried to show Mr. Armitage the impracticalities of his ambitions. There was a young, newly appointed head of English and a recently appointed director of studies and I could not therefore see what head of department post Mr. Armitage thought he might be given. I also pointed out that a move from his present scale 2 post to a scale 4 post was perhaps too ambitious without an intermediate move. I suggested that Mr. Armitage was creating his own difficulties rather than others creating them for him. We spent some time talking about applying for posts in other schools but Mr. Armitage said he wanted to stay at Borecross and thought by virtue of his qualifications he deserved to be a head of department. Mr. Armitage also had personal reasons for wanting to stay in this part of London.

Mr. Atherton spoke for his colleague and presented his views of Mr. Armitage's situation in a very kind and considered way. Mr. Atherton said he recognized Mr. Armitage's problems were largely of his own making but his situation in the school was becoming untenable. Finally, Mr. Atherton said that in his own opinion Mr. Armitage's passionate desire to institute changes in the school was causing him positive hurt and distress.

During the interview Mr. Armitage had several times to be checked when making scathing comments about other people; governors and the headmaster. Mr. Armitage raised the question of the headmaster's treatment of his memo on the subject of the head of English post which the headmaster had rebuked as canvassing. I said I thought the rebuke to be reasonable. Mr. Armitage also took exception to the fact that the headmaster had not attended the governors' meeting on March 13, 1978, when he put his case to the governors.

Mr. Armitage considered he had been unfairly treated and said that the governors should know that their resolution of March 13, 1978 had not been fully carried out and he had not discussed fully with the divisional inspector and headmaster the development of his career. Mr. Armitage also asked us to request another meeting with the governing body.

Mr. Atherton had to leave before the end of the meeting which was taken up with a discussion between Mr. Armitage and Dr. Kinship on the curriculum evaluation paper which Mr. Armitage had prepared. We ended the meeting by assuring Mr. Armitage that we would meet him again if he wished to talk to us.

After Mr. Armitage had left, Dr. Kinship and I agreed that we should investigate the allegation that the governors' resolution had not been fully carried out and we decided that we would ask our colleagues to see Mr. Armitage again. I wrote to Mr. Armitage (23.5.79) to tell him of our decision.

I wrote to the chairman (16.5.79) who was able to satisfy himself that the governors' resolution of March 13, 1978 had been fully carried out and at the governors' meeting on June 18, 1979, Dr. Kinship and I, with the support of the chairman, obtained the agreement of our fellow governors to a meeting with Mr. Armitage. I asked for a report from the Inspector of English since few of the governors, myself included, had any knowledge of Mr. Armitage's classroom teaching.

On the evening of July 16, Mr. Armitage telephoned me at home to talk about the meeting the next day. I expressed my concern at the contents of the document he had written for the governors, particularly the references to colleagues and the remarks about the headmaster.

On July 17, 1979, the governors met Mr. Armitage for a second time. I spoke to Mr. Armitage for a few minutes before the meeting and he outlined to me arguments he proposed to use in the meeting. At the meeting, upon advice from Mr. Moore, much of the document prepared by Mr. Armitage was excluded from the discussion. Mr. Buckley, inspector of English, reported to the governors. At the end of the meeting the governors were very concerned by Mr. Armitage's behavior and felt he had not justified his allegations of unfair treatment. In view of Mr. Armitage's recent behavior the governors also felt he should be seen by the Authority Medical Advisor.

On the evening of July 17, Mr. Armitage telephoned me again to ask to meet me and I agreed but again I insisted that Dr. Kinship accompany me and advised Mr. Armitage to ask a friend, perhaps Mr. Atherton, to come with him. Eventually a meeting was arranged during the summer vacation.

On August 13, 1979, Dr. Kinship and I met Mr. Armitage, who had chosen not to bring Mr. Atherton (Mr. Atherton had telephoned me before the meeting to say he had been willing to come).

I began this meeting by telling Mr. Armitage that I felt he was becoming more and more obsessed with his case and his failure to sway his colleagues and the governors with his arguments was leading him to more extreme action.

Mr. Armitage did not agree with my assessment and said it was preposterous. We then talked for some time of the meeting on July 17 with the governors and then about career prospects. Mr. Armitage said he was looking for another post and felt his qualifications stood him in good stead. I think he also mentioned that he was applying for posts in higher education too. I gave my own personal view that he should take a complete break from the educational world, for a term at least, so that he could get things into perspective, but he rejected this idea.

We talked briefly of the posts Mr. Armitage had applied for and he said he could not agree with the reasons Mr. Buckley had given at the recent meeting of the governors for his not being appointed to these posts. Mr. Armitage seemed to feel there was a conspiracy against him and the failure to secure a post was part of the victimization he had suffered.

Several times during the meeting Dr. Kinship was forced to stop Mr. Armitage making bitter comments against his colleagues, particularly the headmaster and deputy head.

When Dr. Kinship asked about his class discipline and how he got on with the boys he said his discipline was good and he got on well with the boys. (Mr. Armitage did write to me a few days later to ask (17.8.79) if the letter of complaint from a parent had been produced at the governors' meeting. My last letter to Mr. Armitage (31.8.79) was to tell him that any discussion at governors' meetings is confidential.)

The meeting was not as constructive as that in May. Mr. Armitage seemed to be seeking from us agreement that he was right and when we could not give this he seemed at first confused and hurt and finally angry. He felt the part of the martyr keenly and toward the end of a very long meeting said something about history showing men of courage opposing the establishment always suffering.

When Mr. Armitage left the meeting Dr. Kinship and I were so stunned by his rambling and illogical arguments, his failure to grasp what we were saying at times, and his agitated behavior when we could not agree with his views, that we felt concerned on his behalf and more particularly on behalf of the school. We decided that we were sufficiently worried after the interview to write to the Divisional Officer, Mr. Flood. We wrote the letter on 20.8.79 and sent it to Divisional Office.
Signed
N. R. Hall, B.Sc., Ph.D., A.K.C., F.R.G.S.
Encl. correspondence

Letter to Mr. Armitage dated 10.4.79
Letter to Mr. Armitage 23.4.79
Letter to Mr. Armitage 26.4.79
Letter to Chairman dated 16.5.79
Letter to Mr. Armitage dated 23.5.79
Note of argument given by Mr. Armitage 17.7.79
Letter from Mr. Armitage dated 17.8.79
Letter to Mr. Armitage dated 31.8.79

Critical Analysis of Dr. Hall's Evidence

On day 1, page 15, Dr. Hall says, "I was not prepared to discuss anything prior to the meeting with the governors on March 13, 1978. I felt I was not competent, or was it proper to consider matters before March 13, on which I was not familiar." Hence, since this matter started in 1972, it was quite outside Dr. Hall's knowledge and competence. It was therefore a political mistake for her to be involved unless she were prepared to go into the history of the case. She prevented discussion of the complex history of this case as I have recorded it. She had no way of putting perspective on her judgments. Hence political misunderstandings were inevitable. If she was going to be involved, she would have been better informed if she had allowed discussion of matters prior to 1978 since they were historically relevant. Dennis Moore used Mr. Stephens's letter as a historical precedent when it suited his argument. It is also politically noteworthy that Dr. Hall was not in agreement with other governors who didn't want a meeting. This is a criticism of the inadequate machinery for communication in the system.

On day 1, page 16, Dr. Hall said, "When Mr. Armitage telephoned he was anxious to talk about the next day, and I said that I wished he had shown me a copy of that statement, and I would have then been able to express my views, and asked him to remove certain statements, which I felt would do him 'no good at all.' " I couldn't do this since I didn't have the document.

Dr. Hall, on day 1, page 21, commended Tim Atherton as "a very acute and intelligent" person. "I have great faith in Mr. Atherton." He had understood the situation. Tim Atherton had clearly pointed out to Dr. Hall that my political "situation in the school was becoming untenable" and my "passionate desire to initiate changes in the school was causing" me "positive hurt and distress." Well, of course, it had become an "untenable" situation since the authorities resisted dialogue and political participation. Dr. Hall was being asked to support a rational and democratic politics. Instead she really made the political situation worse by not supporting democratic opposition and by suggesting I was mentally unstable.

Dr. Hall says, in her written evidence, "I suggested that Mr. Armitage was creating his own difficulties rather than others creating them for him." Here she expressed her political ignorance of schools. She didn't seem to realize the problems I was dealing with were the school's political and educational problems which couldn't be dealt with in any other way. Yet, she also says elsewhere that the interests of the pupils must come first.

Dr. Hall blamed me for taking part in democratic politics and ignored all events prior to 1978. She was out of her political depth in this situation. The explanation can only be that either because she didn't know me or know the school, she completely misjudged my character and the situation in the school. Her acquaintance with me was extremely superficial. Her attitude and judgment were completely contradicted by the other witnesses who had known me for years. There was never any suggestion of instability. I did, however, have strong feelings that "something was wrong in the state of Denmark." There was a lot to be concerned about. Since she was the governor I had had most contact with, this shows how seriously uninformed the rest of the governors must have been.

On the question of discrimination, Dr. Hall was also wrong. I hadn't been interviewed for either the head of English post or the director of studies. I hadn't been interviewed for any post in the school for several years. The process was halted at the shortlisting procedure. There had been blatant manipulation of short-listing procedure by the head teacher and chairman of governors in relation to the math appointments and probably English appointments. It was political appointments which had partly produced this situation. It had also happened under Brian Fellows when Alfred Wellberry had delayed a promotion. There was a history and a pattern of manipulating appointments so that the full governing body wouldn't be involved in making decisions which individual governors couldn't control.

Dr. Hall confronted a difficult political situation. If she had accepted that I had a rational point of view, she herself would have had to face a conflict of opinions with her fellow governors. I gave her the opportunity to act politically. She declined it.

It was unfortunate but hardly surprising that I couldn't find a governor with sufficient understanding of Borecross School and education to help me effectively in both representing my case and improving the government of the school. The governing body was the heart of the problem. They had to be persuaded to think things through and to change the situation in a positive direction. I had originally contacted her because she was a woman and might have been capable of handling a difficult situation, and because I thought she might have the ability to stand up to the other governors.

I asked Dr. Hall (day 1, page 22) why she had said nothing in her evidence about my "strength of character." She replied, "I do not recall him (Mr. Tim Atherton) expressing any views of your strength of character." I do, and on day 3, page 33, I asked Tim Atherton the following question: "Do you remember saying I was a strong person?" "Yes, I did," he said.

Since Dr. Hall hadn't heard Atherton's point and had heard him use the word "distressed" she would seem to have picked up an erroneous view of my character. This would explain her misunderstanding of the situation. Dr. Hall didn't seem to be a very good judge of character.

Then how could she judge someone on the basis of a short acquaintance in a particular situation. She said of me, "I found him rather a bizarre character." This is a general and unanalytical view of another person which says more about her perhaps than it does about me. Her specialism was geography whereas Atherton's was English and mine was English and the social sciences. Perhaps that was where the difference between us lay. She had plenty of formal qualifications but formal qualifications may or may not work in everyday, micro-politics. What matters is talk and performance.

Dr. Kinship's Statement

Statement for Tribunal of Enquiry
D.H.W. Kinship, School Governor, January 1980
Mr. P. Armitage, Borecross School

In July 1978, I was invited to join the governors of the Borecross school. I volunteered for this post following a request from the school for a governor from the polytechnics. I hoped that as a governor I could assist in fostering links between the secondary and further and higher educational sections of the CEA system. I had also had some previous informal contacts with Borecross School and was anxious to assist what I considered to be an enthusiastic, committed and successful school.

On November 14, 1978, I attended my first governors' meeting and in April I was asked by Dr. Hall to join her in a meeting with Mr. Armitage. It was explained to me that Mr. Armitage had met the governing body a year before to present a grievance and that he had not been satisfied with the outcome of this meeting but had been refused a second meeting with the governors. As a result of this he had made a direct appeal to Dr. Hall who had agreed to meet him but had asked me to join her. She explained to me that she thought it sensible for more than one governor to talk to Mr. Armitage and felt that as a new governor I would not be prejudiced by any previous meetings or decisions.

Before agreeing to meet Mr. Armitage I discussed the matter briefly with Mr. Tottenham, the headmaster. He thought that my presence would be of assistance to Dr. Hall and I was impressed that he made no attempt to present me with any particular view but was anxious that I should meet Mr. Armitage with an open mind on the case.

Dr. Hall and I met Mr. Armitage on May 14 at the school; he was accompanied by Mr. Brown, Head of the English Department. Dr. Hall had forwarded to me before the meeting a letter from Mr. Armitage with a document he had written on curriculum development. I was particularly interested in the latter since not only had I written papers on curriculum design and development but I was also chairman of a UNESCO working party on the topic. Also, parts of the paper related to research methodology which was an important aspect of my own Ph.D. studies.

My notes of that meeting confirm the very strong reactions it left with me. The first was that Mr. Armitage initially presented a very sincere, well-prepared and comprehensive case to justify his sense of persecution, but that as the meeting progressed and he was pressed further he became increasingly vague and ill-considered and less convincing.

Mr. Armitage's main grievance was that he had not been appointed as head of department. He was convinced that the reason for this was that he had been victimized and discriminated against because he did not agree with the headmaster on how a comprehensive school should be run. It became apparent during our meeting that he was quite unable to accept, or even discuss the fact, that there were other acceptable reasons for his not obtaining the post, or that it was not now possible for the school to make such an appointment if they so wished.

My second strong reaction was that his knowledge of curriculum design and research methods was quite superficial and even naive. This contradicted his written submission which I had found impressive. I suggested to Mr. Armitage that in academic circles it was necessary to convince by discussion and performance and not to depend solely upon written statements which could have been copied without real understanding. To my surprise he took this as a personal attack on his ability and it became impossible to discuss the matter further.

As the interview progressed I became increasingly concerned at Mr. Armitage's sense of persecution and the language he was using to describe his colleagues. I pointed this out to him, and was again disturbed to realize that he was unable to accept any criticism, however considered and helpful it was intended to be.

Following the meeting with Mr. Armitage, Dr. Hall and I recommended that he be given a further opportunity to meet the governors. My reasons for this were that I began to sense that Mr. Armitage would not be able to accept any suggestion that he was in the wrong and that therefore the governors would eventually be forced to take more serious action. In this case it was essential that every opportunity was afforded to him to present his case. Also I was concerned at his allegations that the recommendations agreed by the governors at their last meeting had not been implemented.

The governors subsequently accepted our recommendation that Mr. Armitage should present his case to them again. Unfortunately a special meeting had to be arranged at short notice for July 17 and I was not able to be present. I did, however, discuss and agree with Dr. Hall's report to the governors.

In August 1979, I received a report of the meeting between Mr. Armitage and the governors. This included an assurance that the recommendations of the governors at the previous meeting had been carried out and that Mr. Armitage's allegations to the contrary were incorrect.

I also received a letter from Dr. Hall asking me to join her in a second meeting with Mr. Armitage. We had agreed to this during our first meeting with him and, although by now I had serious doubts about Mr. Armitage and his case, I agreed to meet him again on August 13. I hoped that with Dr. Hall I might convince Mr. Armitage that our objective unbiased view was that he was doing harm to himself and the school by continuing to insist that he was being discriminated against and by vilifying his colleagues.

We met Mr. Armitage for the second time on August 13, 1979. It soon became clear that he was not prepared to accept any of the criticisms made of him, was obsessed with the view that he was being victimized and that he was entitled to a head of department post. In spite of our assurances he was convinced that the governors had not given him a fair hearing and had made up their minds, before he met them, to reject his case.

Toward the end of the meeting it became impossible to reason with Mr. Armitage and he became angry that we were not prepared to accept his interpretation of his situation. I asked Mr. Armitage a general question concerning his relationships with his colleagues and whether he had any difficulties over class discipline. He assured me that his record was excellent in both respects. Dr. Hall and I were both very disturbed at Mr. Armitage's lack of stability, intense but unjustified feeling of victimization and his spiteful attitude toward the headmaster and colleagues, which became evident during this meeting. Each of us had reached the same conclusion independently and from an initial position of some sympathy for him.

In view of this and the strength of our concern, we felt obliged to make it known to the CEA inspectorate. We therefore wrote to Mr. S. M. Flood, Divisional Officer, on August 20, expressing our view that Mr. Armitage's obsessive and disturbed behavior could present a threat to the children in his charge.

On August 21, I received from Dr. Hall a copy of a letter she had received from Mr. Armitage concerning a letter from a parent to the headmaster. Mr. Armitage had asked whether my question on his relationship with his pupils was related to this letter. I confirmed to Dr. Hall that I had no knowledge of any such letter from a parent and my question had been general, not specific.

On November 8, 1979, the governors met and reconsidered the case of Mr. Armitage. The headmaster informed the governors that there had been a formal written complaint from a parent about Mr. Armitage's alleged assault of a child; he also reported the result of a meeting between members of the inspectorate and Mr. Armitage.

Dr. Hall and I also gave the governors an account of our second meeting with Mr. Armitage and informed them of the extent of our concern and of our letter to Mr. Flood. The governors after some debate agreed on the Resolution in Item 23 of the minutes of the meeting held on the November 8, 1979, in which they recommended that Mr. Armitage be suspended pending further necessary action by the Authority.

Dr. Kinship, January 1980

Analysis of Dr. Kinship's Evidence

Dr. Kinship's evidence was insubstantial since he misunderstood the situation entirely, which was hardly surprising since he was a new governor with no knowledge of the school. But, also because, like Dennis Moore, he took a paternalistic view of a head teacher's relations with his subordinates and was unprepared to accept any criticism of authority.

The governors should have appointed someone who had known the school since the amalgamation. Hence, they made a political error of judgment and had not given enough thought to this matter. Dr. Kinship reacted irrationally to my use of the words "underhand," and "corrupt" as if this was unthinkable. Yet, they were not an inaccurate description of many events that had occurred, such as the issue of the maths appointment. In this case, the following letter was sent by the chairman of the common room to the chairman of governors:

July 21, 1978

Mr. J. Pickett
Chairman of Governors

Dear Mr. Pickett,

At a meeting of the common room, held on Tuesday July 18, the following motion was passed unanimously:

"This common room deplores the procedures used in the non-appointment of the 2i/c Maths Department. However we accept those assurances made by the headmaster at the meeting of the common room, and expect that all future appointments will be made following accepted procedures."

This motion followed a lengthy discussion about the series of unfortunate events surrounding the shortlisting and eventual non-interviews for the above mentioned position in the school. It would appear that the accepted procedures regarding appointments were not adhered to, and that members of the Maths Department were not treated with the courtesy that they warrant. In short the whole affair was described as being "shabbily conducted."

Members of the common room, and their professional associations, are not prepared to be treated in this way. It would appear that the loyal commitment to the school given by the staff is not being returned. We have accepted the assurances given by the headmaster regarding future appointments, and would ask you formally to fully support the view that the accepted procedures regarding appointments are properly followed in future.

Yours sincerely,
D. Shore
Chairman of the Common Room

The staff common room had little real power to do anything other than write a letter. However, the letter revealed a very disturbing situation, since the authorities had been caught manipulating appointment procedures and this behavior was consistent with previous behaviors of certain governors. It destroyed trust in the integrity and veracity of the governors. Teachers have to maintain trust and confidence with their students if their work is to prosper. Teachers were at the mercy of politicians who were manipulating them behind the scenes. While teachers had to set an example and behave to the best ethical standards, the people who were controlling their livelihoods and careers were taking advantage of their situation. The City Education Authority should have set up an inquiry into this situation and taken appropriate action after investigating the facts. This is where Dennis Moore and Mr. Stephens should have been paying attention. The fact had been established that the chairman and headmaster were manipulating appointments so that they could select candidates of their choice. There was every reason to suppose that political merit was the major consideration, certainly not educational qualification. I recall asking the first critical question that led to the head teacher admitting that procedures had not been followed, a question that no one else had the courage or verbal skill to ask. I also remember the chairman of common room, David Shore, pressing the question home so that the head teacher in front of many members of staff had to answer the questions truthfully. This led to the letter. In evidence at the tribunal (day 3, page 25) Alan Tottenham said:

The governors are quite prepared, for instance, in the case of staff appointments, for me to make a short list and come to agreement with the chairman of the governors rather than appearing as a corporate body and going right through it; they are prepared to let scale 2 appointments be made by chairman action rather than insisting on full governors' meetings.

It is clear that the head teacher could leave someone's name off a short list so that he would never be interviewed by the governing body. He had that power and could use it in a corrupt way if he so decided. And this had happened once and was found out. How could teachers trust a head who was known to have behaved in this way? Without the tribunal inquiry, this information would never have been made known. Dr. Kinship was unaware of the above situation and hence made a wrong judgment.

The situation had become complicated because schools are complex places and the matter in question had a long history. Dr. Hall had put up a barrier to communication and comprehension since she refused to have events that took place before she became a governor discussed. Dr. Kinship was a new and untrained governor with no school experience, let alone comprehensive school experience, who rushed in where angels fear to tread.

My well-controlled frustration and exasperation with Dr. Kinship came from the fact that he had the wrong idea. It was a pity (with hindsight) that Tim Atherton only attended the first meeting with him and not the second. When he started to question my relationships with colleagues and pupils, I knew he was getting on the wrong track and was making the issue psychological, not logical. What he was attempting was character assassination or at least professional assassination, since personal relationships are an important part of teaching. My interest was in arguments, not personalities.

Brian Buckley, the English inspector, gave independent evidence that my discipline and personal relationships with students were good. He observed two 40-minute classes. How else would I have had the confidence to pursue this case?

The depth of Dr. Kinship's and Dr. Hall's misunderstanding of the situation is seen in their exaggeration of a slight and justified irritation on my part. The basis of my teaching was being unfairly attacked without evidence by uninformed and unqualified people, who were transforming it into a case of mental instability and taking it upon themselves to write a letter, which must have led the governors as a body to recommend a medical inspection.

The question has to be asked: Either Dr. Kinship and Dr. Hall were correct in their views, or Tim Atherton, I, and other members of staff were correct. Both could not be. The evidence is all against Dr. Hall and Dr. Kinship.

In his statement to the tribunal Dr. Kinship said, "I began to sense that Mr. Armitage would not be able to accept any suggestion that he was in the wrong." The point here is that Dr. Kinship had, on brief acquaintance and knowledge, concluded uncritically that I was; not that there was some doubt, that there are two sides to every question. It was this belief that naturally caused a difference between us. If I was not in the wrong, then Dr. Kinship was in the wrong about the view he had formed of the situation. He had reached a definite, even hostile position about this matter.

Furthermore, Dr. Kinship raised questions about my intellectual ability. On page 59 he said, "The essence of good methodology, particularly in the participant observation situation is the classic dilemma between validity and reliability. I began to discuss this with you (Mr. Armitage) and you really were not on the same wavelength." On page 65, Dr. Kinship also said, "the real test of ability and understanding is the discussion that follows it (a paper), the preparedness to submit yourself to the debate and to accept the criticism without it being personalized. This is why I was interested to discuss this aspect of it with him to find out the difference between what was written and real understanding. I felt that there was no real understanding."

First, Dr. Kinship had indeed personalized the discussion. I believe I showed remarkable stability under personal, direct attack. Second, the purpose of the meeting was to advance my case for meeting the governors, which I achieved. There was absolutely no purpose served by entering an irrelevant discussion, from my point of view. Perhaps Dr. Kinship was an expert and a specialist but that didn't make him politically aware or make him a person of common sense. Dr. Kinship had also failed to notice the important point I had made in the paper, which was that its purpose was to promote debate, not prove that my view was right or correct. The curriculum evaluation paper was supposed to demonstrate competence. It certainly represented an attempt to introduce curriculum studies into the school. It is a mistake to set oneself up as an expert authority in these matters. It seems to me that Dr. Kinship simply failed to understand the situation, yet he accused me of a lack of understanding. Moreover, I did not use personal abuse against Dr. Kinship, even under gross provocation. It is ironical that he claimed objectivity for his opinion.

On day 1, page 51, Dr. Kinship was asked to describe his impression of the first meeting I had with him, and he replied as follows:

My first impression at the beginning of the meeting was that he presented his case very coherently, very sensibly and very sincerely. . . . but that as the meeting progressed and Mr. Armitage was pressed a little, he began, I think, to demonstrate a certain tenseness, unease, lack of rationality, and I became a little disturbed at his behaviour at that time.

What Dr. Kinship meant by "pressed a little" was that it became clear he didn't accept any aspect of my case and was trying to dismantle it completely. Therefore, there was nothing to discuss. We didn't have time for discussion of educational issues and the whole background to the case, which couldn't possibly be covered in a short meeting.

Dr. Kinship was also asked whether I was "prepared to accept arguments that you (Dr. Kinship) were putting to him?" He replied, "Basically, no. If any argument I presented suggested that his sense of persecution, which became obsessive as the meeting went on, was not justified, then he became quite angry at the suggestion that his sense of persecution was, in fact, false."

There is, of course a distinction to be made between an imagined sense of persecution and one that is real. I would use the word discrimination. I certainly felt discriminated against and for good reasons. So my sense was not false. This is another example of how, in not giving credence and respect to my position, Dr. Kinship misunderstood the situation as it really was. Dr. Kinship seems to exaggerate normal human feelings of irritation and frustration into extreme feelings of "obsession" and "persecution." Borecross School was an authoritarian institution and didn't really like differences of view openly expressed. Social pressure to conform backed up by subtle forms of coercion such as withholding communication, co-operation and so on were ways of expressing the real situation.

Dr. Kinship's sense of exaggeration was also evidenced in his assessment of my document which he said was "a diatribe against my colleagues" (day 1, page 52). If he calls it a diatribe, I can't see he knows the exact meaning of the word. In the whole of the document there is hardly a reference to my colleagues and then only in a descriptive sense. If I am to use supporting evidence for any point I make, I am forced to use a descriptive example, as there is no other way.

Dr. Kinship also said in evidence that:

By the time we reached the second meeting, we were beginning to suspect that what we were concerned with was a man who was, perhaps, unwell and totally obsessed— unjustifiably in my view—with the idea that he had been victimized. The meeting fairly quickly degenerated, because I pressed Mr. Armitage a little harder and a little sooner than I had at the first meeting, and I felt on the second occasion I should make it clear to Mr. Armitage that I was coming to the conclusion that I felt his case was not justified.

Well, if it wasn't justified, either Dr. Kinship had got completely the wrong end of the stick or Tim Atherton had. Dr. Kinship had formed a view on little information, and he was not there to form a view, just to recommend a meeting with the governors.

Two points arise from these statements. First, Dr. Kinship uses words like "press" and "a little harder." What he seems to have wanted was for me to say I didn't have a case. Naturally, I was put on the defensive by the way he was conducting himself. He had come to an unjustified and wrong conclusion after one meeting. I think he mishandled the case totally. On day 1, page 55, Dr. Kinship says he had formed the view that Alan Tottenham, the headmaster, "was, perhaps, a rather rigid headmaster." If his assessment is correct, this might have led him to suppose that it was the lack of flexibility in the situation which was a cause of the problem. Dr. Kinship himself seems to have taken an inflexible attitude.

It is important to note that in my dealings with Dr. Kinship and Dr. Hall I dealt with arguments and kept personalities out of the way. He very clearly, on the contrary, made the issues personal. In this respect I consider he abused his position of power as a governor, and yet he claims a higher intellectual status for his arguments. On the basis of meeting me in one highly specific situation, he generalizes to make judgments about my whole personality. I have, for example, a good sense of humor which is an outlet for any frustrations I might feel; I learned in my first year of teaching never to take work problems home with me, and I am well able to discipline myself to cope with difficult situations. It is a sign of weakness to argue by attacking the other person's personal qualities, yet this is what Dr. Kinship did. There was absolutely no need to "press" me further. His job was to listen, not dissuade me from exercising my rights. The purpose of the meeting was not an inquisition nor was I prepared for one.

Yet when the chairman of the tribunal put it to Dr. Kinship (day 1, page 58) that "The point here is, Dr. Kinship, that Mr. Armitage is doing good sound work and getting no recognition or credit. It is the sort of brush-off behavior of those who were his superiors which is causing frustration" Dr. Kinship replied, "but you did say that Mr. Armitage was doing good sound work." The statement took him by surprise as it hadn't occurred to him.

On page 56, Dr. Kinship said that "I would agree with you that it would be very difficult for a new governor who had attended two meetings to have firm and reliable views about the quality of the school." Then why did Dr. Kinship dismiss my case so readily? He is admitting his own lack of understanding and experience in this matter. So why did the governors choose a new governor to deal with this matter? That says something about their own collective judgment.

On page 63, Dr. Kinship agreed that he and Dr. Hall had suggested that I should prepare a brief, succinct statement of my case, so it was the two governors who asked me to put something on paper.

Another statement of Dr. Kinship's reveals that he had formed a negative opinion of me. On day 1, pages 65 and 66 he says: "The concern that a devoted teacher was being continuously frustrated was the image that was being presented to us for most of the first two meetings." And later, "It was then there seemed to be a layer beneath. I wonder just how sincere the plea from the heart and the devoted thing was." The point is really to establish an unbalanced view of my character which he had formed, surely without justification. As Tim Atherton said with admirable insight, "We are all more or less misunderstanding of each other," a point I don't think would have crossed Dr. Kinship's mind. Yet he claims that he had reached an "objective unbiased view" of these events. In my opinion he completely misperceived my character. My own explanation is that he objected to a complaint of this nature on principle which was a quite normal attitude in his generation.

There is no evidence to suggest that Dr. Kinship had any understanding of organizational theory. Consider these brief extracts on organizational evil:

That organizations can be construed as moral primitives has been explained at length elsewhere (Hodgkinson 1978, 171ff). The crux of the argument is that only an individual can possess consciousness and will. Only an individual can experience value. What passes as group decisions and collective judgements and actions are at best pseudo-conscious, quasi-willful and typologically distinct with respect to value (see Chapter 2). It follows that organizations *qua* organizations cannot be morally responsible. Nevertheless organizations are collectively more powerful than individuals and they do act in the world. Though such action can be directed to ostensibly benevolent ends its potential for corruption cannot be ignored. (Hodgkinson 1983, 60)

Analysis of Mr. Bright's Evidence

Mr. Bright was a City Education Authority inspector with particular responsibility for discipline. The first point he made on day 3, page 4 was that it was not unprofessional to criticize the head depending on the way it was done, and that it was "primarily in not informing the head teacher first." The original charge formulated by Mr. Stephens was "criticizing" the head teacher. So the City Education Authority's inspector of discipline, Mr. Bright, disagreed with the authority's original charge. The second part of his statement relates to the distribution of the document. Since it was distributed by the divisional office, it had not been under my control in any case, and since the headmaster was a member of the governing body there was no question of withholding the document from him and acting secretly behind his back, which is the purpose of having the rule. Therefore, Mr. Bright seemed to be attempting to salvage the case for the CEA by saying the head had not been informed, and they hadn't thought out their case properly from the beginning.

On day 3, page 58, Mr. Bright was asked by Mr. Benford of the tribunal whether in the meeting with him and Mr. White and my union representative, Mr. Arnott, I had agreed to withdraw the document. He replied, "I am sorry. I have to say I do not recall. I know that Mr. Heather was very much involved in the discussion at that stage, but that is all I can say." Mr. Bright also said that as an officer of the education authority he did not make recommendations. I remember clearly what happened at that meeting. I did offer to withdraw that document. If that offer had been accepted the tribunal would never have taken place which, in my view, would have been the sensible thing. It seems that Mr. Bright had failed to pay attention to the conversation. Is it good enough to just say you're sorry? What may have happened was that Mr. Bright had not pursued the matter and the education officer made a poor decision in recommending a tribunal without Mr. Bright's advice. In any case, it shows up considerable confusion in the way matters were handled.

Mr. Bright was also asked to comment on sections of the document I wrote which he considered unprofessional. He said with reference to day 3, page 6:

But, it has been significant that *no comment* or action has come from either headmasters, and it would seem from their comment that they have neither understood it properly [referring to a document published by the CEA] nor implemented it in an acceptable way. Roger Bright, presumably in the name of the head, even said that it should be ignored. The implication there is that the head teacher and others have not digested an attempt to implement suggestions that have been put by the authority.

The point to note here is that these statements were accurate and that indeed the authority's suggestions in its document on the internal government of schools were ignored. Dennis Moore, the CEA divisional inspector, condemned the document as "undemocratic."

The second point is that I agree with Mr. Bright that the accusations were very serious and that, in my view, the meaning of professional conduct is that the school is there to serve its pupils, so I had a professional duty to do what I could to help the situation. As it happened, the complaint of unprofessional conduct against me completely shielded my critical document to the governors, and these serious accusations, which I consider true, were in fact side-stepped. This was behavior consistent with Dr. Gardner's analysis of the original situation at Borecross School.

Concerning the distribution of the document on cross-examination (day 3, page 10), I asked Mr. Bright whether he thought the divisional officer "had a responsibility to inform me that he considered it unprofessional, and if he considered it unprofessional indeed not to have distributed the document at all." Mr. Bright replied, "I am not aware the divisional officer saw the document." So Mr. Bright couldn't answer this significant question and clearly hadn't enquired into this matter. He had thus failed to carry out his responsibilities in two important respects.

Mr. Bright was asked on day 3, page 4, by Mr. West of the tribunal, whether, in his view, if I had presented Mr. Tottenham with a copy of this document prior to sending it to the divisional office for circulation to the governors, his conduct would not have been unprofessional. Mr. Bright replied that he quite agreed with this statement and it would *not* have been unprofessional, but the unprofessionalism came "in not informing the head teacher first."

Mr. Bright was also asked (day 3, page 5) if "supposing a teacher was not aware of this formal procedure" (under the staff code) "and it had come to the attention of an officer of the authority that there was a matter which, in the view of that officer, did amount to a complaint; Would you think it part of the responsibility of that officer to advise the teacher of the method by which the complaint should be pursued?" Mr. Bright did not answer the question except to say that the officer was in a difficult position. The point here is surely that the divisional office was not given the document by me, and distributed it under its own authority and therefore was a party to its distribution. Neither did it inform the head teacher. So it was as much guilty as I was, in one sense.

Analysis of Mr. Buckley's Evidence

Mr. Brian Buckley had been asked to observe my teaching, at the request of the divisional inspector, Dennis Moore. I didn't mind this as I was confident of my abilities in the classroom and had made a thorough study of all aspects of classroom teaching. One of my most valued texts was *Interpersonal Relations and Education* (1972) by David Hargreaves, and anyone who has worked out the theoretical implications of that study in practice over a period of years could only be confident in knowing what he was doing in the classroom. The style of teaching based on symbolic interactionism is an informal, interpersonal style, hence I was practicing an informal style in a formal, bureaucratic organization, which was a compelling reason to change the attitude of organization at the macro level.

In his written statement to the tribunal, Buckley wrote, "during both lessons discipline was good, with a friendly relationship between Mr. Armitage and the pupils."

This is evidence by actual observation of my classroom strategies and tactics, and contradicts the evidence presented by Dr. Hall and Dr. Kinship. It suggests that the governors believed what suited their points of view and that they took a partisan view on inadequate evidence. If they had consulted

Brian Buckley, as they should have done, they could not have recommended a medical inspection, because mentally unfit people do not maintain good relationships with others.

Brian Buckley made one criticism of me, which he says was that the "discussion" he had with me "revealed a gap that exists between Mr. Armitage's use of ideas at an abstract level and his inability to translate them into practice." This was a false judgment, as shown by the previous pages. Contextualizing this criticism, no teacher is perfect or without weaknesses of one kind of another. Buckley had pointed out a great strength, which was an ability to be friendly and to maintain good discipline without sanctions. I possibly made a misjudgment, but when I heard Buckley was attending two lessons, I played safe and put on two fairly formal lessons. He then mistakenly concluded that I was a "very formal" teacher. In this he was quite wrong, since my teaching is a combination of formal and informal methods based on my judgment of the particular situation in the classroom, the time of the week and so on. Tim Atherton, who had never seen me teach, said, "Mr. Armitage has a similar approach to teaching as myself. It is a variable approach, not a consistent style that he communicates." "He varies his approach quite a lot."

In the tribunal evidence, Mr. Buckley (Chapter 8), the inspector of English (day 2, page 28), made the judgment that the author was unable to relate theory to practice. His statement was more political than educational since the issue of the house and year system was basic to the practices and ideology of the school. The house system was an ideological system with no rational basis. The best way to solve the problems of the house system, was to change it to a year system, as the arguments showed.

Yet, Brian Buckley answered this question as follows:

Mr. Graham: He loves his profession really. Would you disagree?

Mr. Buckley: No, I think he does.

The word "love" is an emotional word and it is significant that it was recognized in a positive light, because emotions belong to the informal aspects of a person. Teaching should be an enjoyable activity, yet formal organization doesn't recognize emotion even though it is the basis of teaching. Even the learning of science requires love of the subject matter.

DEFENSE WITNESS

Critique of Tim Atherton's Evidence

I called Tim Atherton as a witness because he was my head of department and we had enjoyed many Habermasian conversations together. He was a Cambridge English graduate with an acute and sensitive understanding of people, and he understood the educational situation at Borecross well. He signed the school evaluation in Chapter 3. He was a person of independent mind. I could not have anticipated what he would have said. However, he understood the situation well beyond my expectations, and did a fine job.

Tim was recognized by Dr. Hall as an "acute and intelligent person" "in whom I had great faith." I considered his evidence analytically competent and well judged.

March 5, 1980
P. B. Armitage

I have been Mr. Armitage's head of department for nearly five terms. I have always found him cooperative and communicative and quite unresentful of my position. His optimistic preoccupation with improving the school system is impressively sincere if, sometimes, a little unnerving.

Obviously, Mr. Armitage's position in Borecross School has, for too long, been an unhappy one. I must take the opportunity of this statement to declare that I am horrified that the present troubles have been allowed to occur. In my view, a caring authority and *several* of its officers (that is not to say any single headmaster) would have seen, some years ago, that an unfortunate and potentially difficult situation was developing. Had Mr. Armitage been counseled to seek, and then helped toward, promotion out of Borecross School, his career would not be in its present condition.
T. Atherton
Head of English.

By describing my behavior as "communicative" and "cooperative," he refutes Dr. Kinship's idea that I had difficulties in personal relationships with staff or pupils caused by an inability to communicate. He himself had been promoted over me and found me "quite unresentful" of his "position." Second, Tim Atherton made the point that my efforts were devoted to "improving the school system" and were therefore moral in purpose. Third, Tim Atherton's evidence contradicts Dr. Hall's evidence that the difficulties of my position were of my own making. On the contrary, they were caused by my involvement in the educational problems of the school. Teachers should be involved in their work. Fourth, in stating that a "caring authority" would not have allowed this situation to have developed, a point I quite agree with, he is putting the point that the authority hadn't acted competently. Fifth, Tim could also see that the present condition of my career prospects, which had been in the hands of the authority, made my position a difficult one, since I was well qualified, hardworking and underpromoted.

On day 3, page 32, under cross-examination by me, Tim was asked whether, when he met Dr. Hall with me, he wished to give her the impression that I needed to see a psychiatrist. He replied, "certainly not, no." I also asked him whether he remembered saying I was a "strong person." He said "yes." The point of these answers is to support the view that Dr.

Hall had misread my character. It was because I was a strong character that I was able to act as I had done at Borecross School. If Dr. Hall had read me as a weak person who was suffering from hurt and distress, then her decision to ask for a medical inspection was more understandable, but even then misguided. It may also have reflected her own attitude that she couldn't do what I was attempting.

Tim was then asked the following question:

Armitage: So if Dr. Hall heard "strong person" alongside "hurt" she could not be confused about your intentions on that occasion?

Atherton: I would hope not. We are all more or less confusing of other people whenever we are talking. I would like to comment on why I used the word "strong." It does clearly connect with the word "hurt." It also connects with the second paragraph of my statement that you asked me to make. Is it fair to mention this?

Chairman: Of course it is. I have this very much in mind. Would you like to see your statement?

Atherton: No, I think I remember it well enough. I meant to indicate to Dr. Hall and Dr. Kinship, who was also present, that, consistent with the second paragraph of my statement, it struck me that what I have come to call in my own head "the Peter Armitage problem" should not in fact exist at present, and I meant to, when I used the word "strong," suggest that you had supported and contained the effects of the problem, which was of some years' duration, extraordinarily well. I meant, and I think I was communicating it, to indicate to Drs. Kinship and Hall that a lot of people would have become very disturbed by the problem. I did not wish to indicate that I thought that a well-qualified analyst would imply that you were disturbed by it. I used the word "hurt" quite deliberately because it seemed to me the position of people in relation to institutions, large institutions, is quite often much more hurtful than any of us realize or any of us habitually realize. I do see a connection between those three. I do not want to run the risk of rambling on too much.

Here was a problem which needed to be resolved, which is part of the reason why I was seeing the governors. Yet Dr. Hall, Dr. Kinship, Mr. Moore and Mr. Buckley didn't grasp the problem.

I also asked Tim Atherton the following question:

Armitage: Am I the sort of person who tries to get to the bottom of things, tries?

Atherton: I certainly do think you are someone who tries to get to the bottom of things with a dedication which I find quite extraordinary.

Tim Atherton, who is a very humane fellow, also said: "I am well aware that Mr. Armitage was unhappy with the way in which Borecross School was developing as a comprehensive school, before he began to feel that promotion for himself was appropriate within the school, and there is a long and consistent approach to the problems of the school." This is the answer to Dr. Hall's suggestion that I had been making my own problems. The school had problems and anyone trying to solve them was personally involved. The importance of Tim Atherton's evidence was his practical analysis of the situation, which was contrastive with Dr. Hall's and Dr. Kinship's views. They could not have both been right.

Finally, perhaps the most important comment of the entire tribunal was made by Mr. Atherton, who said:

Is anybody going to tell me what unprofessional means, because I am very depressed about the state of the teaching profession. I am very depressed about the state of the profession because I think it is a profession almost unprofessional not in the sense of the behaviour of the people who participate in it, but in the way it views itself.

Written Evidence

A number of my former colleagues, for whom I had a high regard, wrote letters of support and I quote them here for two reasons. First, they had known me on a daily basis for several years, unlike the opposing witnesses whose knowledge of the school was extremely limited. Second, they understood the real situation at Borecross School. Jim Shaw wrote, "What I can only call his moral courage has been very considerable. Many a time he has defended alone, or in a minority, an educational viewpoint in the Common Room. Indeed, he pioneered the issue of a year system—which we have now adopted—at a time when the house system seemed unalterably entrenched."

Alan Harkness, the head of maths, was, in my view, a master teacher of mathematics who achieved outstanding results even after the school had become a comprehensive. He contextualized the problems the school faced:

I have been a teaching colleague of Mr. Armitage for over nine years. We have often talked of the changes which have taken place during this period and I share his views of the necessity to maintain standards wherever this is possible. He has been genuinely concerned about some aspects of the present system and has felt that he should make this known to the Governors and Senior Management.

My impression of him is that he is a dedicated teacher who is very concerned at the boys' progress and, because of an excess of zeal and also because he could not put many of his theories into practice, has become frustrated in his present position.

The essential difference between the defense and prosecuting witnesses was that the former were insiders and the latter were outsiders. And the outsiders did not understand the situation and didn't put in the necessary imaginative and empathetic effort in order to do so.

In the tribunal there emerged two distinct points of view relevant to the practical context of this case. As the chairman of the tribunal, Mr. Graham said on day 1, page 4, "Your own professional standing and integrity themselves are in issue in this case." But equally so was the system's.

THE AUTHENTIC STORY

Why did the tribunal take place? The examination of witnesses revealed the stories behind the tribunal.

Why did Dennis Moore bring a charge of unprofessional conduct? He said In evidence he didn't want the governors to discuss the document. Why didn't he want them to discuss the document? There are a number of possible reasons. In a formal system of education, discussion is minimal. It was an anti-intellectual system. Second, he was worried about sharing power with the governors and that the situation would get out of control. Dennis Moore was defending the power of the head teacher to be unquestioned and total.

In the Auld Report it says that "the headmaster is in effective control of the school, its aims, policies and methods of teaching."

Ball writes: "The legal responsibilities of the head place him in a unique position of licensed autocracy" (Ball 1987, 80). These reasons were behind Dennis Moore's initiative to stop the governorns from discussing the document. His evidence established the point that because he had a certain authoritarian view of human relationships, his attitudes were influenced by that view and it led to the judgments he made. This was probably a situation quite new to his experience. His view of human relationships was basically adult–child, senior–junior. As he reminded me, I was a "junior member of staff" in the formal structure. On two occasions in the evidence, he makes out that I myself didn't understand as I hadn't had the experience at a senior level and also that Tim Atherton, a colleague, was inexperienced. Dennis Moore was pulling authoritarian rank and apparent superior experience. He didn't accept complaints against authority by definition and so, not accepting them, he couldn't deal with them rationally on their merits. Since the authorities of the City Education Authority supported him, he was carrying out their wishes. He must have been fearful of a "crisis of authority" if the governors discussed the document, which is why he took it from Mr. Lewis and devised the plan to distribute it without permission and charge the writer with misconduct. That way the head teacher didn't have to answer any questions. Attack was the best means of defense.

On day 1, page 70, Moore admitted that he instituted the charge of unprofessional conduct. He said, "Yes." But he contradicted himself when he said the real decision came from the education officer, which meant he didn't want to accept the political responsibility for the charge since the education officer must have acted on his advice. He also says he made "certain assumptions about the way a complaint should be made" and "certain assumptions about the relationship which a junior member of staff should have with his headmaster."

Dr. Cathy Hall didn't want or was unable to take on a political struggle to democratize the school and allow for criticism and opposition. She chose

loyalty to her fellow governors as her priority and her action aided the maintenance of the political status quo. She positioned herself incorrectly since
she had no knowledge of the history of the amalgamation and Dennis
Moore had not informed her. She didn't understand the connection between history and identity. The historian Eric Hobsbawm argues that "an
a-historical, engineering, problem-solving approach by means of mechanical
models and devices" is relevant to certain fields but it has no "perspective"
and "it cannot take into account" "anything not fed into the device or
model from the start" (Hobsbawm, 1997, 35). That is, Hall lacked perspective and information. She played a formal role in the system and had a
systems theory of organization. Dr. Kinship took a similar attitude to Dennis
Moore and considered democratic opposition and democratic politics as not
within the authoritarian system. He acted to prevent change and improvement. He also positioned himself incorrectly in relation to the realities of
the situation.

Mr. Bright and Brian Buckley were not central figures politically. Mr.
Bright supported the proposition that criticism was not unprofessional.
Brian Buckley took a politically ambiguous position.

The defense witnesses were dominated by outsiders who were in positions
of greater political power, and although the insiders' view of the educational
state of the school was more informed and based on experience, it was
simply rejected. Tim Atherton's evidence provided a correct view of the
situation. He noted that large organizations are hurtful of individuals since
they dominate and dehumanize them. He implied in his remarks concerning
cooperation and communication that the micro-political model is the basis
of school organization (Ball 1987).

The evidence of the defense showed that the school had serious problems
which were a reality that could not be addressed because the political process
of communication was distorted. It was distorted because the system was
authoritarian and dominated the lifeworld, leading to its "colonization" and
"fragmentation." Organization had taken over from people. Science dominated. This was why the school could not change and improve. This was
why it could not produce effective education.

CONCLUSION

How has the plot developed from the analysis of the stories of the witnesses to the tribunal? Dennis Moore plotted to prevent discussion. Dr. Hall
and Dr. Kinship were angered that I did not accept their view of matters
and used medicine for political purposes. They were overruled by the expert
opinion of the psychiatrist who declared me medically fit. I achieved my aim
of meeting the governors, which they tried to prevent.

The true picture to emerge from the stories was that the tribunal was
based on a defense of formal bureaucracy against participative and deliber-

ative democracy and freedom. The old view of education as formal learning prevailed against a modern view which includes informal aspects of a learning and educational situation. That was the true meaning of the tribunal evidence. The structure of the school was static and rigid. Any change or view of the school as a process of development was disallowed. Science and history were in conflict and the scientific view of the world was dominant.

Brian Simon (1994) has argued that historical analysis is relevant to the cultural emancipation of educators because it assists them in understanding the real nature of their work as "human development" and "human empowerment." It is difficult to see the educational system they inhabit objectively without a historical perspective and to understand how educational principles have a historical component (16).

A historical perspective produces "critical awareness," such as our own problem of authoritarian domination, which should become critically apparent through this study. It is easy to live uncritically in the present and adopt an attitude of uncritical and dominative routine to everyday "occcurrences." Educational systems are conservative by nature. A historical awareness "can provide the motivation for that innovation and change which is essential if education is to make the contribution to social advance which is its raison d'être." It makes teaching an exciting job and gives society the confidence that educators make a useful contribution to "human objectives" (17).

Chapter 5

The Politics of Domination

This chapter concerns the outcome of the tribunal. I record the findings and recommendations of the tribunal in the first part. In the second part, I conduct a critical analysis of their report. In the third part, I record the findings of the appeal committee. In the final part, I analyze the events into a plot theme and draw the wider implications from an educational point of view.

Findings and Recommendations of the Tribunal

The following is the complete report of the Findings and Recommendations of the Tribunal.

1. This Tribunal sat on March 17, 18 and 19, 1980 in County Hall and heard the following complaints against Mr. Armitage:

a) that he inflicted irregular corporal punishment on July 13, 1979 upon Barry Kirkland, a pupil at Borecross School;

b) that he was guilty of professional misconduct, and thereby misconduct, in that he caused to be put before the Governors of Borecross School for their meeting on July 17, 1979 a document (Appendix C) which strongly attacked the Headmaster of the School, Mr. Tottenham, without giving any due notice beforehand to Mr. Tottenham.

2.1 The complaint of irregular corporal punishment was presented by Mr. Tottenham, the Headmaster of Borecross School. He was accompanied by a friend, Mr. Black.

2.2 The complaint of unprofessional conduct was presented by Mr. White on behalf of the Education Officer.

2.3 On the morning of the first day of the hearing before us, Mr. Armitage attended accompanied by a friend, Mr. Clee. However, before the proceedings commenced Mr. Armitage said that he did not wish to avail himself of the services of

Mr. Clee and indicated that he was happy to do the case on his own. When asked why, he said he did not want an adjournment.

2.4 By consent both complaints were heard together. It was said then, as later became apparent, that matters arising in each complaint intertwined. As a matter of convenience the complaint of professional misconduct was presented first by the calling of all witnesses solely relevant to that complaint: then the complaint of irregular corporal punishment was presented by the calling of the witnesses relevant to that complaint. Thereafter, Mr. Armitage after calling one witness, gave evidence himself in respect of both complaints. At the request of Mr. Armitage, Mr. Tottenham was not present during the cross-examination of Mr. Armitage upon the complaint of professional misconduct.

2.5 The following witnesses gave oral evidence before us and are here named in the order they were called:

a) *for the Complainants:*
Dr. Hall
Dr. Kinship
Mr. Moore
Mr. Buckley
Barry Kirkland, a pupil
Michael Bly, a pupil
Mrs. Lee
Mr. White
Mr. Tall
Mr. Tottenham

b) *for the teacher:*
Mr. Atherton
Mr. Armitage himself.

2.6 In addition to this oral evidence we considered and gave due weight to all the documentary evidence placed before us by both the Complainants and by Mr. Armitage.

3.1 In respect of the complaint of irregular corporal punishment we make the following findings of fact.

3.2 On July 13, 1979, Barry Kirkland arrived late for a lesson by Mr. Armitage. When he did so, the lesson was already in progress. He arrived wearing sunglasses which he did not take off. He sat in the second row from the front, and almost immediately was asked to read a passage from the book the class was reading together. When he had finished he turned round to the boy behind him and asked the time. (We think such an enquiry to those within earshot was possibly intended to indicate that the lesson was boring.) Mr. Armitage was standing nearby. We are satisfied that he hit Barry Kirkland on the back of the head. We are not satisfied, however, that this happened more than once. At or about this time we believe Mr. Armitage made some attempt to take Barry Kirkland's sunglasses off, having previously told him to take them off. We are also satisfied that as the incident developed Mr. Armitage brought the book he had in his hand very close up to Barry Kirkland's face and by flicking the book from side to side taunted the boy in a menacing way without hitting him with it. We also find as a fact that when the boy got up intending to leave the class, Mr. Armitage knocked the boy's chair in some fashion in an attempt to stop him leaving the class. We also believe that during an attempt to stop the boy leaving the class, his bag got kicked.

3.3 We do not believe that the single blow which we find was struck, was in any way a hard blow. We were told by Michael Bly, and we accept from him, that the class were jeering and laughing during the incident and that for some boys it was a welcome amusement in what otherwise was a boring lesson. We do not think the class would have reacted in this way if the blow was hard and seen by the class to constitute a serious assault. As it was some boys in the class are unable to recall any assault. We further note that no boy followed Barry Kirkland out of the class to comfort him which we would have expected if he had been struck with any real force or viciousness.

3.4 We have reached our view of the facts primarily upon our assessment of Barry Kirkland and of Michael Bly, a fellow member of the class. We have also taken account of the reports afterwards made to Mrs. Lee, Mrs. Kirkland, Mr. White and Mr. Tottenham. We do not think it strange, as was suggested to us, that the later reports contain detail absent from the first report to Mrs. Lee. Mr. White's report was obtained by question and answer on his part, following a request to report by the headmaster, after Mrs. Kirkland's serious letter of complaint. Mrs. Lee on the other hand took no notes, and thought the matter would blow over when she first heard of it. We have also taken into account Mr. Armitage's reaction to the incident at the time. He let Barry Kirkland leave the classroom in an admittedly disturbed state of mind and made no enquiry after him. He reported the incident to no-one. In our view, he then deliberately evaded investigations and when he did respond— within a time when he may reasonably be expected to remember—he did so in a deliberately unclear fashion. On the other hand, we are not prepared to say that in his evidence before us upon this complaint that he was being deliberately untruthful. On the contrary, we feel that he has now convinced himself that the account he gave to us, which we have rejected, is a true account.

3.5 Before leaving this complaint we record here that we feel that there was some small degree of provocation present in the circumstances which faced Mr. Armitage. These circumstances include the late arrival of the boy concerned, and his wearing of sun-glasses and his apparent disturbance of a class quietly intent upon the reading. However, we feel the degree of provocation arising was hardly exceptional. It was of a kind which we would expect a teacher to take in his stride. It is not without significance that at the time of this incident the forthcoming Governors' meeting was imminent and that Mr. Armitage's anticipation of the meeting placed him under some stress.

4.1 In connection with the further complaint that he was guilty of professional misconduct, we make the following findings of fact.

4.2 Mr. Armitage wrote the seven page document (now before us as Appendix C) sometime before July 9, 1979. He gave his manuscript to the clerk to the Governors on about Monday, July 9. The submission of his manuscript on this date allowed ample time for its necessary typing, copying and circulating to the Governors before their meeting on July 17. We are perfectly satisfied that when he submitted his manuscript he wished it to be brought directly to the attention of the Governors either by being posted to them after typing, or by being laid on the table. We entirely reject Mr. Armitage's evidence that he required only that his manuscript be typed, and that he should receive back a copy for further perusal and reflection over the weekend; and that in no sense did he authorize or anticipate circulation of his manuscript without further reference back to himself. If this was so the clerk to the Governors was allowing himself to be used as a free typing service to Mr. Armitage, which we cannot accept. We were told by a Governor, Dr. Hall, and accept from her that Mr. Armitage expressed no surprise or regret on the night before the Governors' meeting that the manuscript had been circulated. We also note that if it had been Mr. Armitage's intention to present a final draft of his manuscript on the Monday following the weekend there would then have been insufficient time for the circulation of the document to the Governors for their meeting the following morning. The document takes a considerable time to read. It would have been quite impossible for those referred to in the document to prepare any defense to the matters raised in the time available. In view of his relationship with the Governors, Mr. Armitage cannot have reasonably imagined that the Governors would have granted him facilities for yet another meeting. As for the alternative suggestion made that Mr. Armitage may never have submitted his manuscript had he had time to reflect upon it over the weekend, we reject this also. Mr. Armitage plainly spent a considerable time upon his manuscript and we are convinced that it was his ardent wish at the time that the Governors should read it.

4.3 The Articles of Government of Inner London County Primary and Secondary Schools provide at Article 3(3) (d) that:

> Members of the teaching staff shall be entitled, either personally or by their representative under suitable arrangements made by the governors, to make representations to the governors on matters affecting the school, provided that the head teacher be given due notice of such representation.

4.4 Mr. Armitage in his written submission refers at page 103 to a resolution passed by the Council of the A.M.M.A. Association:

> that this council considers that it would be injurious to the rules, interests or objects of the Association for any teacher to make a report on the work or conduct of another teacher without at the time acquainting the teacher concerned with the nature of it, if it be an oral report, or without showing it, if it be written, and allowing the teacher concerned to take a copy of it.

The Rules of the N.U.T. make very similar provision.

4.5 It was not seriously disputed before us that neither Mr.'Tottenham the headmaster (nor those senior staff who may be identified from the document circulated) received any due notice of the representations. Due notice requires that Mr. Tottenham (and the senior staff affected) be given notice before circulation to the governors. For this reason we rejected in the course of argument the suggestion made that the condition of notice was satisfied by the receipt of the document by Mr. Tottenham in the course of circulation to governors.

4.6 In the circumstances we find that Mr. Armitage was guilty of professional misconduct.

4.7 Whether an act of professional misconduct amounts to misconduct within the terms of the Staff Code we regard as a matter of fact and degree in every case. In the present case we consider that professional misconduct clearly amounts to misconduct; and that the misconduct is grave in character for the reasons that now follow.

4.8 In our judgment Mr. Armitage by his circular intended to hurt and harm Mr. Tottenham, the Headmaster and possibly some senior staff as well, in the eyes of the Governors. The relationship between a Head and the Governors is a delicate and difficult one and we regard the circulating of this document written in scurrilous language without notice or opportunity given for reply as potentially most damaging to that relationship. We emphasize that in our view Mr. Armitage intended to damage that relationship.

4.9 In reaching our conclusions about Mr. Armitage's intentions we have taken into account many circumstances (apart from the impression he made upon us). These circumstances include the malicious tone and language of the circular and its timing and the way it was circulated without notice, as already found.

4.10 In the event, the publication of Mr. Armitage's document and its circulation disgusted the Governors. That is the language used by Dr. Hall. It also seriously upset Mr. Tottenham the Headmaster who we feel has been troubled by it ever since. We consider too that the publication of the document was detrimental to senior staff as well, and that it had an unsettling effect on the school.

5.0 When considering our recommendation upon the complaint of irregular corporal punishment we have taken into account the stress Mr. Armitage was probably under at the time, the slight degree of provocation that was present, and the degree of force used which we have already found was not great. We took account of Mr. Armitage's obvious anxiety to minimize further harm to the two boys caused in any way by their attendance to give evidence before thus.

6.0 When considering our recommendation arising upon the complaint of professional misconduct, amounting to misconduct, we bore very much in mind Mr. Armitage's intention, as we have found it to be, to cause hurt and harm to the Headmaster and possibly senior staff; his deliberate neglect to use other means of complaining open to him; the complete absence of remorse that he displayed to us; and the certainty we feel that such events that have now occurred, with all the attendant ill-effects on staff and the school, will occur repeatedly in the future in any school in which Mr. Armitage teaches.

7.0 Our recommendations are as follows:

(a) upon the complaint of irregular corporal punishment—that Mr. Armitage be REPRIMANDED;

(b) upon the complaint of misconduct that Mr. Armitage be DISMISSED WITH NOTICE to expire on the last day of the Summer Term 1980; and that meantime he is not employed in any teaching or other employment at Borecross School.

8.0 Mr. Armitage is to be reminded of his rights of appeal as provided for in the Staff Code.

Discipline X at 10(h).

G. Graham: (In the Chair.)

P. Southern: Deputy Head, C.E.C. Branch

H. Scotland: Staff Inspector, Home Economics

P. Benford: Head Teacher, Coventry Park School

R. West: Teacher, Edgehill School

CRITIQUE OF THE FINDINGS AND RECOMMENDATIONS

The tribunal failed to consider the alternative explanation of the distribution of the document to the distribution of the document by myself. This was that Mr. Moore and Mr. Flood took the document without the knowledge or authorization of the owner and authorized its distribution in order to hurt and harm me. They do not consider this possibility since it would have meant considering the implications of such an action. As a consequence their judgment is partisan and entirely biased. What they should have done and failed to do was to consider both sides of the case, the defendant's and the CEA's, and weigh the evidence for each bearing in mind that the prosecution had to prove its case beyond a reasonable doubt. Since they failed to weigh both sides, their verdict was unreasonable.

Once this point is understood, it is easy to understand the unreasonable case they made for blameworthiness and the numerous errors in their reasoning.

The tribunal were entirely misled by failing to note Dr. Hall's evidence concerning the distribution of the document, which was truthful, and by rejecting Armitage's evidence, which was also truthful. There was no conflict between the witnesses. It is clearly stated in paragraph 4.2 of the findings and recommendations: "We entirely reject Armitage's evidence that he required only that his manuscript be typed, and that he should receive back a copy for further perusal and reflection over the weekend: and that in no sense did he authorize or anticipate circulation of his manuscript without further reference back to himself." "We were told by a Governor, Dr. Hall, and accept from her that Mr. Armitage expressed no surprise or regret on the night before the Governors' meeting that the manuscript had been circulated."

This statement in the findings must clearly be wrong and contrary to evidence, since Dr. Hall stated in evidence on several occasions that Mr. Armitage expressed surprise and regret and annoyance at the distribution of the document, as can be shown.

Dr. Hall says on day 1, page 17, "I also that evening asked him not to make unkind comments to the clerk of the governors, Michael Lewis, because he was placing the blame for the circulation of the document on Michael Lewis and I was not prepared to accept that." Dr. Hall was wrong not to accept it because it was true. I clearly did express my views that the document had been distributed against my wishes. Also on day 1, page 39, "do not make unfavorable comments about our clerk, because I will not tolerate that." And on day 1, page 40, "not make disparaging remarks against our clerk." All these remarks were a response to my comments about the distribution of the document which was done without my knowledge.

Furthermore, Mr. Moore also confirmed Dr. Hall's evidence on the distribution of the document. On day 1, page 1, I asked him:

Q. *(Mr. Armitage)*: Did Mr. Lewis tell you that I had given him this document to be typed in confidence, and that it was to be returned to me?

A. *(Mr. Moore)*: No, that was not said at all.

Q. *(Mr. Armitage)*: He did not tell you that I had given it to him on the Monday and wanted it back as soon as possible to have the whole weekend to reconsider it, read it, consult various other people about it, before it was distributed?

A. *(Mr. Moore)*: No. *I think he told me that after the governors' meeting itself.* I did not know at the time of the governors' meeting that it was so. I had assumed you had sent the document to the office to be typed and distributed to the governors.

When Mr. Moore said that, "I think he told me that after the governors' meeting itself," he confirmed my evidence to the tribunal and the evidence Michael Lewis could have given, had he agreed to appear as a witness.

Asked about the distribution of the document, first, Moore said that Lewis did not tell him what my instructions were. Asked a second time, Moore says that he was told what my instructions were after the governors' meeting. He said he didn't know it at the time and before the governors' meeting. He could easily have lied or been mistaken on this point, especially since he used a hearing aid. He then says he "assumed" I had authorized the distribution of the document. So, he didn't know but only assumed.

What is the significance of the above evidence? It means that the tribunal said they were told by Dr. Hall and accepted from her that Armitage expressed no surprise or regret on the night before the governors' meeting that the manuscript had been circulated. Yet, she didn't say that. On the contrary, she said I had expressed dissatisfaction on this point and discouraged me from mentioning it. It was also clear that in a lengthy and complicated case the members of the tribunal had not read the evidence properly and had ignored vital evidence. Therefore, on this point alone, they can't have made a finding of guilt without being unreasonable and unjust. It also meant that their finding was incorrect and unjust in its entirety.

The tribunal also failed to note that Dr. Hall had no direct evidence regarding the distribution of the document since she was not concerned with it. So to accept her evidence and not to consider the absence of key witnesses as significant was unreasonable.

On day 1, page 16, Dr. Hall said, "When Mr. Armitage telephoned he was anxious to talk about the next day, and I said that I wished he had shown me a copy of that statement, and I would have then been able to express my views, and asked him to remove certain statements, which I felt would do him no good at all." In paragraph 4.2 of the findings it is written: "As for the alternative suggestion made that Mr. Armitage may never have submitted his manuscript had he had time to reflect upon it over the weekend, we reject this also." They rejected it though against the evidence since I was seeking Dr. Hall's advice and her statement here confirms my evidence.

When the tribunal say they "entirely reject Mr. Armitage's evidence," they were entirely wrong and it is clear that they concluded that I lied about the distribution of the document. Yet, Dr. Hall's and Dennis Moore's evidence supports my evidence. They had no evidence to entirely reject my evidence. They appear to have indulged in wishful thinking. The use of the term "entirely reject" is strong and implies that there was no doubt in their minds. However, even if they arrived at this conclusion because they hadn't noticed Dr. Hall's and Dennis Moore's evidence on this vital point, which they had not, it is clear they didn't entertain reasonable doubts as to why the key witnesses to the distribution of the document didn't give evidence and that Mr. Moore's evidence was confused on his role in the distribution. He *could* also have been lying. In addition, if they thought wrongly that I was lying, it would persuade them against my case.

The tribunal should have trusted my evidence and accepted my view of the events concerning the document's distribution. I was the only person who could have known my own intentions. In fact, I always work in a step-by-step manner. But to have done so would mean that they would have to consider that the City Education Authority inspector was being deceptive and they didn't seem to want to entertain this.

On a further point, in the Findings and Recommendations of the Tribunal, paragraph 16, the complaint against me was as stated:

that he was guilty of professional misconduct, and thereby misconduct, in that he caused to be put before the Governors of Borecross School for their meeting on July 17, 1979, a document (Appendix C) which strongly attacked the Headmaster of the School, Mr. Tottenham, without giving any due notice beforehand to Mr. Tottenham.

The tribunal altered the charges during the course of the proceedings and came up with a new charge in the findings. This was a deceptive and therefore wrong practice. Why did they need to do this? The logic must have been that when they found that the original charge had no foundation, the only way they could secure a finding of guilt was by changing the charge. This was why they introduced the complaint of "strongly attacked" rather than criticized the headmaster "without giving due notice beforehand to Mr. Tottenham." It was an unfair principle of procedure, since my defense was directed at the original charge and criticism it was agreed by the tribunal was not unprofessional conduct. The essential points of the initial charges as formulated by Mr. Stephens were:

a. "criticism of the previous headmaster"
b. "continued to criticize"
c. "the document was considered to be unprofessional in content"

None of these charges was unprofessional. Criticizing a head teacher is not unprofessional as Mr. Moore and Mr. Bright testified. Since the headmaster is responsible for the management of the school, he is primarily accountable. Therefore, from the argument of incorrect procedures alone but also from the argument that the charge was not a charge of unprofessional conduct, the charge ought to have been dismissed. Not to have done so was unreasonable.

However, the injustice was much worse and more irrational than this. Since the tribunal couldn't prove that I caused the distribution of the document, they were not justified in making a finding of guilt. Since I didn't distribute the document, the question of due notice did not arise. Furthermore, the fact that I did not give due notice to Alan Tottenham is further evidence that I did not control the distribution of the document, because I knew the correct procedure and carried it out in the case of the criticisms concerning the first head teacher, Brian Fellows. The tribunal have tried to say that I distributed it to the governors but not to Tottenham. But, the head teacher *was* a governor, so how could I have distributed it to all the governors but not to him? There was no question of his not being informed and this is the point of the rule. There was no question of going behind his back and acting in secrecy. In addition, since the divisional officer distributed the document, he distributed it with the knowledge that its distribution would result in a charge of unprofessional conduct. Therefore, why did he distribute it? Wasn't this act irrational? Why didn't he and Moore come to me and say they thought that there were certain problems with the document and I should make changes before they distributed it. Then I would have known what was happening. They ought to have done so, but why didn't they? Why didn't Mr. Flood appear as a witness at the tribunal if he had nothing to hide? I gave evidence in full because I had nothing to hide, yet the tribunal did not take this into account.

Since there was only one rule of professional conduct which is clear, the tribunal introduced it so that a charge of unprofessional conduct could stick. The tribunal plainly took sides in the issues and supported the authorities against the evidence. The tribunal therefore assumed a political character. It was determined to convict irrationally. Three members of the tribunal held positions of authority as a deputy head, a staff inspector and a head teacher, and therefore were likely to be prejudiced in favor of the authority and were unable to weigh the issues fairly.

The tribunal didn't consider the fact that the three important witnesses to the distribution of the document, namely Michael Lewis, the divisional officer Mr. Flood and Mr. Leburn, did not appear before the tribunal. Michael Lewis was the key witness after me. Yet they accepted the evidence of Dr. Hall who didn't know about the matter. The handling of the tribunal findings amounted to irrational incompetence.

The intention behind the distribution of the document was to hurt and harm me since, as a result of its distribution, Mr. Flood and Mr. Moore both knew that Mr. Moore was going to charge me with unprofessional conduct and the governors would be prevented from discussing the document. That was why they wanted it distributed. They wouldn't accept criticism of authority. This was irrational. However, it showed that there was a "crisis of authority."

The main reason why the members of the tribunal must have acted in this way was the political consequences which would have resulted from dismissing the case. The tribunal had a clear political motive in a finding of guilt.

In paragraph 2.6 the tribunal claim to have given "due weight to all the documentary evidence placed before us." Yet, they did not mention the evidence of Tim Atherton and have disregarded the alternative explanation of these events put forward by me and supported by the weight of evidence. The tribunal took the side of the authority in this issue and clearly acted in a biased way.

The tribunal failed to evaluate Moore's evidence. A rational analysis of his evidence is as follows. Armitage had heeded no advice given by Moore. Moore agreed that criticism was not unprofessional. He complained about a few words in the document which he considered emotional. Moore authorized the distribution of the document. Moore could have informed Armitage that he had seen the document without Armitage's knowledge and he considered certain remarks unprofessional. Moore considered Armitage's behavior "presumptuous"(day 1, p. 70). It didn't conform with Moore's idea of the proper relationship between a headmaster and a teacher, which he assumed was one of domination.

Moore didn't want the governors to discuss the document. He said, "it seemed to me extremely important at that governor's meeting that the governors should not be allowed to discuss this document"(day 2, p. 9). He told the governors he was bringing a complaint of unprofessional conduct in order to prevent them from discussing it. Moore said, "I had to tell them that to save them from discussing it." This seems to have been connected with Moore's observation that there had been a "nasty political battle" during the amalgamation. In reality, he was using professionalism to prevent politics.

In acting as he did, Moore deliberately encouraged what he apparently considered an act of unprofessional conduct. Yet, it was clearly a political act with political motive. He prevented the governors from discussing the document. He assumed an authoritarian relationship between a headmaster and a teacher. It is extremely vague and unsatisfactory to say that it is the "totality of the matter" which constitutes unprofessional conduct. By Moore's own standards of unprofessional conduct, he didn't consider criticism unprofessional. He seems to have brought the charge for other reasons not to do with professional conduct.

The tribunal failed to evaluate the background to the case as partly explained by Tim Atherton's evidence. Atherton said (day 3, page 33), "the Peter Armitage problem should not in fact exist at present, and I meant to, when I used the word strong, suggest that you had contained the effects of the problem, which was of some years duration, extraordinarily well." He also said, "In my view, a caring authority and several of its officers (that is not to say any single headmaster) would have seen some years ago, that an unfortunate and potentially difficult situation was developing." Atherton also said, "I had recently heard a statement by an inspector in which he said that he did not think the inspectors could do very much, and I passionately disagreed with that as a statement of possibility." From this viewpoint, it was the lack of political action within the City Education Authority which had led to the problem.

The tribunal demonstrated political bias by failing to evaluate Armitage's claim that Alan Tottenham, the headmaster, brought the charge of assault against Barry Kirkland for political reasons. It was a sign of poor judgment on Alan Tottenham's part because he took the political side of a pupil who had been continuously harming the education of his fellow students by regular absence and disruptive conduct, as I reported in written evidence. This charge was evidence of the lack of judgment which had produced the approach to the governors and the authoritarian relationship which Alan Tottenham had with his fellow professionals. He treated and punished them them like children. The Barry Kirkland incident was a minor incident, blown up out of all proportion, which was brought to the attention of the tribunal out of anger and the "crisis of authority" engendered by the critique of his leadership.

Concerning the charge of irregular corporal punishment, the tribunal based their finding on the evidence of two individuals, Barry Kirkland, the pupil who claimed he was struck, and Michael Bly. On day 2, page 52 of the verbatim report, the following questions were asked of Michael Bly:

Q.: Mr. Armitage hit him where?

A.: Well, I was not watching. I sort of heard the hit.

and on page 53:

Q.: Now, where did you say that Mr. Armitage hit Barry?

A.: I mean, if he knocked his glasses off, I suppose it was on the head, I suppose.

Further on Michael Bly says:

"Yes, I assumed it."
"I would have suspected that he did hit Barry."

and

Q.: You did not actually see Mr. Armitage hit Barry at all?
A.: No.

The members of the tribunal considered the above evidence of one witness in a classroom of boys sufficient to claim that "we are satisfied that he hit Gary Kirkland on the back of the head." This was insufficient evidence and evidence of biased judgment. For the classroom was full of boys, four of whom wrote in evidence that no assault occurred. Hence, the case was not proved. Also the members ignored the evidence that one other senior teacher had written a letter of apology to Kirkland's mother, which suggests that her complaining was not an unusual occurrence. Tim Atherton said in evidence that Armitage was "against corporal punishment" and not the sort of person he would expect to administer irregular corporal punishment.

It is remarked in the tribunal findings that the lesson was boring yet it was also remarked that when Barry Kirkland entered the room the class was intent on reading and obviously quiet. Is this a contradictory position? Could I have reasonably been expected to give Barry Kirkland an interesting lesson within a minute of entering a class which he had disrupted. Furthermore, I reported to the tribunal that Barry Kirkland had missed on average two or three classes out of five every week and this is why the classes were ineffective for him individually. The tribunal ignored this evidence.

My analysis of paragraph 4.2 is, first, it is correct to say I gave the document to Mr. Lewis on Monday, July 9, as I testified in evidence. So the tribunal believed my evidence on that point. But, I gave it to him in his capacity as Michael Lewis, a friend, not as clerk to the governors. I gave it to him to type because I met him accidentally on the road leaving the school and, because of the unreasonably short notice of the meeting, nothing to do with "ample time." My weeks were always busy. It was due to the short notice that Dr. Kinship said that he couldn't attend the governors' meeting, hence he confirmed my evidence. I asked Lewis to assist me since I normally type my own documents. Why should the tribunal reject my evidence that I required the manuscript to be typed and returned to me for perusal and reflection over the weekend? They had no reason to do so. That was my intention since I had no time during the week. Why did Mr. Lewis, Mr. Flood and Mr. Leburn refuse to testify? The tribunal didn't take into account their unwillingness to give evidence. In no sense did I authorize the distribution of the document. It is quite untrue to say "without reference back to myself." This was my responsibility. I didn't think of it as a free typing service. That's a purely accounting way of looking at things. I have frequently given hours of my time to the CEA without payment. The tribunal ignored Dr. Hall's evidence, as I have mentioned elsewhere. The tribunal simply didn't evaluate the short notice of the meeting. As Dr. Kinship testified, "Unfortunately, the meeting was arranged at very short notice." I needed the weekend to peruse matters carefully and decide what to do. The document was a first draft.

The following criticisms of Armitage made in paragraph 4.9 are unjustified. The tribunal complained about a relatively few number of words out of a total of 4,800 words approximately. The language of the document was rational. The document has to be judged as a whole. Armitage neither circulated nor timed the circulation of the document. Armitage had not ignored "channels of communication." He had used them as much as he reasonably could have. He had seen Mr. Cohen and Mr. Buckley.

The tribunal halted the proceedings abruptly and prematurely (see day 3, page 79). I objected to this at the time because I had no time to analyze the evidence and make a summary of my case. This was a procedural error with consequences.

The burden of proof was on the CEA since they brought the charges. They failed to prove their case. With reference to paragraph 6 of the findings, the concluding paragraph, the tribunal are unjustified in saying Armitage intended to hurt and harm the headmaster. His concern was the school's well-being. Tim Atherton said there was a long and consistent approach to the school's problems. The other points made are also unjustified. In particular, they are unjustified in saying that this would happen in any school in which Armitage taught. They ignored the evidence put before them that the head teacher was an unqualified teacher whereas Armitage had professional qualifications in education. With a competent and qualified headmaster there could be no grounds for complaint.

The tribunal operated on a very narrow and inadequate definition of professional. A teacher concerned with good education is acting professionally. The tribunal failed to analyze the background complexities of this case. Their analysis, such as it is, is superficial and blatantly biased. To have dismissed the case would have raised questions about the competence of those individuals who brought the charges since it would have meant they hadn't thought through what they were doing in the first place. This seems to have been the principal political motive behind the tribunal's recommendations and findings.

When matters reached the tribunal, they had gone a long way and too far to stop easily because someone would have had to admit that mistakes had been made. We seemed to be in a system so lacking in confidence in its own ability that it couldn't admit any mistakes. As I pointed out to the governors in Chapter 3, authoritarianism collapses as soon as questioning gets under way and the whole effort had been to question what we were doing. The governors including the headmaster and the CEA couldn't tolerate the opposition. I had in effect been forced to and felt it necessary to bring the issue to a head. I had no other choice since the authorities had denied my promotion, had refused to accept realities and had refused to discuss the situation with me and negotiate a solution. That was hardly surprising since the school had a communication problem. The two inspectors who came to the school said, in a report,

Consultation:
The way in which decisions are arrived at is of great importance to staff morale. Most of the teachers we met considered that they had opportunities to express views, but a disturbing number of them expressed the opinion that consultation is a facade for decisions which have been taken in advance.

Note the use of the well-chosen word "facade." It echoes Dr. Gardner's surface-stability and its opposite deep instability mentioned in Chapter 1.

To have given a verdict of not guilty was filled with political implications. Politically, it would have strengthened the opposition. I could have gone back to Borecross School considerably strengthened politically. That would have been a humiliation to all who had opposed me, including the head teacher, Alan Tottenham, Dr. Hall and Dr. Kinship, Dennis Moore, and the governing body. That was the probable reason why the members of the tribunal felt forced to find me guilty. In not dealing with this problem in its early stages, the authority had allowed me to build up a position of power and influence within the school in opposition to the official authorities. If they had handled the matter competently, this situation would not have occurred. Morally and politically, they had been defeated.

It is significant that the appeal ordered that I not return to Borecross School. This was an intentional political intervention. It meant that all the work I had put in over many years was null and void. It was a deliberate suppression of democratic and constitutional politics.

As for imagining out of an irrational feeling of persecution that opposition was not wanted and gave rise to irrational action, the evidence on these pages is clear. At the time I saw Dr. Hall and Dr. Kinship and had decided to appeal to the governors once again for justice, the evidence had been mounting. I had applied for and not been interviewed or shortlisted for the head of English or the director of studies. The deputy chairman of governors had approached me personally in my classroom and said, "The system of promotion just isn't fair. My father was a teacher and he had similar sort of problems as you've got. The best thing to do is seek promotion elsewhere." Since I hadn't been interviewed by the board of governors as a whole for years, it was reasonable to be suspicious that the exclusion was intentional and irrational, since it wasn't based on knowledge or evidence. Second, I had performed well in my job and was responsible for the change to the year system which had now been adopted. I was involved in several innovations designed to raise standards in the school. I had been informed by Peter Tall, the deputy headmaster, that I would not have a class group the following year with the year system. This was a studied insult if ever there was one. It could only be interpreted as a punishment by the house masters for having the system changed and an implicit recognition that I had been the main person responsible. I was not going to be allowed to benefit from a success. On the contrary, I was demoted. Furthermore, when I went to see Peter Tall, the new deputy head, with Tim Atherton, he refused to discuss the matter. Communication had been ended. Yet, the tribunal of inquiry claimed that communication was both welcome and possible within the school. The headmaster, Alan Tottenham, also supported the decision, as he mentioned in writing. The whole thing was done without discussion. Tottenham also said on day 3, page 15 that he would only talk to me if a deputy head were present, which seems to be connected with his statement that "I know my English is deplorable," although he claims I misinterpret things and "I get the feeling that you are often unable to perceive the truth." Mr. Tottenham also said, "I think you live in a world of fantasy, sometimes, and you do not know what you are talking about." This was his assessment of me and yet we had never had an extended conversation in all the years I had known him, so his knowledge could not have been from firsthand experience. This is what happens when people won't or can't communicate on an interpersonal level. There is plenty of evidence in these pages that I am a communicative person, yet my relationship with Tottenham was one without communication. I had organized a successful debating society for years and I took assemblies for six or eight hundred boys and was regularly applauded for the telling of stories. I am also a reasonable actor. I had attended two courses on group dynamics which dealt with problems of interpersonal communication at an institutional level, so I was aware of communication problems. Tim Atherton called me "communicative" and, since he had a rare rapport with people, his assessment is likely to be accurate. Tottenham refers on day 3, page 15 to a warning by the acting headmaster when he arrived "that I should see you only with a witness," advice which stems from the meeting mentioned in Chapter 3; such is the link between events over the years.

Tim Atherton was asked at the tribunal why he had come to the conclusion that dedication was "unnerving." He said, "it is an accumulative thing. I suppose one can be cumulatively unnerved! I think others of my colleagues find the same. I may be intellectually more absorbent than most of the staff at Borecross School but I do not like to pay close attention all the time. I think Armitage has to a certain extent unnerved a reasonable proportion of the staff at Borecross School by his dedication to questions of the possible improvement of comprehensive schools besides Borecross. It ought to be said that some of his insistence upon discussion in connection with that has been effective in making people think."

APPEAL

The following is the exact record of the appeal document placed before the appeal committee composed of elected members of the City Education Authority.

IN THE MATTER OF AN APPEAL BY PETER BRAITHWAITE ARMITAGE TO THE STAFFS APPEALS SUB COMMITTEE TO BE HEARD ON THE 29TH DAY OF MAY 1980.

THE APPEAL IS AGAINST THE FINDINGS AND RECOMMENDATIONS OF THE DISCIPLINARY TRIBUNAL OF ENQUIRY IN RELATION TO A COMPLAINT OF PROFESSIONAL MISCONDUCT BY THE APPELLANT.

STATEMENT OF GROUNDS OF APPEAL.

All paragraph references relate to the document of Findings and Recommendations of the Tribunal.

A. Blameworthiness.

(1) There was insufficient evidence for the Tribunal to make the following findings of fact:

(a) That Mr. Armitage had authorized the distribution of the document such finding under Paragraph 4.2.

(b) That there was an intention to distribute the document such finding under paragraph 4.2.

(2) The Tribunal did not fully investigate the facts of the alleged distribution of the document.

(3) The Tribunal failed to observe the Rules of Natural Justice.

B. Proposed Punishment.

(1) In recommending that Mr. Armitage be dismissed the Tribunal failed to investigate mitigating circumstances.

(2) The Tribunal should have considered the following matters:

(a) Mr. Armitage had written the document merely to express his views on a particular part of the educational system.

(b) The interests of the school were always uppermost in the intentions of Mr. Armitage.

(c) There was not an intention to hurt and harm the headmaster or any other member of staff.

(3) Mr. Armitage had explored other avenues of expressing his view in particular staff discussions in the common room.

Dated the 20th day of May 1980
Peter Braithwaite Armitage

The following was the official statement of the result of the appeal:

This letter sets out in writing the decision of the Staff Appeals Sub-Committee on 29 May 1980.

The Sub-Committee dismissed your appeal against blameworthiness, but decided to vary the punishment of dismissal with due notice which had been recommended by the Disciplinary Tribunal of Inquiry and instead downgrade you from a scale 2 to a scale 1 teaching post and to ask the Education Officer to ensure that you no longer teach at Borecross School.

J. R. Wintle
Deputy Authority Clerk

Only one member of the appeal committee claimed to have read the evidence. Mr. Graham, the chairman, had remarked that the appeal committee normally accepted the findings and recommendations of the tribunal. Therefore, in altering the recommendations, they went against normal procedures and implicitly criticized the work of the tribunal. This was a significant act. Therefore, the appeal was successful by implication and a vindication of the defense.

The members of the appeal committee were perplexed by the situation they found themselves in since they could hardly argue with the fact that the tribunal had not fully investigated the facts concerning the distribution of the document and had failed to observe the rules of natural justice. The chairwoman was in an emotional frame of mind and communicated hostility, frustration and anger at the situation. The City Education Authority lawyer remarked that in any case the document that had been written was not unreasonable, a remark which was also very significant. He would surely have advised an acquittal. They knew they had no case if the matter had been taken to an industrial tribunal, which would have been open rather than held in secret.

The appeal committee decided entirely wrongly, knowingly and unjustly to maintain the finding of blameworthiness, since that would save the City Education Authority and all concerned grave embarrassment and further problems. Then, by reducing the punishment to downgrading and removal to another school, they could prevent an appeal to an industrial tribunal against wrongful dismissal and give a minimal punishment which would give the appearance that the City Education Authority had acted correctly. They would have also dodged the problem that would have arisen had the accused been found not guilty and returned to Borecross School.

It was clear that, since they accepted the justification of the defendant's position, the appeal committee acted unreasonably in maintaining the finding of blameworthiness. Hence, they intervened in a political process to prevent its natural outcome. They didn't respect the process. They ought to have ordered an acquittal.

PLOT ANALYSIS

I critically analyzed the evidence of the tribunal proceedings and demonstrated that a finding of guilt for criticizing a head teacher was against evidence, the accusation itself was not unprofessional and the document I wrote was rational in content. Yet the members of the tribunal, Mr. P. Southern, Mr. H. Scotland, Mr. P. Benford and Mr. R. West, who were employed by the City Education Authority, ignored significant evidence and their conclusion was biased in favor of the authority.

The evidence of Chapter 4 demonstrated that Dennis Moore initiated the disciplinary tribunal for an authoritarian motive. Thus, he put the members of the tribunal in a political situation, because if they had rejected the charge of criticizing a head teacher as an unacceptable charge, which they should have done, they would have put the authority in an embarrassing, political situation since a political process between the opposition and the governors of Borecross would have been freed up to the consequences of a democratic, political process. They would have had to have made a politically courageous choice. They faced a choice between avoiding the problem and confronting the problem. They should have made the hard choice for the sake of educational improvement in London which is dependent on a political, democratic culture. The system was underpowered for its tasks and the teachers were powerless to change without the political cooperation of their political rulers.

The appeal committee similarly faced a difficult choice. They had less excuse to make the wrong decision, since the evidence was so clear that the tribunal had committed a "miscarriage of justice." They should have acted in the light of the evidence to ensure justice but they acted politically to support the authority and similarly prevented the natural process of a democratic politics from proceeding. The policies of the opposition should have resulted in educational improvements, if the right people had been in the right place to implement them, but the political authorities all acted to prevent educational change and development in a qualitative direction. Hence, it was the inadequate political practices of the authoritarian authorities which prevented improvement.

Dennis Moore essentially prevented the political process of talk, dialogue, discussion and democracy in favor of secrecy and silence. He wouldn't allow a teacher to talk with the governors. I argued in Chapters 1 and 3 that the amalgamation was carried out without thought, and he was in a leading position of responsibility with a vested interest in maintaining his authority. When problems were pointed out, Moore took a position of defending the status quo. He was wrong not to change the house system and reestablish his authority. He was wrong about the issue of professionalism. He was also wrong about school organization as formal in character. If the authorities had recognized educational qualifications and experience they would not have found themselves in this situation. So this situation was created by the mistakes of those with responsibility for managing the system.

There is a further strand to this issue. It is expressed thus by Mary Warnock:

Another factor of a different kind prevents the general public from respecting teachers as professionals. Besides being increasingly unionized, teachers are also thought to have become increasingly politicized, especially teachers in London and the inner cities. It is very hard to judge the accuracy of this sort of accusation against teachers. Certainly the Local Authorities, up till now their employers, and the City Education Authority in particular, are highly political, and this was the basis of the Conservative determination to diminish the powers of Local Authorities to vanishing point. It is certainly true, as well, that many parents fear that their children are being indoctrinated at school with political views which they, the parents, do not share. And even if they do share them, they may well feel that teachers ought not to try to get their pupils to adopt any political views at all, left-wing or right. Teaching, it is felt, ought to be distinguished from indoctrination and propaganda. (Warnock 1988, 112)

The relevance of this quotation in this context is to lend support to the view that the City Education Authority had put politics before education and here is a concrete example. There was a connection here with the politicization of teachers in the comprehensive system and the blurring of the distinction between education and indoctrination. This was political theory and practice rather than educational theory and practice.

This tribunal and appeal committee was guilty of the erosion of freedom. Nor is that a case of special pleading, because the following quotation provides evidence that it was recognized as a serious problem in Britain:

The area that particularly concerned Pinter was her undermining of what he saw as fundamental liberties. He was far from being alone. *Index on Censorship* in September 1988, in the first ever issue devoted to a western democracy, examined the state of freedom in Britain. In the introduction Ronald Dworkin, the American legal philosopher and Oxford Professor of Jurisprudence, warned: "liberty is ill in Britain . . . the sad truth is that the very concept of liberty is being challenged and corroded by the Thatcher government." He argued that freedom of speech, conviction and information were among fundamental human rights and that the protection of those rights was essential to "the culture of liberty" which had been part of Britain's national heritage as handed down from Milton through John Stewart Mill. (Billington 1996, 306)

It is interesting to note that in this case it was a left-wing local government that denied the freedom of speech and the culture of freedom but that a conservative government followed their example in retaliation.

The teaching profession needs a teaching council to ensure autonomy from political interference. A local education authority has a vested interest in a political policy and cannot be expected to act impartially, as this verdict demonstrated. In the grammar school, educators were independent because freedom was respected. Left-wing views at the time emphasized equality of educational distribution but at the expense of freedom. Peters argued, in *Ethics and Education*, that equality was a necessary but not a sufficient condition of an educational theory (Peters 1966). Freedom is an essential part of an educational ethic and an educational theory. Moreover, freedom is a difficult attainment and not an automatic condition as Eric Fromm argued in the *Fear of Freedom* (1960).

The charge of criticizing a head teacher was an attack on free speech. Authoritarian non-freedom had won over democratic freedom. Authority dominated power. Organization dominated the individual.

Chapter 6

Discourse, Policy, Politics

Narrative and educational argument come together in this chapter. I present two discourses which represent two contrastive views of education, a social scientific and a natural scientific view. These two views are the source of the conflict between freedom of thought and choice versus authoritarianism that has run through these pages. I record the policy document in the first section, which was the subject of the disciplinary tribunal. I analyze its content as an educational philosophy of theory and educational enlightenment. In the second section, I record a policy statement written by the head teacher which revealed his style and practices. I analyze them as based on the theory of scientific discourse and management and expressing an instrumental philosophy of education. I critically analyze it from the point of view of the culture of education. I implicitly compare and contrast the two documents. In the third section, I juxtapose the policy and practices of secrecy and revelation and argue for the politics of revelation. In the fourth section, I examine theories of discourse and policy practice. In the final section, I analyze the critical approaches to political theory and practice which inform this study and are a basis for action.

THE CONFIDENTIAL REPORT TO THE GOVERNORS OF BORECROSS SCHOOL

I wrote the following document but did not authorize its distribution. It became the subject of an expensive and lengthy City Education Authority tribunal of inquiry on the grounds that it was considered unprofessional.

I'd first like to thank the governors for agreeing to meet me. I know that there are some people (including inspectors) who think that governing bodies are made up of amateurs who shouldn't be informed or consulted, but I take the view of the Taylor Report that if they are part of the system making important decisions they should be informed, particularly about the results of their actions. I have two main aims. One is to put the argument that the school is not being managed as a comprehensive school. Second, to argue that the spirit and resolution passed at the last meeting has not been carried out and that the evidence which I gave then has been added to and reinforced by developments since.

First, my point about the school not being managed as a comprehensive. There is now a considerable body of literature on the comprehensive school, what it is, and what ought to be happening in them, which ought to be the starting point for important and intelligible discussion. But, for the moment I shall refer to the CEA document on the internal government of schools presented to the Education Committee on March 5, 1974. I take this to be a very good and relevant document, based on the experience of several schools in the CEA which have got themselves into difficulties in recent years. It was distributed to all staff by the authority and passed by the staff in a common room motion. But, it has been significant that *no* comment or action has come from either headmaster, and it would seem from their conduct that they have neither understood it properly nor implemented it in an acceptable way. Peter Tall, presumably in the name of the head, even said that it should be ignored.

To take but a few points from this document. "Full and successful involvement of heads and assistant staff" "is a complex matter!" This is particularly true of the large secondary school! Complicated matters I take to mean that detailed discussion is necessary, yet the staff seem to have only the very vaguest notion of the headmaster's ideas and plans for the school, if he has any. A special meeting during the holidays was called by senior staff because people wanted more information. He remained almost totally silent throughout the house system/year system debate. If the head isn't prepared to commit himself in public, who is? He says very little except on trivial administrative points, and very little of any significance during informal meetings, or whole common room meetings, thus undermining the importance of these occasions. He has announced that since he can't talk to all the staff all the time, he can't talk to any of the staff, which I take to mean he is unwilling to discuss the real issues within the school. He seems to have no interest in educational ideas or principles or any ability to analyze and evaluate the problems of the school, an ability which could only come from recognized courses in advanced educational studies. Another paragraph in the C.E.A. document says that "effort stems naturally from democratic leadership and from discussion of issues and plans." We seem to have authoritarian leadership so far as we have any leadership at all, yet the pupils and society are demanding democratic style teachers. For example, the head announced his decision to change the policy regarding corporal punishment at a stroke, in a manner which produced unnecessary controversy and conflict, and then invited discussion. Anybody acquainted with Leila Berg's book on Risinghill Comprehensive will recall that this decision by the head resulted in the closing of the school. When such an authoritarian decision is made, any discussion or questioning is a threat to the authority, competence and dignity of the head, as happened on this occasion. It was even the case that he had not consulted his deputies, so that there was considerable resentment at the way it was implemented and the wisdom of the action.

A further remark in the C.E.A. document is the importance of a "genuinely re-

ceptive attitude of senior staff to the ideas and views of others," "an attitude exemplified in the conduct of the head." I would say the headmaster is unreceptive to
ideas. His ability to argue and criticize arguments is rarely tested in practice because
he dodges out of all such situations. For example, he missed the last meeting I had
with the governors for a reason I couldn't understand, and it was impossible to
discuss the matter properly the next day. I have indicated on several occasions subjects
which I wished to discuss and he has refused. Other staff make similar observations.

Another point is that "heads reserved the right to make some decisions themselves
after consultation." In this school the practice seems to be decide then consult.
Examples of this are the decision to get the staff rooms in the central administrative
building. When staff complained afterward, as much out of an affront to their dignity
as anything else, their fair complaint was criticized, resented and misunderstood. This
is hardly the way to cultivate good relations. Since the thinking behind the decision
was not explained, making a decision in this thoughtless, careless way could only
further undermine the head's credibility and authority. Since it came so soon after
the maths appointment confusion, it could only point to something seriously wrong.
The C.E.A. document says, "Reaching a consensus may take longer but the extra
effort may be worthwhile in gaining fuller support and cooperation." The decision
to change from a house to a year system took seven years to effect, and was a model
almost of the consultative process, so that nobody could argue in public that it wasn't
fair. Incidentally, I first took the initiative for this change at the time of the amalgamation and in spite of putting a lot of thought and work into it, have received no
recognition, even though anyone can see that this school has been chaotically disorganized for years. With hindsight, it would have been better if I said nothing,
which is what most staff have concluded in this school.

A further point is that "real democratic involvement means recognition of the
views of other reasoned argument before decisions are taken." Now, reasoned argument is not possible in an atmosphere of mistrust and suspicion and the knowledge
that the head finds argument and reasoning as threatening and unacceptable. The
head is not a public speaker and therefore does not manage staff meetings effectively;
he stopped the end-of-term assembly last term and speech day has also been stopped,
important occasions in the life of most schools for a very long time.

The document also mentions "the importance of courses" and of "updating
courses for those who have held positions for some years, cannot be emphasized too
strongly." The benefits of in-service training are not implemented here because new
ideas, attitudes and methods are not welcome. Discussion is at a very superficial level.
The pastoral side is run on the basis of rudimentary psychology and social work
theory in an almost uncritical way. The main problem of the school amongst the
pupils is possibly the relationship between authority, discipline, freedom and equality
which the school doesn't have a clear, proper policy on, even though the area has
been thoroughly explored by educationalists. Freedom here, for example, often
means freedom to be as lazy as you like, to answer back as rudely as you can, disrupt
lessons and be a continuous nuisance and expect to get away with it. If you don't
like the teacher or his teaching methods you can complain to the deputy head who
will sympathize and blame an inadequate teacher. Rights come before obligations,
and generally when that happens obligations go by the board! The senior staff at this
school do not clearly have adequate training. Advanced educational qualifications are

clearly essential. Yet, when properly qualified people apply for a job they're not even given an adequate hearing, let alone an interview.

In the section on communications it says that "there must be provision for a flow-back of ideas, comments and reaction from staff to head." The headmaster has a well-known inability to communicate, so discussion and dialogue are not possible in this school. Moreover, there are many serious problems which ought to have been looked at years ago, which haven't been. I'm thinking of a multi-ethnic policy and a language policy.

In the conclusion, it says that consultation means having "an organization which exists in good working order and not merely on paper." A reasonably and widely held view is that we have an organization on paper, but it doesn't work in practice because the informal human relationships side doesn't work. The Taylor Report on governing bodies says, "it is the human involvement which makes for a successful school." This school discourages participation, even though participation is an important comprehensive value.

Finally, this C.E.A. document repeats that "There is a special responsibility on the head and his senior staff to be accessible and to show a readiness to listen to ideas about the running of the school." The message that comes to me from senior staff is that we don't know what's going on and they have no real confidence in the head. The implicit suggestion is bumble along as best you can.

In a book on accountability in education there is an authoritative article on a secondary head in a maintained school. Listed there are thirteen functions of management as follows:

1. Perceiving the needs of society.
2. Responding to national and local directive.
3. Determining school ethos through curriculum and pastoral care.
4. Counseling problems.
5. Providing leadership.

Communication
6. Relating to the immediate community.
7. Appointing staff and developing their skills.
8. Teaching children.
9. Communicating with parents.
10. Arbitrating in matters of discipline.

Housekeeping
11. Administering a large and complex institution.
12. Deciding issues where priorities conflict.
13. Planning future needs.

Out of these thirteen points perhaps the headmaster is carrying out two or three functions effectively. Even his main strength, which is administration, it could be argued is a fault since this school may well be overadministered and overbureaucratized. A great amount of staff time, better spent on preparation, marking and teaching is taken up with administration, but, the boys do not feel the benefit of it. Staff have complained and hinted, but nothing has been done.

To turn now to the problems of the school. In a book on *The Politics of Educa-*

tional Change, Maurice Kogan, on page 161, writes, "There is a gap between feeling out of the comprehensive issue by the early seers and its implementation by Fred Mulley and Ashley Brammell." "In secondary education, however, only a few practitioners have been speculative about what ought to happen—Margaret Miles, Margaret Maden, for example—in their own schools, and they have had to rely too much on the sociological and psychological cases against selection." In this school, for example, we have never discussed what a comprehensive school ought to be doing. We may have merely been drifting in the dark. There is now a body of literature available which anybody seriously interested in comprehensive education on the inside would need to consider. But, where do you find that consideration here? There is now one widely recognized man of genius (whose ideas the headmaster apparently rejects), Michael Marland, M.B.E., a practicing head, who has edited a whole series of professionally competent books on different aspects of school organization and management, and he regularly runs management courses. So there is a literature and standard against which to measure the practices and achievements of this school.

Now, I would ask, though it is hard to see anything which is genuinely comprehensive about this school, where does it so clearly fall down? First, in his book *Comprehensive Values*, P.E. Daunt, possibly the leading authority in this area, says, "the eliminating of competition from the organized modes of the school will leave a gap in motivation which must first be filled if there is not to be a severe loss of purpose." We may well have abandoned competition but not replaced it with anything better, hence the severe loss of purpose we see around us in the boys who often complain of boredom. And boredom of course is one cause of violence and dropping out of society. Daunt says that cooperation is the only alternative to competition. Cooperation is a softer word than competition, so it is easy to suppose it implies "tranquility and freedom from conflict." He suggests we must "distinguish firmly between passive cooperation (Borecross style), which is the hallmark of an autocratic system, and active cooperation." He describes passive cooperation as "a wilderness of peace based on the inert cooperation of those under discipline" (the staff of Borecross), and active cooperation as "a continuing stir of controversy as a necessary factor in a creative cooperation in which all are involved." Two or three years back, I started a staff newspaper using school funds, to promote involvement of staff in school issues. The new head stopped the funds, so it collapsed.

As regards the virtual abolition of corporal punishment, it is of no value unless it is exchanged for some better form of keeping discipline. There is incidentally a body of very good quality literature on discipline, as you would expect, but the policy we have is certainly not based on a practical understanding of the theoretical issues in the literature. No real alternative forms have been discussed or promoted by those responsible. The result is a poorly disciplined school, so that the work in class can't be done properly since it requires self-discipline, which most of the pupils haven't been taught either at home or in school. Common staff complaints are the passing of responsibility from the center to the class teacher while reducing his powers and undermining his authority by passing the buck. The areas where the center has to lead in maintaining reasonable control, areas such as corridors and areas surrounding the school, are often areas where control has broken down. This last year there have been three very serious incidents. There were two muggings of old ladies near the school, in typical semi-organized gangs. Also, a large number of boys (70 or 80) went on a semi-rampage in the local area, and the whole school was cautioned by the police at an assembly. There was also a serious incident involving a female member of staff. In *Fifteen Thousand Hours*, a study of twelve C.E.A. schools published this year, the point is made that poor discipline outside the school results from poor discipline within the school, which is further evidence for the view that discipline here is not on a practical and sound footing. The connection between size and discipline has never been discussed adequately. The head's handling of the school on these occasions was widely criticized, yet it is his opportunity to demonstrate his authority and control of the situation.

Another problem I would like to have brought up (and have studied in some depth myself), but have had no chance to do so, is the question of how values are taught and what the values are. But even though there is a considerable body of literature on moral education worth consulting, nothing has been done to replace the teaching of Christian and religious values, except perhaps in the isolation of the classroom. The pastoral side, in some respects, could be, totally unawares, promoting anti-educational values in any well-understood meaning of the term "education." Some people have commented on the possibility that the English exam results are less good than that of other departments. One major cause may be that English depends upon the quality of relationships and the ethos within the school more than other subjects, and will reflect the quality of moral values.

In *Fifteen Thousand Hours* there were significant differences between schools along a range of factors. The main factor was the ethos of the school, which an outsider would not easily perceive in a short visit and could easily be deceived about. I suggest that this may be the key to the problem of this school, and only a head can create the ethos, by talk, performance, motivation and persuasion. As one member of staff remarked the other day, it would take at least two years' work by a really dynamic head to put this school on its feet again, and he would need the support of an understanding and properly informed governing body.

In the attached evaluation (based on modern approaches), I list some of the other problems, most of which seem to be to be largely reasonable judgments. Clearly, it would be useful to discuss them in greater detail, since fuller evidence and observation are necessary.

Turning to the treatment of staff in the school, it has become school policy (since presumably the center doesn't feel it had the power to share the responsibility) to pass responsibility to the classroom teacher, who may be being placed in a position of extreme conflict, since he has to manage increasingly vocal attacks from pupils, and many of his traditional powers have been removed, without being replaced by anything tangible enough.

A democratic classroom teacher maintains his authority by rational methods and by respect and confidence in his abilities. Yet, many teachers are not trained for this situation. It is unfair for the head to hold the staff in authoritarian subjection by using the sanctions of promotion and career prospects, in other words, to have a master–servant relationship between head and staff, while demanding implicitly a democratic relationship between staff and pupils. Things can't and don't work out this way. Anyone with a training in the sociology of the classroom and the sociology of the school would know this. Democracy must start from the top, not from the bottom with little-educated second formers, for whom freedom and equality mean license to do what they like in the name of their democratic rights; who don't regard their teachers, at least in one way, as their betters, from whom they can learn. I have yet to meet a parent who would hold to the views this school is sanctioning.

To give two examples of the head's attitude to his staff: A formal note was received by a teacher in difficulties with his class which said:

> "I was surprised to find two boys playing chess and three other boys noisily watching on in your library period with 4(9) today period 6. I was also surprised at the general lack of application of the other boys in the class.
>
> "The class is under your direct supervision and you are responsible for what goes on in it, it is clear that you were not following the agreed syllabus and it is my belief that the class is not making good use of its time. You are to ensure that this does not occur again."

Is this really the best method of treating a teacher in difficulties? Much of the business of this school is carried out in writing. Talk and chat is a much quicker and better method. Notes lead to misunderstanding. The tone of this note is domineering, threatening and unhelpful.

Second, I have spent a number of years practically in the school and in two years of an in-service course dealing with language and communication difficulties of boys in the school. When I suggested it would be in order to discuss my ideas and attitudes to them (since I hadn't had an opportunity) when the head of English post became available, I was written a letter and accused of canvassing. I regarded the letter as symbolic and absurd, symbolic of a head who couldn't really care less. I have watched professional standards go down since I have been here, but this really was the ultimate evidence of what I had already been suspicious of. I know of a least one other teacher who received a similar note. I also know of a teacher who felt forced to resign as a result of psychological pressure of an unfair character. These kinds of incidents are highly damaging to staff morale and confidence. Since it is no part of an overall and long-term policy of staff relations; it is totally unsatisfactory and half-baked.

Turning now to the second aim of this meeting, which is my treatment and position within this school. It is the duty of a head to represent a fair and unbiased view of his staff to the governing body. It is also an opportunity for heads to abuse their considerable powers over staff. I do not myself believe that interview techniques have kept pace with the changing complexities of society and education. Most staff consider the interview system as amateurish, too much dependent on luck and out of date. Much better methods are available. The evidence suggests that the head has been using short-listing procedures unfairly. The maths appointment was the clearest case which came to light. As one member of staff pointed out, there is no reason to short-list when there are only three candidates to interview; therefore, the English head of department appointment was another example of an irregularity in the short-listing. Since the head is a mathematician, and not conversant with current trends in English teaching, I wrote a paper evaluating the problems of the English Department. He would neither talk about it nor read it. If then the problems of the English Department are not sorted out in the next year or two, he has only himself to blame. How can you run a school if you ignore relevant facts and you're not willing to discuss different attitudes and points of view?

The head dodged the last meeting with the governors. As in so many matters I have mentioned, I am sure he has the wrong end of the stick regarding the series of circumstances which led to my making a complaint to the authority about the pre-

vious head, a complaint which was fair and was upheld. One member of staff commented at the time, "This school would have fallen apart in another term if
something hadn't been done." Mr. Creech, the deputy head at the time, who was
present at meetings I had with the inspectorate and the head, told me that his view
was that the head had been manifestly incompetent. All the staff knew it. If the
governors had worked to encourage responsibility in the school, they would have
commended my action. Any unpopularity I have suffered has been perhaps either
staff guilt at not having done something themselves, or the cowardly and stupid
action of the panic stricken head in placing my letter of complaint on the staff notice
board, in an attempt at public humiliation. Incidentally, I believe it would have been
much better to have faced the facts at the time so that the school could have begun
on a firm footing. Like most problems in the school, it was covered up.

I believe that the head has been carrying out a policy of revenge on behalf of the
previous head, since he knew him when he was director of studies in this school. I
have recently obtained further qualifications and he just doesn't want to know, even
though the school obviously needs the skills I can offer. I would define his attitude
as uncompromising, unhelpful, prejudiced and dogmatic. He has not carried out the
spirit and resolution of the last meeting. The inspectors who have visited the school
recently have criticized heads of department for not being strong enough in speaking
out about problems. Most staff know what has happened to me. This school is essentially privatized. The decision-taking is carried out in unknown and secret channels, with a committee structure as a front.

I would request that a suitable role and position is created for me, so that this
matter may be concluded and I can look to the future instead of the past.
P. B. Armitage

A probable reason for the charge of unprofessional conduct was that in
the first paragraph I said my aim for the meeting was "to argue that the
spirit and resolution at the last meeting has not been carried out" and since
it was Dennis Moore's responsibility to execute it, I was challenging him to
account for his actions and submit to questioning. Hence, his motive for
the charge of unprofessional conduct was to avoid his responsibility to account for what had happened. He didn't want the governors to have the
opportunity to judge the matter impartially. Hence, the document was rejected for political reasons.

The arguments which were advanced in the above article have not been
commented on or answered. They were entirely dodged. It contained a
practical analysis and understanding of the school's situation supported by
relevant literature. Dennis Moore and Mr. Bright selected one or two
phrases which they used in order to reject the theme of the article as a whole.
It suited Moore's political purposes since the tribunal was designed to prevent criticism and opposition. The article should be judged as a whole in a
rational form of critical analysis. What they could have done and didn't do
is require that the criticisms be answered so that there could be rational
dialogue. Or they could have accepted that the article as a whole presented
an accurate analysis and then made a rational decision concerning a course

of action. If the issues that were raised yet again had been dealt with several years previously, this situation would not have arisen. It was the authority's failure to act that had caused the situation; it is always better to deal with problems at their early stages. But then the authorities did not seem to have any problem-solving abilities.

The case history is understandable within the bureaucratic system of management. "Bureaucracy is a form of domination." "It errs on the side of the task function" (Ball 1987, 99). In erring on the side of the task function, it narrows life down to the physical realities of the everyday like "hot dinners" and "fire practices." It excludes ideas and the processes of question and answer, which are the bases of knowledge. It excludes knowledge and understanding. As the method of organizing a school, it does so by taking the emotional and intellectual heart out of people.

Mr. Graham, the chairman of the tribunal, asked Dr. Hall what was the harm in this document if the governors didn't see me as a credible person. They could just ignore it and nothing would happen. The following dialogue took place:

Mr. Graham: I am now going to turn the matter, as it were, on its head and ask you this: all the governors have the interests of the school at heart, have they not?

Dr. Hall: Yes.

Mr. Graham: Their meetings are private?

Dr. Hall: Yes.

Mr. Graham: The document was a private document?

Dr. Hall: Yes.

Mr. Graham: It is, indeed, headed, if I can remind myself, on the first page "Confidential to the Governors," is it not? I cannot immediately find it. It came through the post so it was not left around for any person not connected with the school to read. In the privacy of that relationship of governors and the school, what damage was going to be done by this document?

Dr. Hall: The damage, as far as I can see, was that anyone reading the document may have had grave doubts about the headmaster because of the comments made, and it would, I think have upset the governors.

Mr. Graham: Dealing with the first point, why should they be upset by comments made by someone who on past showing they do not believe? Was not this a case of "we don't accept what Mr. Armitage says?" So why did it hurt so much if he said it again? You see what I mean? Here is someone whom you reckon to be someone you do not give much credence. So why should you be upset by this?

Dr. Hall: I think they would be upset that any member of the teaching staff could so criticize their headmaster. It is upsetting to governors to feel that there is this distrust among the staff of the school and an expression of disharmony of this kind. It is to my mind—and I am sure to my other governors—very unprofessional. It upset me very much.

It is useful to examine Dr. Hall's thinking and reasoning. She ignored the public interest. Here was a confidential document which was solely for the governors to read at a private meeting as part of their role as governors. There was no question of public distribution or public damage. Yet, Dr. Hall says the damage consisted of "grave doubts about the headmaster" which could be caused and it would have upset the governors. Dr. Hall says that the document "upset me very much," which could imply that she substantially believed the arguments put forward. She need not have been upset if she had confidence in the abilities of the head teacher. The governors should have been upset if the school was indeed not being run as a comprehensive, and if hundreds of children were not getting an adequate education or hundreds of children and their families were being upset. Dr. Hall seemed to be saying it's unprofessional to upset the people in positions of authority and responsibility. This was fallacious, practical reasoning resulting in poor judgment.

Dr. Hall's position is comprehensible within the formal, scientific theory of organization. When she says "this expression of disharmony," she implies that consensus is the norm of organization and conflict is harmful. Yet according to the micro-political model conflict is normal and also healthy. Thus, she didn't understand organizational theory nor the complex organization of schools. She could also have reasoned that if there was a level of distrust, then the leadership has the main responsibility for taking action.

At the appeal the comment was made by the City Education Authority lawyer that there was nothing seriously to complain about in the document. This was an independent opinion. The main complaint had been concerning a few emotional words. But, schools are emotional places. Formal organization doesn't recognize informal organization and thus the evidence reinforces the position that the governors as a whole believed in formal organization as the way to run a school. But, they were wrong, since there is an alternative theory.

A SCIENTIFIC, BUREAUCRATIC STYLE OF LEADERSHIP

The purpose of the following account is to gain insight into the thinking and practice of the head teacher and to examine it critically for an understanding of his educational philosophy. I obtained this article from a colleague years after I left the school:

A Day in the Life of Alan Tottenham, Head (Borecross School)

My day begins at 6.25 A.M. when the radio switches on and I listen to LBC news before breakfast. It usually is an uncooked breakfast, fruit or fruit juice and I aim to be away from home at 7 A.M. Most days I walk across the common from Reading to Herndon and arrive at school shortly before 8. Then the day begins. The first hour is a race between the mail coming into my "in" basket and being sent on its way through the "out" basket. Large booklets, reports by inspectors and difficult letters are put on one side to be dealt with later. This is the time staff know I will be in my office so the phone will ring, heads are put round the door, deputies call in and we review yesterday, look forward to today, before a general move to the staff room about 8.45 A.M. This is the time that staff look at the notice board, empty their pigeon holes, check on cover arrangements before moving to their tutor groups.

9 A.M. and school starts, perhaps with an assembly to one of the year groups or a walk round the school at tutor group time. Sometimes a visitor or the telephone prevents this, but it is always heartening to see how quickly the school settles down to work. I try to walk round the whole of the school at least twice a day, calling in at class rooms and delivering messages to teachers personally rather than using the written memo. Occasionally, very occasionally, I find a boy out of class without permission but one can hope that all will be well till break time.

Morning break sees me in the playground, near the tuckshops or in the staff room catching up on my chores and listening to others' problems. Maybe after break I will have a visitor; inspectors, advisors, governors, visitors from overseas, all come to Borecross quite frequently and fill up my diary. On a quiet morning I will be able to go back to those items in the "in" tray which deserve studied and careful consideration.

Lunchtime means school dinners, which I think are very good. We have solved most of the problems except keeping the food hot and we're working on that one. The boys have an enormous choice of items on the cafeteria menu. I have my favorites which include chicken, chili con carne and many of the vegetarian dishes of the day. School dinners are meant to help boys grow, so I leave out the pudding. After lunch and a leisurely walk through the dining room and playgrounds, I make my way back to the staff common room or my own room ready for the afternoon session.

If I'm in school I may be covering for an absent colleague or more visitors or at long last getting down to the morning's mail. Letters have to be dictated, checked, and signed; statistical returns have to be completed; planning for the year ahead goes on all the time, and there appears to be a steady stream of annual administrative tasks to perform. Perhaps there is an outside meeting. Secondary heads in Herndon meet frequently amongst themselves as well as with the primary heads. We have scheduled meetings with the divisional inspector and divisional education officer. There are management meetings for the support unit and for the 6th form consortium, as well as the tertiary education board; there are conferences and CEA-wide meetings too. Some of the meetings are extremely productive, others are less so but it does mean that I see and hear what is going on elsewhere.

After school we have so many meetings. The management team meets once a week, and in addition there are staff meetings, senior staff meetings, working parties and year evenings. All get their share of attention. Later there may be a parents' evening and the eagerly awaited show or concert. Sometimes there are none of these and I can be away by 6 P.M.

I consider myself very fortunate to be the head of such a dedicated school. Of one thing I am sure: It is not the head who is important but the staff and the pupils; the head can do nothing without the cooperation of all.

My role is to give everyone confidence in what they are doing and to help when things get difficult.

Allan Tottenham, Head.

This is the bureaucratic language of reporting, not communicating. Alan Tottenham's article revealed his leadership style. It is by listening to someone talk that their thinking becomes visible. Here was a technocratic head in political terms who converted all political problems to technical problems. His very choice of subject matter is important for understanding him, because every word almost adds up to a culture of instrumentalism, of ends converted into means. He reported his work day which is about means not ends, about process not content, for there is little content. He reports all his instrumental duties and "chores" including his mail, reports, letters, daily routines, meeting visitors, walking around the school regularly, meetings and so on. But, what was talked about in all these meetings? There are generalities but there are no specifics so what was there to understand?

The instrumental position assumes a direct relationship between theory and practice and is manipulative, since it assumes a cause-and-effect relationship between the head and the teachers and students. By controlling staff and students through instructions and organization, it assumes that learning will take place (Fay 1987, 86–88).

Alan Tottenham was certainly a hardworking and capable manager of a "large and complex institution" who evidently practiced "scientific organization" and "top-dog" management theory (Chapter 2). However, he missed out on his administrative role and provides no rationale for a school policy. He doesn't seem to understand that a school is a culture in which meaning is central rather than something like a computer, a car factory assembly line or a machine.

At the end, which is a reflection of his priorities, he mentions his educational role in three short statements, for example, his role is to give everyone "confidence in what they are doing and to help." But how can his article give anyone a sense of confidence? That is an internal feeling and an end value which comes from the quality of a relationship with oneself and others. It is not an external matter like an in and out tray. There is a sense of trivializing anything important by mentioning such material things as an uncooked breakfast and his favorite lunches. It helps to have a full stomach when attending an English lesson but more than that a student needs language ability, interest, morale, motivation, stimulation, good teaching and the ability to study.

What is significant is what the head doesn't say. He has nothing to say about the meaning of school and education and where he wants the school to go. Moral leadership and meaning are entirely absent.

What is the purpose of the school? Why go to school? The head doesn't say and may not even know himself since it is a theoretical and a practical matter. This article was an opportunity for the head to talk and inspire the whole school who needed him to lead. He could have said, for example, that the aim of the teachers is to teach maths and science, history, English and business studies and that the curriculum was central to the school's activities. That is why we were all here, to learn and to grow. For we can learn if we study. School is about preparing for adult life and it is a serious business. Reading books is important because reading and thinking go together. He would have had in mind numerous students who could not read and did not value education and learning. He could have talked positively about the value of good work, of taking an interest, of honesty and friendship, of music and art. He could have talked about his passion for mathematics or reading Shakespeare and left his audience in no doubt as to what education stood for and what he expected and indeed demanded. Education is not a "race" with the mail. The head could have talked about the opportunities the school offered in return for cooperation and effort. He could have said in everyday language that success comes through effort. He could have told a story or two about Borecross or some historical figure and how they succeeded against the odds, and the moral qualities such as courage, patience and perseverance which they exemplified. Here was an opportunity to state what the school valued and why it existed. The students didn't come to school for hot food but good and hot education, for mental and emotional stimulation. The head was required to bind the school together by talk and moral example. He was needed to articulate the meaning of a good education and boost the morale of teachers and students alike. The moral and psychological aspect of education was entirely missing and his article is boring to read. Its interest is derived from the fact that he was the head and the designated leader and he had nothing of importance to say.

"Of one thing I am sure. It is not the head who is important but the staff and pupils; he can do nothing without the cooperation of all." This statement missed the point and could be interpreted as false modesty. The moral and authority relationship between the head and the rest of the school was fundamentally important and here he denied a relationship, implying that there was none or the relationship was meaningless. He passes the relationship over to the staff and pupils but then ambiguously brings himself back into the picture by saying he can do nothing without the cooperation of all.

The head implied that there is no such thing as leadership. This raised a serious issue. There are two approaches to leadership which I will call the old and the new. In the old style, leadership was moral and intellectual leadership as examined in the work of Christopher Hodgkinson (1983) and *Leadership and Organizational Culture* (Sergiovanni and Corbally 1984). The head created the culture and the symbolic meanings. In the new style, leadership is based on management theory. The issues in this dissertation can be read as a conflict between the old and the new styles of leadership. There is, however, room for a combining of both styles.

It is not possible to understand the meaningful intentions and rationale of Alan Tottenham's leadership from his statement. The article can only lead to questions and intellectual confusion. What does the head expect from his followers in the school? What was required was intellectual clarity from him and this he did not provide. Hence, the school could only have been in a state of intellectual and moral misunderstanding and confusion. This was another reason for the school's educational failure.

SECRECY AND REVELATION

The rationality of the document in section one was irrelevant since Dennis Moore perceived revelation, even internal revelation, as outside the rules. Why was this? The answer is that he needed to maintain the secrets of the organization even from the governors. This is what determined his political practices. The following theory explains what was really going on in the situation I have analyzed and demonstrates why theory is essential to the understanding of practice.

Sissela Bok has theorized the nature and dangers of secrecy in her book *Secrets* (1989a). Her concern is with the practical ethics of secrecy and revelation. Her analysis is relevant because the power struggle within Borecross was about issues of secrecy and openness.

Bok defines secrecy as "intentional concealment." She analyzes both the need for secrecy and its dangers and its close connection with moral choice and ethical considerations. Secrecy takes us to the heart of organization and its ethical life. Secrecy harms by debilitating judgment, shutting out "criticism and feedback," and leads to "stereotyped, unexamined, often erroneous beliefs and ways of thinking" (Bok 1989a, 25). It can "affect character and moral choice." It is particularly dangerous when linked to political power without accountability because secrecy removes accountability. Without accountability, responsibility is weakened (102–112). Secrecy creates discrimination between the insider and the outsider. It results in noncooperation with others to reduce shared burdens. It is connected with self-deception which can lead to "error, ignorance, bias and avoidance."

Bok has illuminated the ethics of revelatory whistleblowing, and I want to explain the principal arguments to show why whistleblowing is ethical and necessary in certain extreme, authoritarian situations; I consider that the Borecross situation was extreme. A whistleblower "is a recent label for those who make revelations meant to call attention to negligence, abuses, or dangers that threaten the public interest." They speak out from a position of inside knowledge within the actual organization they work in. "With as much resonance as they can muster, they strive to breach secrecy, or else arouse an apathetic public to dangers everyone knows about but does not fully acknowledge" (Bok 1989a, 211).

The whistleblower is in a situation of ethical conflict because:

In many professions, the prevailing ethic requires above all else loyalty to colleagues and to clients; yet the formal codes of professional ethics stress responsibility to the public in case of conflict with such loyalties. (211)

In certain circumstances the whistleblower is justified in speaking out. It is ethical professionally. If she were not, then the door is open to political suppression. (213)

Bok analyzes three aspects of whistleblowing which a whistleblower must consider: dissent, breach of loyalty and accusation (214–215). In the case of individual moral choice, the above three factors need to be weighed according to circumstances. The element of accusation assumes that someone can be held responsible for "danger or suffering." The whistleblower needs to be sure that the case to be made is specific and justified.

The whistleblower is motivated by an "urge to throw off the sense of complicity that comes from sharing secrets one believes to be unjustly concealed," or "hope for revenge for past slights or injustices" (216). Hence, in applying this analysis to the case history, I argue that the expression of dissent, breach of loyalty and accusation were justified. If Dennis Moore's evidence, for example, is viewed with these three elements in mind, it is clear he disapproved of dissent, breach of loyalty to a head teacher and accusation, out of a need for secrecy, power and irresponsible unaccountability.

DISCOURSE AND POLITICAL STRUGGLE

Why did Dennis Moore and the governors react so strongly to the discourse of the confidential document? I will give a theoretical and practical explanation. It was not the one or two emotional words, as was said at the tribunal. If it was, it was an attempt to make all expression of emotion culturally unacceptable. This may have been true because scientific rationality represses emotion as irrational (Albrow 1997, 93–108). But, there is an alternative way of seeing the document in context. It was because they could not answer the discourse without revealing their ideological thinking and because the discourse was connected with matters of politics. The theoretical explanation derives from the Foucauldian connection between power, discourse and knowledge. I want to briefly examine this connection to show that the negative power of silence as practiced by the governors, and which probably concealed an egalitarian discourse of comprehensive education, could not compete with a powerful and positive discourse supported by educational research. Silence is incapacitating and self-protective. It has "power over" when used from a position of authority but not "power to." The discourse challenged their knowledge and power and they refused discussion, because to discuss is to be ready to share and distribute power.

First, what is discourse for what I wrote in the confidential report was discourse. Discourses consist of expressions at the "supra-sentential" level which connect the linguistic with the extra-linguistic. They make statements and "embody the meaning and use of propositions and words" (Ball 1994, 21). They construct "certain possibilities for thought" and "prohibit others" (22). They order and combine words and displace other combinations (22). They have an eventful and meaningful character, eventful because language is situated in power relationships and meaningful because we were all participants in a community situation (14–27).

Second, what are the uses of discourse? Discourse is the "conjunction of knowledge and power" (Sheridan 1980, 113–134). Through discourse power and policy are communicated which are important since they "guide and control practices." "Discursive practices produce, maintain or play out power relations." They constitute subjectivity and power relations (Ball 1994, 22). They can contain "policy ensembles" (22). A discourse is a practice that "systematically forms the objects of which they speak." They "constitute objects." They "decide what can be said and thought and who can speak, where and when" (14–27).

Third, what are the consequences of discourse? The effect of policy is discursive. There are "real struggles over the interpretations and enactment of policies" (23). A discourse "speaks us" (23). "We are the subjectivities, the voices, the knowledge, the power relations that a discourse constructs and allows" (22). "We are what we say and do." "We are spoken by policies." "We take up positions constructed for us through policies." Policies are "a system of practices and a set of values and ethics." "Discourses get things done, accomplish real tasks, gather authority" (22). This is the nature of discourse that is important, powerful and productive of consequences.

Fourth, how is discourse connected to power and knowledge? Language in use produces discourse. To name and articulate by discourse is to know. Power brings into "play relations between individuals" (Dreyfus and Rabinow 1982, 217) and is "a way in which certain actions modify others" (219). "Power relations are rooted in the system of social networks" (224). Power is connected with knowledge because nothing can be known without an agent to know them. Knowledge "lives only through its agents, who themselves employ ideas and techniques selectively as their tasks and perspectives dictate" (Wrong 1988, xii). Knowledge is communicated by discourse. "Forms of power are imbued with knowledge." And "forms of knowledge are permeated with power relations." Hence, I conclude my theoretical explanation that the governors reacted to a powerful discourse by dismissing rather than analyzing and evaluating it.

Now for the explanation from the point of view of practical reasoning. There were two kinds of discourse in this chapter. The confidential report was written in the language of educational discourse which I had acquired in advanced courses in educational studies paid for by the City Education Authority. The discourse carried power and knowledge. I have written throughout that there was silence concerning school policy and there was no educational discourse, which left a power vacuum, and the school needed power and policy to operate successfully. Educational discourse is what theoretical studies in education provide. The rejection of the document was a rejection of educational discourse and educational theory. This chapter has shown two discourses in competition, educational discourse and the beginnings of management discourse.

The scientific style of discourse presented in section two is remarkable for an absence of educational discourse, not even discourse about learning and teaching, which is the purpose of the organization. The language of management discourse communicates a particular view of education, a technical view and a particular form of authority. The view of education communicated by the head, Alan Tottenham, has now clarified into the management view. I acquired the statement by Alan Tottenham in 1994, fourteen years after I left the school, and have included it here as a fair reflection of his educational view as I had known it.

The governors rejected a power struggle as illegitimate. But, they were probably wrong in the situation. There was no golden age of the comprehensive school. "The discourse of comprehensive education was a discourse of vagary, of uncertainty and of polarity" (Ball 1990, 31). "The meaning and practice of comprehensive schooling remained a focus of conflict and indecision" (30). The comprehensive movement failed to bring off a "meaningful discursive formation" (31). The Borecross governors prevented discussion and the development of a discourse of comprehensive education and thus contributed to the failure of the system to develop. Their authority had to be infallible.

The power struggle was between "locals" and "cosmopolitans." The locals controlled Borecross. A local is characterized as someone with local interests and involvement. Locals are "company men" with loyalty to superiors and to the organization. Their knowledge base is local. A cosmopolitan usually has more formal education. He has lived in a succession of communities and so has wider horizons and reference groups. His loyalty is to his fellow professionals (Musgrove 1971, 133–135). In the background to the power struggle was the "power implications of recruitment policies" (135). A weak head can recruit all locals to shore up his own power and there was a pattern of locals being appointed to positions of authority.

A need for power may be due to the needed to bolster up self-esteem and insecurity. Or the need for power may be the motivation to achieve a task. Only an agent can wield discourse. There is no knowledge in the abstract. It can only be applied (135).

The rejection of educational discourse by the City Education Authority and the governors raised issues of power, and it is my argument that schools need to expand their power in order to be successful, and in order to do so they have to have the know-how, and this comes from educational discourse. There is a relationship between power, discourse and knowledge. First, knowledge through the curriculum is the central business of the school. The various discourses of the curriculum communicate knowledge and power through language. Second, educational discourse is also knowledge. The discourses of the philosophy, psychology and sociology of education constitute educational knowledge. The linguistic sign and the signifier are connected by the power of meaningful language expression which makes language constitutive. There is no knowledge without meaning and therefore no knowledge without language. The critique of Borecross was meaningful to the governors. It caused a meaningful reaction because it was communicated to get their attention and to influence them. Language, meaning and power are connected. Power is the capability to achieve outcomes. Language is a form of action in order to achieve an outcome. Language communicates meaning and meaning is "saying something about something."

The power struggle also related to the public role of the teacher and the student in the comprehensive school. Henry Giroux has conceptualized the role of the teacher as a "transformative intellectual" in contrast with the teacher as technician and instrumentalist (Giroux 1988, 121–128). The notion of intellectual conceptualizes the meaning of teaching as engagement in thinking and thinking in practice. The school is not simply an instructional site but a cultural site and hence it has a political role. Teachers as intellectuals play a political role because ideas are powerful. Giroux shows how learning to write empowers students to engage in the curriculum in a critical way so that they are transformed by what they know and hence become educated (54–73). Writing is an intellectual pursuit of understanding. It is an active learning process which requires the active and public participation of students in schooling and contrasts with the passive absorption of facts by memorization.

POLITICAL UNDERSTANDING AND PRACTICE

The practical analysis of the political practices of a school have demonstrated that it was a misunderstanding of the nature of politics that was partly at the heart of the school's problems. So I will examine critical theories of political practice which would promote educational change by fair political practices.

I will consider first the general idea and "implications" of power. Dennis H. Wrong, in *Power: Its Forms, Bases, and Uses* (1988, Preface), has analyzed power as a skill, a mental capacity, a capability and thus an ability to achieve an outcome or a consequence. There is power because individuals are agents and can act freely. Power happens in a political and social context of specific social relations. It is "intentional," "distributive" and "relational." There is "power to" and "power over." Power is derived from the use of resources (Wrong 1988, 1–20).

Power is an "ability to activate commitments," an intention to cause something to happen. Power is subjective and precedes agency. Authority is tied to a status but power is a property of persons. A person in a top position of authority has authority but may have no power if s/he is afraid to use it or has limited capacities. Power works through language and discourse by naming and articulating, which produces knowledge. It is "a way certain actions modify others" (Dreyfus and Rabinow 1982, 219). It exists only when it is put into action. "The exercise of power consists in guiding the possibility of conduct and putting in order the possible outcome" (221). Power is a property of society and is "ubiquitous."

Power pervades all social relationships in the form of "micro-politics" (Wrong 1988, x). It is "something that is exercised from innumerable points, in the interplay of non-egalitarian and mobile relations." "Power is everywhere, not because it embraces everything but because it comes from everywhere" (x). It is "ubiquitous because it inheres in every social interaction" (xi). The power to bring about "outcomes" is expressed by Foucault as follows: "What makes power hold good, and what makes it accepted, is simply the fact that it doesn't only weigh on us as a force that says no, but it traverses and produces things, it induces pleasure, forms knowledge, produces discourse" (xi).

This analysis implies that my own political practices in the case analysis were normal political practices. The political conflict in the case analysis was between my own valid understanding of politics and the politics of force and misunderstanding.

Bernard Crick defends politics within the Western tradition of culture in his *In Defence of Politics* (1962) and argues that its importance as the "master-science" has been neglected. His intention is to articulate the true claim and nature of politics, to criticize misunderstandings which have made politics unpopular and to "praise" politics for what it can do. He also analyzes the "price to be paid" for a political society. I appropriate his theory as an explanatory, critical social theory of political practices in the context of this narrative case analysis.

Crick starts with an analysis of the nature of political rule from "the truth . . . that the *polis* is an aggregate of many members" (17) which "arises" "in organized states which recognize themselves to be an aggregate of many members, not a single tribe, religion, interest, or tradition" (18). This is important because it is widely thought that the aim of politics is unity, unity of thought and belief and the unity of conformity, an attitude most clearly exemplified in twentieth-century Nazist and Stalinist totalitarian politics. However, politics is not conformity and uniformity but diversity, and it arose from the need to reconcile the differing interests of groups in a complex society. From the reality of diversity it follows:

Politics, then, to Aristotle, was something natural, not of divine origin, simply the "master science" among men. Politics was the master-science not in the sense that it includes or explains all other "sciences" (all skills, social activities, and group interests), but in that it gives them some priority, some order in their rival claims on the always scarce resources of any given community. The way of establishing these priorities is by allowing the right institutions to develop by which the various "sciences" can demonstrate their actual importance in the common task of survival. Politics, are, as it were, the market place and the price mechanism of all social demands—though there is no guarantee that a just price will be stuck; and there is nothing spontaneous about politics—it depends on deliberate and continuous individual activity. (Crick 1962, 23)

Politics then is the "master-science," the "market place" and "price mechanism" controlled by talk and discussion and needs the "right institutions." It is the activity of discussion and the dialectic of opposites. It follows from the diversity of society that persons and groups have social and individual identities. Therefore, central government must rule by talk and by reconciling the differing interests of groups in society if it is to rule politically and not by coercion force or other means. Politics is freedom in the sense that free speech must be allowed in a diverse and complex society so central government can see where the differences lie and reconcile them in the interests of unity, that is, unity in variety. Politics is "conciliatory." "Where there is politics there is freedom" (184). "A political system is a free system" (184). "Politics are the public actions of free men; free men are those who do, not merely can, live both publicly and privately. Men who have lost the capacity for public action are not free, they are simply isolated and ineffectual" (186). "Freedom, then, is the manner in which political action is conducted" (186).

Politics, Crick argues, needs to be defended against its enemies which are "ideology," "democracy," "nationalism," "technology" and three "false friends," namely, the "non-political conservative," the "a-political liberal" and the "anti-political socialist," in order to preserve politics as the master-science and prevent its intellectual corruption. Politics has many enemies and that is why politics is so badly conducted in modern bureaucracies and institutions.

I will briefly consider the enemies of politics and freedom and why they are enemies. Politics has to be defended against ideology. Ideological thinking is the enemy of political thinking because it doesn't believe that politics is necessary. It is the end of politics (34–55). Politics precedes democracy and is not democracy. When democracy becomes the rule of the majority and a "matter of principle," it is a perversion of politics. Democracy is a very diverse term meaning very different things, but politics has a very specific meaning. It comes down to talk and discussion. Democracy can be a tyranny, since Hitler was democratically elected. When democracy denies freedom and opposition, it denies political differences.

Politics also has to be defended against technology, which includes science, and administration, which regards politics as technique rather than the conciliation of differences by talk. The scientist has closed the theory and practice gap by technique (92–110). The non-political conservative is an enemy of politics by considering her or himself "above politics" because of a concern for order and the state as "a ship which needs firm handling" (111). He "trusts" himself but takes a "cynical view" of others. The "apolitical liberal" makes the opposite mistake of trusting too much in human nature. He wants the fruits of politics but is not willing to pay the price. He is willing to take the benefits of liberty and democracy but trusts too much in the ability of people to be reasonable (123). The "anti-political socialist" arrives at his position by criticism of the "narrowness" of conservatism and the "generalities" of liberalism (130). S/he wants to see the liberties and privileges of the few extended to the many since freedom doesn't mean much if few enjoy it. The problem with this position is "a quest for certainty and a contempt for politics" (131). It reflects an unwillingness to be bothered with the methods and work of real politics.

Politics, argues Crick, is a "preoccupation of free men" and "a test of freedom." It is conservative, liberal and socialist, to take up the positions of three enemies of politics which are represented in society. He praises it as a way of ruling divided societies without undue violence. He praises it as a "type of moral activity." He argues that diversity of resources and interests is "itself an education" and an education necessary for politics. He takes account of the problematic relationship between science and politics in which politics is condemned as "unscientific." He praises politics for a "political ethics" and a "constitutional ethics." He praises politics for being hypothetical like science so that it is always flexible and amenable to change. Politics relies on the test of experience.

Politics, positively, is not deception but authentic relations between real people who are other and different, a praiseworthy activity which involves "compromise, conciliation, uncertainty, conflict" (165). It is a "blending of elements." A political system consists of an "empirical generalization" that society is diverse and an "ethical commitment" that diversity is normally good (170). Politics recognizes the importance of group diversity and the affirmative individual (53). Politics is concerned with limited purposes (41). Politics means that the person has some "ability to call his soul his own."

Crick understands politics as a good. He calls politics "a bold prudence," "a diverse unity," "an armed conciliation," "a natural artifice," "a creative compromise," "a serious game on which free civilization depends" (161).

Politics is the "creative dialectic of opposites" (160). It depends on "procedural values" (148). Politics requires a "minimal respect for freedom, toleration, respect for truth, empathy, disputes and discussion" (247). There is "nothing above politics." It is freedom. "Politics can prevent the vast cruelties and deceits of ideological rule." It is the "interaction between the parts and the whole." Political education needs "diversity of resources and interests." Politics, like true science, is "open-minded, inventive and skeptical."

The key to a free politics is constitutionalism (148). But, there is "no constitution better than the men who work it" (148). Democracy is not the answer to everything. No compromise is the destruction of normal politics. Politics is inevitable. All commitments should take a political form. Knowledge of politics only thrives in political systems. "Representative government" is no guarantee of liberty "if all posts are filled by men of the same mind" (35). In totalitarian and ideological societies free activity is "hunted down." In totalitarian societies everything is "sociologically determined."

A "clear contrast to politics" is a totalitarian ideology (47). It purports to explain everything. "The totalitarian destruction of intermediary groups only points to the relative naturalness of some of these groups" (48). The two totalitarian regimes of greatest importance had one man as the head (44). The ideologist knows that political habits are his greatest enemy.

Crick argues that the price of politics is the need to give up, even by activists, the attitude of "winner-take-all" (255). The only way to maintain peace and politics is to practice politics continuously. Power rests on "legitimate authority"(259). Authority comes from doing a task which others respect and realize needs to be done. Governments retain authority by ruling legitimately.

I shall now consider another view of a critical, social scientific politics explained by Brian Fay in *Critical Social Science* (1987). It arises from the view that a critical social science can inform people about the "oppressive" conditions of modern culture by offering a critique of culture. A critical social science is scientific, critical and practical (Fay 1987, 36). It is scientific because it explains conditions in society scientifically. It is critical of current conditions. It is practical since it is a "catalyst" for change. It is scientific in the sense of a social rather than a natural science. There are two views of science, the instrumental view and the social scientific view. These views are in conflict, the former derived from the model of the natural sciences, and the latter from the human sciences. The educative social scientific view regards its task as to give people the knowledge so that they can understand their situation and it produces enlightened self-knowledge so that people can change their circumstances. It does not seek to enlighten people by giving them the causal variable to change their situation, but rather by illuminating them about the real meaning of their practices and why they are oppressive and self-defeating (Fay 1987, 89).

People who are powerless could do something about it if they understood the reasons. They need to understand the politics of their situation. The central concepts of power are force, coercion, manipulation and leadership (120–121). Force is the power to make another person take an action against his/her own voluntary will, by fear and the threat of punishment. Coercion is a weaker form of force. Manipulation is a weaker form of coercion. Leadership, however, is a positive power since it enlists the cooperation and willing consent of the led. It is a "power to." Power in leadership is essentially shared and consensual; a leader cannot enforce what his followers do not wish to be enforced. It entails agreement by the led. Hence, leadership power is "dyadic," mutual and shared (Fay 1987, 120–121). "What defines a relationship of power is that it is a mode of action which does not act directly and immediately on others. Instead it acts upon their actions: an action upon an action" (Dreyfus and Rabinow 1982, 220). It is the kind of power appropriate for a transforming kind of education, since leaders and led cooperate. The dyadic educator is a leader who cannot force others to learn but leads them into it (Fay 1987, 120–121).

Force, coercion and manipulation, the other concepts of power in addition to leadership, are also dyadic and consensual since they also depend upon the agreement of the forced, the coerced and the manipulated, in theory and in fact. Hence the forced, the coerced and the manipulated do have power even though they don't realize it (122). This knowledge can be used successfully in power struggles between oppressed educators and oppressive organizations to achieve justice.

Lukes (1974) theorized power as "subtle manipulation" which works to keep "the conflict between the oppressors and the oppressed latent." The "self-understandings" of the oppressed are "subtly manipulated" "in subtle manipulation." He argued for the following result:

Is it not the supreme and most insidious exercise of power to prevent people, to whatever degree, from having grievances by shaping their perceptions, cognitions, and preferences in such a way that they accept their role in the existing order of things, either because they can see or imagine no alternative to it, or because they value it as divinely ordained and beneficial? To assume that the absence of grievance equals genuine consensus is simply to rule out the possibility of false or manipulated consensus by definitional fiat. (Lukes, quoted in Fay 1987, 123–124)

The main elements of Lukes's Radical Theory of Power as subtle manipulation are as follows:

1. the real interests of the oppressed are often disregarded in a particular social system.
2. (1) often occurs as a result of subtle manipulation; subtle manipulation transpires when the political system is so structured that the interests of the oppressed are

not considered to be part of the political agenda even by the oppressed themselves.

3. (2) obtains because the oppressed, as well as the oppressors, consent to the legitimacy of a particular set of social arrangements, including the right of some to benefit more than others and to be in a position to make decisions which affect everyone.

4. (3) is the result of the systematic ignorance of the oppressed as to their needs and capacities.

5. (4) is the causal outcome of socialization processes in the society which prevent people from discovering their true identity.

6. (5) is sometimes the result of the conscious manipulation by the oppressors, and sometimes the unwitting result of the social arrangements and cultural values of the society. (Fay 1987, 124–125)

To free educators to assume the free and political role necessary for education in a modern democracy, they need to be politically educated. This would involve methods of "non-violent resistance" which Sharp has classified into three types: (1) non-violent acts of protest and persuasion, (2) non-cooperation, (3) intervention (i.e., sit-ins, alternatives to power structure) (131–133). This resistance would have three purposes, namely, to alter the behavior of those in power, to remove people from power and to alter the distribution of power. The non-violent approach requires "genuine solidarity" and "strong determination." The education of educators must be from submission to self-respect. They do not have to understand the theory so much as learn "to conceive of" themselves "in terms of the theory" and to see the theory as describing their situation.

They can do this by realizing that they have some power in their situation and that they can overcome the domination of their oppressors. Gramsci has formulated three propositions at the basis of revolutionary emancipation:

1. *Consent is a fundamental ingredient of all power.*

2. *Consent derives from a structural context which is manipulative and which ultimately rests on the capacity to coerce through violence.*

3. *Political action, including revolutionary action, can only be understood in terms of a dual perspective which includes both consent and force, persuasion and violence.* (Fay 1987, 138–142)

From these propositions Gramsci suggested a strategy which can be adopted by oppressed people which can undermine the power of the oppressors. This is the "war of position." In this strategy, one seeks to undermine the consent of the oppressed and thus weaken the power of the oppressors. The intention is to create a "crisis of authority" by "undermining the legitimacy" of the leaders in power "by calling into question its capacity to lead, the direction in which it wishes to proceed, and the basis on which it claims the right to lead" (Fay 1987, 140).

Fay has suggested three methods for coping with the problem of resistance to a critical theory among the teachers who have most to gain from it. First, the theory must be translated into the language and experience of educators. The second method is by ideological-critique and the third method is by demonstrating that the "social structure" can be altered (98).

The example of the women's movement is a successful example of critical theory in practice. It has relied on three strategies. First, the womens' movement has used social scientific texts to educate women about their real situation. Second, consciousness-raising groups have enhanced political awareness. Third, it has dealt with problems of resistance (113–116).

What is the practical situation in schools which could be helped by a critical education scientific politics? In *The Challenge for the Comprehensive School* (1982), David Hargreaves has argued that the culture of teaching is individualistic and involves an abnegation of political responsibility by teachers in regard to their responsibility for the kind of society they are educating for. They leave political responsibility to the head teacher in exchange for autonomy in the classroom. Hargreaves based his argument on the decline of the community and the rise of individualism. However, using Durkheim's work, he argued that individuality must be based in group life. Hence, he identifies an irresponsible individuality within the culture of teaching (Hargreaves 1982, 77–112). Musgrove argued that the teaching profession was underpowered for the tasks it needed to perform (Musgrove 1971, 13–28). Hence, the remedy is political (Fay 1987, 117–142).

The problem is, how can a critical education science educate educators for empowerment? First, what is needed is a critical education science directed at teachers which explains how the system functions politically, to show them why they are unhappy and frustrated in their situation. I analyzed this In Chapter 1 and this case history has modeled a critical education scientific politics. Educators in large, formal organizations are in a situation in which they are oppressed in good part by manipulation. They need to empower themselves and take more responsibility for the educational process. If they have more power then their students will have increased power. "The process of education is in part a process of empowerment" (130).

The problem of a critical social science then becomes a problem of execution.

CONCLUSION

I started the chapter with two discourses in competition for meaningful practice. They are meaningful within the narrative of the story which is to comprehend the significance of the events as a whole. One discourse was informed by educational theory on practice and was put to the governors as a critique of existing policy and the need to change the narrative. The other was a commonsense practical view of educational practice informed by a teaching ideology and an instrumental view of education, and stood for a view of education and the narrative of the school from the point of view of the head teacher. I then put the confidential report in terms of a theory of the ethics of secrecy and revelation. I also put the issues of the case history in a theoretical framework of discourse analysis and its connection to politics. Finally, I articulated understandings of the nature of politics and political understanding, understandings which have been theorized from practical understandings in order to influence the "self-understanding" and "self-definition" of politics in practice. This is to put an orienting perspective on the political practices of the case history and to demonstrate that institutional change demands change in political practices. Political relationships are "dyadic." There is no need to submit to political manipulation and to do so is to submit to an instrumental view of education which is philosophically and socially insupportable.

Chapter 7

Authoritarianism versus Authority

Sadly, another 30 years was to pass before the UK woke up to the idea of its being the worst-educated nation among the modern industrial states.

—Lawrence 1992, 24

I continue the story with an appeal to the Department of Education and Science against the outcome of the tribunal. What kind of culture and society were we living in? There was the principle of a free and responsible society at stake. A society and culture which combines freedom, responsibility and communication is one worth struggling for since it allows people to live with human dignity, which is the only human way to live.

I exhibit in this chapter the practical reality of Habermas's thesis that the bureaucratic system in modern culture dominates the "rationalized life-world" of communication and culture. In Chapters 4 and 5, I produced the evidence for the argument that the authoritarian use of power distorted communication because in a relationship between formal unequals in a chain of command, the more powerful can use their position to dominate the less powerful. This happened according to the evidence. I test in this chapter the micro–macro political relationship of reciprocity, trust, fair exchange and moral consideration to see whether power preceded justice or justice preceded power. I analyze the culture of the Department of Education and Science. I conclude that power preceded justice and democratic principles and ethics were irrelevant.

COMMUNICATION WITH THE DEPARTMENT OF EDUCATION AND SCIENCE

The political purpose of an appeal to the Department of Education and Science was to test at the macro level the democratic and constitutional politics within the educational system as a whole. The Rt. Hon. Christopher Smith, member of parliament for Kingston-upon-Thames, referred me to an official at the Department of Education and Science. I met a junior official on one occasion and he agreed to raise the matter with higher authority. He refused further meetings.

In March 1981, I had asked the Department of Education and Science to adjudicate the matter narrated and analyzed in these pages. They sent the following reply:

In cases of complaint his (the Minister of Education) main concern is that the Articles of Government have been complied with.
and,
I have seen a copy of the report on the proceedings of the Disciplinary Hearing which took place on 17 March 1980 and noted the Tribunal's conclusions. Also, I understand from CEA that you took up your right of appeal against the Disciplinary Tribunal's recommendations in accordance with the provisions of the Authority's Staff Code. There appears to be no evidence to suggest that the agreed procedures were not followed correctly and, therefore, there are no grounds on which the Secretary of State could be asked to intervene. April 2, 1981.

There are three points to be made in reply to this letter. First, an article of government was broken since Dennis Moore's intervention caused the disciplinary tribunal because he said he had to stop the governors from discussing the document in question. Hence, a meeting with the governors was prevented. Second, there were three breaches of agreed procedures. One, the charge was changed during the course of the proceedings. Two, the tribunal was brought to a premature conclusion on day three so that I did not present a summary of my case. I registered my disagreement on the abrupt ending. Three, all the evidence and the historical complexity of the case was not considered in the verdict.

I also asked the secretary of state to intervene under section 68 of the Education Act, which is as follows:

68. Power of (Secretary of State for Education and Science) to prevent unreasonable exercise of functions. If (The Secretary of State for Education and Science) is satisfied, either on complaint by any person or otherwise, that any local education authority or the . . . governors of any county or voluntary school have acted or are proposing to act unreasonably with respect to any power conferred or the performance of any duty imposed by or under this Act, he may, notwithstanding any enactment rendering the exercise of the power or the performance of the duty contingent upon the opin-

ion of the authority or of the . . . governors, give such directions as to the exercise of the power or the performance of the duty as appear to him to be expedient.

The following four extracts from letters from the Secretary of State for Education and Science give the arguments for their refusal to intervene under section 68.

1. This is essentially an issue for resolution between employer and employee rather than an education related matter. Alaisdair Butcher, January 6, 1988.

2. Section 68 only applies if there are clear grounds for believing that an authority has acted in a way that no sensible authority could possibly act in the exercise of any power or duty imposed by the Education Acts. I do not believe that there is sufficient evidence in your case to justify action under section 68. July 4, 1989.

3. He may intervene only if he is satisfied that a local education authority has failed to carry out a statutory duty or has acted unreasonably. The courts have interpreted this to mean conduct which no sensible LEA, acting with due appreciation of their statutory responsibilities, would have decided to adopt.

   As Mr. Armitage is aware, the Secretary of State has considered the evidence and has concluded that there are no grounds on which it would be appropriate for him to intervene. Alan Freeman, October 25, 1990.

In reply to the Department of Education and Science letter of 1989 in 2 above, I wrote the following reply:

Thank you for your letter of July 4.

You say in your letter that "you do not believe that there is sufficient evidence in your case to justify action under section 68."

There are a number of questions which arise from this statement:

1. What is the evidence so far in your view?
2. How much evidence do you think there is so far?
3. At what point does the evidence become sufficient?
4. What evidence do you regard as insufficient?

Please will you answer these questions specifically so that I can understand the reasoning and evidential criteria that has led to the value judgment you have made, and so that I can see how you have applied the act to my case. This is only reasonable. Your letter is too general and doesn't discuss the evidence and therefore is most unsatisfactory from my point of view. July 10, 1989.

The reply to this letter amounts to a refusal to discuss the matter further. It reads:

I am afraid that there is nothing I can usefully add to what has already been said. As you know the Secretary of State, having considered all the evidence, has concluded that it would not be appropriate for him to intervene. August 17, 1989.

This has remained the consistent position of the Department of Education and Science.

Since 1980, I have on several occasions asked the City Education Authority to have the finding of guilt quashed. Their main arguments for refusing to take action are as follows:

1. There is no question of reopening the disciplinary case. Under the Staff code the decision of the Staff Appeals Sub-Committee in such cases is final. April 21, 1988.

2. The events leading to the Disciplinary Tribunal took place a decade ago, the personnel involved are no longer employed by the authority and, in accordance with general practice in such matters, many of the papers have been destroyed. In view of current demands upon officers' time—it is not practicable for me to require one or more officers to reinvestigate the case, etc. April 25, 1988.

This matter was addressed to the Department of Education and Science shortly after the tribunal proceedings in 1980 so it could and should have been dealt with properly then. That means that the time lapse of ten years is the responsibility of the Department of Education and Science. Second, I have on several occasions since 1980 asked the City Education Authority to reopen the case and they have refused on the grounds that it is against their rules. Therefore, the only alternative is action under section 68 of the Education Act. Section 68 is democratic in intention and was passed by Parliament as a democratic safeguard; it is clearly applicable to a case such as this. An article of school government was clearly broken since the charge of unprofessional conduct was designed to prevent a meeting with the governors of the school, as was stated in evidence. The finding of guilt was clearly unreasonable since the witnesses to the distribution of the document declined to appear in front of the tribunal to give evidence. Also, the charge of criticism is not an offense. Therefore, in finding me guilty against natural justice, the City Education Authority was clearly acting unreasonably and for a political motive, and thus section 68 applies, since it is designed to prevent unreasonable exercise of powers. In addition, in refusing to reopen the case their unreasonable behavior has been compounded for at least ten years.

In about 1976, the City Education Authority issued a detailed document authorizing the implementation of democratic procedures in their schools. Therefore, I had their authority to act on democratic principles. It is, therefore, unreasonable of them to charge me with unprofessional conduct for which there is no clear definition and could not be, in times of rapid social and cultural change.

It is hard to understand how the Department of Education and science can say this is not an educational matter. The historical evidence shows that education was central to the case.

The situation between myself and the Department of Education and Science ended in deadlock. They refused to explain the grounds for their decision not to intervene under section 68 and they refused to discuss the matter. Their refusal was unreasonable and undemocratic. I saw my member of Parliament, the Rt. Hon. Christopher Smith, three times about this matter, the first time during the tribunal proceedings, and he took my case up with the Department of Education and Science. But, he has been unable to conclude this matter rationally. I wanted a meeting with a top official to communicate adequately and to satisfy myself that the case was being taken seriously. The political process at the macro level failed and therefore the Department implicated itself in the failure of Borecross School to develop as an educational institution. If they had acted otherwise, they could have changed the political situation and the relationship I had with the Borecross governors. The rational rather than the ideological basis of education would have been restored.

THE CULTURE OF THE DEPARTMENT OF EDUCATION AND SCIENCE

The purpose of this section is to view the Department of Education and Science in a cultural perspective in order to understand why their decision was predictable and why they were bound to make the wrong decision judged from a cultural point of view.

There is a recent study which exposes a half-century of government by the Department of Education and Science. The paragraph that follows argues for the importance of following the political and policy processes to understand who is driving policies and how they are doing it in order to penetrate the realities of educational politics:

The justification for the examination of conference resolutions and manifesto promises rests on the notion of the continuity of intention and practice. It is possible to dismiss such phenomena as containing no more than empty rhetoric, particularly if the rhetoric comes from a party that has been out of office for some time. But rhetoric is one of the key weapons in winning elections, and the winners who form a government are imprisoned in their own rhetoric, at least for the first few months in office. It follows that the grounds for looking more closely at the individual roles of both politicians and civil servants are threefold: that policies are not simply abstractions, but carry some traits of the personalities of their producers; that the exchanges between politicians and civil servants depend as much on the processes of human interaction as one would expect in any other walk of life; and that the career structures within which the politicians and civil servants separately operate contribute to the nature of the environment in which they develop and disseminate policies. As Ball has so aptly put it, there is a need in these matters to "capture the messy realities of influence, pressure, dogma, expediency, conflict, compromise, intransigence, resistance, error, opposition and pragmatism in the policy process" (Ball 1990, p. 9). It is, of course, not possible in a book of this size to do more than sketch in the background of most of the 50 or more politicians and 30 or so top civil servants since 1945 who have been responsible for the development of education. But it is important that the reader does begin to form a picture of *who* was influencing *what* in order to understand the *how* and the *why*. (Lawrence 1992, 3)

Lawrence is saying in a nutshell that it is human beings who control systems, not some abstractions beyond human control and understanding. If individual agents don't take responsibility, then the system is out of human control.

Lawrence gives the verdict on the performance:

The tenure of junior Ministers has been even shorter, their comings and goings marked only in the margins of the media. It is therefore not altogether surprising that the relative permanence of the Permanent Secretaries has provided a degree of stability, or at least, as one of their number has so elegantly put it, has demonstrated "a concern for the continuity of things." There have been only five such civil servants since 1964. During their reigns, the department has grown in size and power, seeking further and further control of an education system that was always on the verge of disintegration. Unfortunately, the DES itself created not the solution to, but the main source of, the problem. The rise and fall of the DES is therefore a tragicomedy of unfulfilled ambitions, humiliating miscalculations and abandoned promises. (Lawrence 1992, 1)

I conclude from these two assessments that it is no wonder that the Department of Education and Science couldn't make a decision requiring courage and initiative. For that is what the new comprehensive system had required. In times of change a "concern for the continuity of things" is inadequate. This study has confirmed the view of a system on the "verge of disintegration" from a school and education authority perspective.

Lawrence argues that the political history of education is necessary to achieve understanding:

The principal justification for such accounting of political events in education is simply that without it our understanding of what happened, and what may be about to happen, is severely impaired. Brian Simon has rightly said that "the historical record clearly shows that there is nothing inevitable about educational advance. Far from progress being linear, advances are more often met by setbacks, by new crises, by ideological and political struggles of all kinds. Our present age is no exception." (Simon, quoted in Lawrence 1992, 52)

The following expresses the scientific, bureaucratic understanding of the Department of Education and Science:

Hierarchical, large, well-disciplined, inbred management structures are excellent for the carrying out of orders, and for the execution of policy . . . they are much less effective as innovators and inventors. And that is indeed my impression of the British civil service. It is a beautifully designed and effective breaking mechanism. It produces a hundred well-argued answers against initiative and change . . . the balance between the negative and the positive ones lies at the center of our problems, and the civil service is the most effective of the negative ones. (Williams, quoted in Lawrence 1992, 137)

Thus, the "hierarchical, large, well-disciplined, inbred" character of the school presented in these pages is a reflected microcosm of the Department of Education and Science.

The following points by a minister of education constitute a critique of the British educational system. First, Shirley Williams lamented the lack of time for thought in the life of a minister. Lawrence comments on the enormous gap between thought and action. Williams comments that, "The debate has centered on systems, not on schools." She saw the need to pay attention to individual schools. But politicians concentrate on systems, not schools, which is only one part of the problem. The divorce between thinkers and doers is an acute problem. She made no provision for the monitoring of teacher performance and though she thought in-service education should be a requirement for promotion, she did not legislate it (Lawrence 1992, 70). That is, the Department of Education and Science could not bend down to consider an individual school on the micro level; it could not combine thinking and doing and it had failed to have teachers monitored or in-service training officially recognized.

The Department of Education and Science's main concern is with "gradualism, consistency, coherence" and not with "idealism and adventure" (92). What the new comprehensive system needed was "idealism and adventure." Thus, we can see the macro-political situation in which these micro-political events took place. It was hopeless from the start. Lawrence's book shows how hopeless. The weakness at Borecross was a reflection of weakness at the Department of Education and Science.

CONCLUSION

The attitudes and actions of the Department of Education and Science are understandable within the formal model of organization, as was my member of Parliament, who, in a democratic culture, should have spoken directly to the minister of education and should have had the decision revoked. The department dealt with the matter in a bureaucratic manner. Communication was completely inadequate and I didn't even meet the person or persons responsible for the decision, hence the decision was "disembodied." Alaisdair Butcher's response was the most disrespectful, since he said it was a formal matter between employer and employee, not between professionals with knowledge and principles of ethics. He took an authoritarian approach to human relationships.

From a cultural perspective, the actions of the Department of Education and Science and the politicians were critically inadequate. They practiced a scientized form of educational administration divorced from a cultural perspective. Educational organizations are committed to "the maintenance, transmission, and recreation of culture" (Sergiovanni and Corbally 1984, 262). So, since culture is a prime educational resource, a theory of educational administration which doesn't take culture into account must be inadequately based.

Chapter 8

The Ideological Domination
and Emancipation of Educators

The critical social theory of Jürgen Habermas takes the view that Western rationality is dominated by an instrumental view of rationality derived from an understanding of knowledge in the natural sciences. His critical view opens up an alternative "moral-practical vision" of the state of Western culture and its "future prospects." It is relevant to this study as a framework, because I claim that the school process was dominated by an ideology of systems thinking and political domination and by the "scientizing of politics" to the exclusion of the practice of communicative interaction. I took this critical view from Habermas's theory. I claim that the situation was bureaucratized and Habermas explains the historical process of bureaucratization as one kind of reason, functionalist reason, which he claims is a false theory of reason focused on purposeful task rather than purposeful concept, which has dominated reason as communicative interaction. In the first section I narrate the development of Habermas's theory derived from a critique of politics and a new philosophy of history in which the past, present and future are continuous and unified. I then summarize his critical view of knowledge and an alternative perspective. I explain the historical development of systems domination in a narrative perspective and the bureaucratization of culture from a system and lifeworld perspective. I then explain Habermas's theory of distorted communication and his proposals for continuing the Western narrative in the future.

AN INTRODUCTION TO HABERMAS'S THEORY OF MODERNITY

Habermas's first major work was *The Structural Transformation of the Public Sphere* (1991). His thesis claim was that the public sphere of speech and political action, which had been vibrant in the eighteenth century, declined in the nineteenth-century. The cause of the political decline of free speech was the rise of a scientific politics and its centralization brought about by the abandonment of the old Greek distinction between theoretical and practical knowledge. Hence, our understanding of knowledge was in an unsatisfactory state and needed reform. Habermas set about this task. His alternative model is based on intentional "will and consciousness." Scientific positivism is not true reflection. Philosophy is true reflection and emancipates the mind from dogma by means of historical and practical critique. Criticism has the power to uncover frozen forms of thinking as in ideological thinking.

Habermas made two important distinctions for the purpose of understanding how knowledge is constructed. One, he distinguished labor and interaction. He also distinguished three spheres of knowledge, namely, the technical, the practical and the critical, emancipatory. He linked knowledge to basic cognitive interests and to reason, arguing that the purpose of knowing is to satisfy human interests. Critical knowledge, the third component, is the knowledge gained from reflection on the other two and arises from them.

Habermas argued for a reclaiming of practical knowledge by relating the past to the future in situation. His theory has a "practical intent." He argued that to understand society, you need to study it through language as social interaction. He then argued that it wasn't enough to understand society through the relationship between language and hermeneutical reflection, since it left out the ideology. It is ideology that controls the mind-set of a culture. Habermas argued that psychoanalysis was a methodology of self-reflection which released the mind from the constraints of the past by critical self-reflection. Psychoanalysis uncovered distorted communication. Hence, there was a form of communication which was undistorted and he reconstructed this in his theory of communicative competence, which I discussed in Chapter 2.

Habermas's overall purpose is a systematic theory of modern culture with a "practical intent." Having examined the past development of Western culture his concern is to "redeem" it for future development. It will be the concern of this chapter to understand his theory in outline for theoretical perspective.

Intention is a central category of the mind along with belief and desire. Our minds intend as well as our actions. Humans are characterized by their intentions and purposes (Bratman 1987).

THE THEORY OF KNOWLEDGE-CONSTITUTIVE INTERESTS (McCarthy 1978, 53–91)

Habermas reexamined knowledge from a human perspective. He grounded knowledge in an intellectual and cognitive interest in living, maintaining and enhancing human life. His main thesis is that the "viewpoints" from which human beings apprehend reality are tied to interests in life. He distinguished three basic interests which have evolved into forms of knowledge:

1. The Technical Interest of the Empirical-Analytical Sciences. (Physical Sciences)
2. The Practical Interest of the Historical-Hermeneutical Sciences. (Cultural Sciences)
3. The Emancipatory Interest of the Critical Theory. (Philosophy and Social Sciences) (McCarthy 1978, 53–91)

Habermas made a basic distinction between labor and interaction. In the former case, knowledge is instrumental, purposive, rational knowledge of the scientific, technical kind. It is tied to work. In the latter, knowledge is intersubjective and cultural. It is tied to the symbolic sphere of mutual understanding in language and socio-cultural forms of life. The third interest is derived from reflection on the other two interests and is a critical interest in continuing the "self-formative process." The following diagram (Carr 1986, 136) summarizes the theory of knowledge-constitutive interests:

Interest	*Knowledge*	*Medium*	*Science*
Technical	Instrumental (causal) (explanation)	Work	Empirical-analytic or natural sciences
Practical	Practical (understanding)	Language	Hermeneutic or "interpretive" sciences
Emancipatory	Emancipatory (reflection)	Power	Critical sciences

Mezirow expresses the educational benefits of the third interest of self-reflective knowledge as follows:

Emancipation is from libidinal, institutional or environmental forces which limit our options and rational control over our lives but have been taken for granted as beyond human control. Insights gained through critical self-awareness are emancipatory in the sense that at least one can recognize the correct reasons for his or her problems. . . . Habermas turns to the "critical social sciences" to find the mode of inquiry based epistemologically in the emancipatory cognitive interest. Critical social sciences have the goal of critique. They attempt "to determine when theoretical statements grasp invariant regularities of social action as such and when they express ideological frozen relations of dependence that can in principle be transformed" (Habermas 1971, p. 310). Examples of critical science are psychoanalysis and the critique of ideology . . . one must be critically conscious of how an ideology reflects and distorts moral, social and political reality and what material and psychological factors influence and sustain the false consciousness which it represents. . . . Dramatic personal and social change become possible by becoming aware of the way ideologies—sexual, racial, religious, educational, occupational, political, economic, technological—have created or contributed to our dependency on reified powers . . . intent of education for emancipatory action . . . would be seen by Habermas as providing the learner with an accurate, in-depth understanding of his or her historical situation. (Mezirow 1981, 5–6)

SYSTEMS DOMINATION: HABERMAS'S VIEW

The purpose of Habermas's *The Theory of Communicative Action* is a general, sociological framework for understanding the causes of oppression in large organizations (Habermas 1986, 1987b). His sociological theory consists overall of three components: (1) A Theory of Rationality, (2) A Theory of Society, (3) A Theory of the Pathologies of Modern Society. (McCarthy in Habermas 1986, translator's Introduction)

The theory of rationality, the first component, is developed from a theory of language communication for the purpose of mutual understanding, as examined and explained in Chapter 2.

The second component is a theory of society (Habermas 1986). Habermas worked from Weber's theory which examined the processes of cultural and societal rationalization during the development of capitalism in Western society. Weber asked why Western rationalism developed into three cultural spheres, distinguished by their "inner logics." The spheres consisted of the scientific-objective, the moral-practical, and the aesthetic "structures of consciousness." These developed from the rationalization of world religious views.

Weber explained the success of rationalization in Western society to the "concomitance" of the active cultural exploration of coping with and finding "salvation" in *this* world rather than a supposed heavenly or external world, together with the cognitive, intellectual achievements of Greek civilization. This led to the evolutionary development of cultural ideas and their rational application. The rationalization of cultural ideas led to the rationalization of society as ideas were translated into interests and hence to practice; that is, theory led to practices.

Habermas argued that the story and development of modern society has been progressive and that it has produced "universal" structures of consciousness in science, morality and art. However, in practice, the development to modernity has been predominantly a "one-sided" development, confined largely to the cognitive-scientific sphere which dominated the other two spheres as a way of thinking. The three spheres of rationalization are developments in the accumulation of knowledge, Habermas argues, but a society cannot be called rational which has only exploited development in one sphere, since the "unity of reason" demands a balanced, across-the-board development. Weber noted the rise of modernity had also been accompanied by a "loss of meaning" and a "loss of freedom." Habermas sought to address these problems in his theory of society.

The early critical theorists endorsed Weber's view that rationalization led to "bureaucratization" and the "iron cage" theory in which people narrowed their lives to the service of formal organizations where human values counted for very little, which consequently led to the "reification" of consciousness as peoples' experience was "commodified" and "objectified," with their lives becoming separated from religion and ritual. Given this result, Habermas is concerned to develop a theory of society to explain what has gone wrong with the rationalization process in order to understand what can be done.

Habermas connected his theory of communicative action with a theory of the lifeworld, since the "lifeworld" is the "background" and "horizon" of everyday communicative acts of speech in a defining context of situation.

Habermas developed his analysis with his two key concepts, the lifeworld roughly meaning the individual perspective, and system roughly meaning the general perspective. But, of course, in reality the two perspectives are related. In traditional societies, the lifeworld and system were coupled together. Gradually, what happened in social evolution was that the system became "uncoupled" from the lifeworld, as the sub-systems of the economy and politics obtained some independence.

As modern society developed, the object of society changed. Habermas argued that the system developed from the lifeworld. What Habermas understands from studying Parsons' positivistic-empirical approach to society is that the media of the economic and political systems, having become largely independent, have reacted back against the lifeworld and "technicized" and "colonized" its communicative and reproductive structures. The lifeworld and system depend upon two different principles of integration, the former social and communicative, the latter material. But, Habermas argued, the systems integration of money and power cannot take over lifeworld principles without causing damage to its communicative infrastructure. Habermas also learned from Parsons that the media of influence and values, unlike that of money and power, cannot be transferred into systems imperatives but remain constituents of the lifeworld.

It is important to note that the system correlates with formal organization and the lifeworld with informal organization.

Habermas could explain and "diagnose" the pathologies of modern society with this model of the lifeworld and the system. He explained the bureaucratization and organization of modern society into systems with the consequent "loss of meaning" and "loss of freedom," a loss of meaning because organizations have no need of communication, a loss of freedom because the lifeworld is narrowed to an organizational mode and the culture of the lifeworld is subsumed and dominated by it. The partial destruction and "fragmentation" of the lifeworld caused the pathologies of anomie, alienation, loss of meaning, problems in "orientation and education," "rupture of tradition" and so on because the lifeworld performs essential reproductive functions which cannot be taken over by the material reproduction of the system.

Habermas's position is that of a "rationalist" and modernist concerned to redeem the project of reason itself and to restore confidence in reason and the modernity based on it. From his critique of instrumental and functionalist reason he developed the concept of communicative reason. The remedy to the imbalance between the system and lifeworld is to create a "public sphere" separate from the political system in which the lifeworld's communicative functions can be restored. This could counterbalance the imbalance in culture and society.

Figure 8.1 shows Habermas's model of the rationalization complexes of modern society.

WEBER'S BUREAUCRATIZATION THESIS IN TERMS OF SYSTEM AND LIFEWORLD (Habermas 1987b, 306–312)

I have summarized parts of Habermas's overall theory. I now explain his theory of bureaucratization.

Weber saw modern society as increasingly bureaucratic. A bureaucratic organization is a formal method of organization which tends to exclude the informal. It consists of hierarchical offices which are formally and rationally organized from the top down so that each individual performs a specific function which is interrelated with other functions. Authority, leadership and communication are positioned at the top of the hierarchy. Communication is mainly downward. Social relationships are formalized leaving little room for informal relationships. There is a system of formal rules. Obedience to authority is implied. Coercive sanctions are applied to office holders who disrupt the system. A bureaucracy is depoliticized, dehumanized and conflict is regarded as pathological and is based on a scientific means-serving-ends view of reality.

Bureaucracy became the dominant method of organization in capitalist and state-organized societies. Modern society is a "society of organizations" (306). Organizations are dominated by purposive-rational action, according to Weber.

Bureaucracy is part of the system since it is coordinated by systems power in terms of Habermas's two-level concept of lifeworld and system. The scientific analysis of systems was first applied to organizations because of its suitability. A bureaucracy follows functionalist Parsonian prerequisites. It "neutralizes" what doesn't apply to its model. Hence, the lifeworld is outlawed. The communicatively structured world of culture, society and personality has no relevance to the aims and methods of a bureaucracy so is

Figure 8.1
Rationalization Complexes

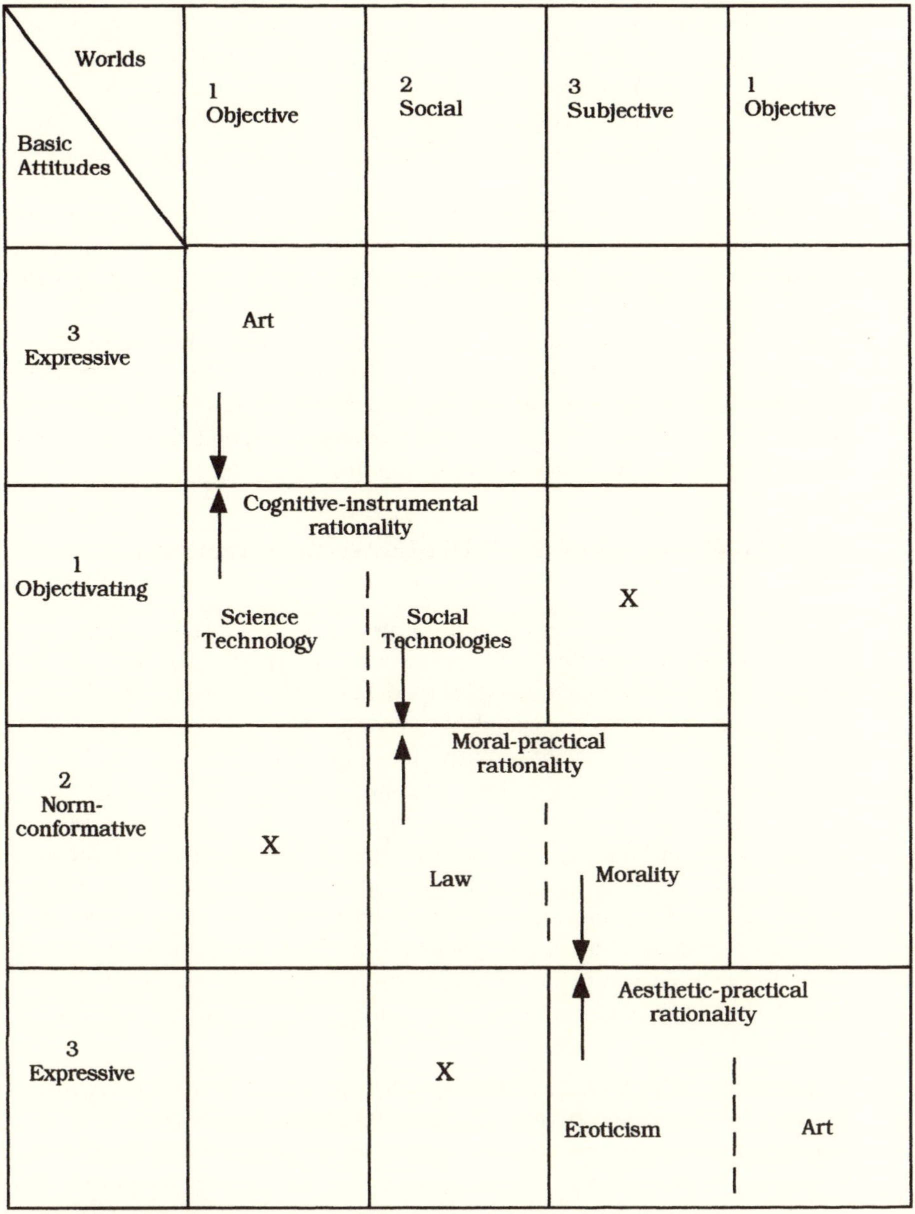

Worlds ╲ Basic Attitudes	1 Objective	2 Social	3 Subjective	1 Objective
3 Expressive	Art ↓			
1 Objectivating	↑ Cognitive-instrumental rationality Science Technology	┆ Social Technologies ┆ ↓	X	
2 Norm-conformative	X	↑ Moral-practical rationality Law	┆ ┆ ↓ Morality ┆	
3 Expressive		X	↑ Aesthetic-practical rationality Eroticism	┆ ┆ Art ┆

Source: Habermas 1986, 238.

"shut out." The informal has no place in a formal bureaucracy. Between the lifeworld and the system there is a "zone of indifference." The bureaucracy is governed by rules which control the actions of participants. The members of a bureaucracy are depoliticized. They can act communicatively only "with reservation." It is necessary to leave the lifeworld behind, which includes one's cultural tradition, including ideology when entering a bureaucracy, ideally. A bureaucracy "dehumanizes" itself by cutting itself off from the lifeworld (307–308). The cultural system is "reified into the environment of a system, is instrumentalized for purposes of system maintenance."

Even though the lifeworld produces the system, it is the bureaucratic system which has "reified," "mediated" and "technicized" it. Systems rationalization is distinguished from lifeworld cultural, societal and personal rationalization. We shall see how this bureaucratization thesis is developed.

In a bureaucracy there is a "norm-free sociality" which is how the bureaucracy organizes itself to carry out its purposive-rational task unimpeded by lifeworld considerations. In this way the "mediatization" is carried out over the heads of the participants, who voluntarily suspend their other interests for the sake of economic considerations.

THE COLONIZATION OF THE LIFEWORLD (Habermas 1987b, 318–326)

Weber's bureaucratization thesis in terms of the "colonization of the lifeworld" resulted from the "*effects of the uncoupling of system from the lifeworld*" within Habermas's two-level model of society. The colonization of the lifeworld cannot be explained by a change from purposive rationality grounded in value rationality to purposive rationality "without roots," nor by a process of secularization from religious views leading to a decline of morality. The explanation must be in terms of two paradoxical methods of sociation or coordination. Systems sociation and integration is achieved when the lifeworld is rationalized and turned over to "objectified linguistic media" so that "*the mediatization of the lifeworld turns into its colonization.*" The objectified media can then turn back on the marginalized lifeworld and neutralize contexts of communication. Habermas developed this idea into the interchange relations between the system and the lifeworld.

INTERCHANGE RELATIONS BETWEEN SYSTEM AND LIFEWORLD IN MODERN SOCIETIES (Habermas 1987b, 318–326)

Habermas proposes a model (see Figure 8.2) to explain the relations between the system and the lifeworld in modern society.

This model explained the "loss of freedom" and oppression in modern

Figure 8.2
Relations between System and Lifeworld from the Perspective of the System

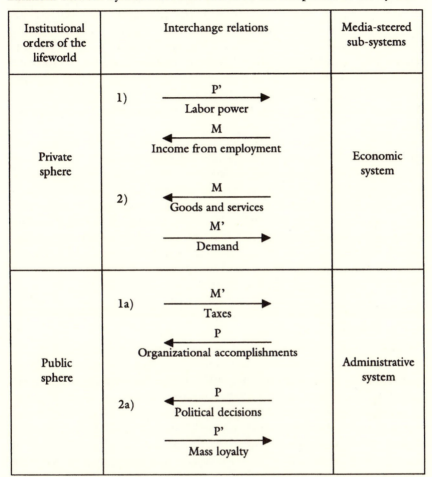

M = money medium; P = power medium.

Source: Habermas 1987b, 320.

society (318–323). The interchange relations between the system and the lifeworld are shown from the perspective of the system. The private sphere of the nuclear family consists of defining relations with the economic system of employee and client in the "institutional orders of the lifeworld." The public sphere consists of relations with the administrative system of consumer and citizen. The public sphere is made up of "communicative networks" such as television, newspapers, magazines and so on. In the interchange relations between the private sphere and the economic sub-system, labor power is exchanged for income from employment as an employee in an organizational role controlled by legal fiat. The consumer relation within the economic system exchanges goods and services for money. This is a non-dependent relation on an organization.

In the interchange relations between the public sphere and the administrative system, in the reciprocal relationship of client to the administrative system taxes are paid in exchange for organized services produced by the state. This is a legally binding relationship. In the public sphere the relationship of citizen with the administrative system consists of the exchange of mass loyalty with political decisions.

In Figure 8.2, 1 and 1a are dependent, organizational relationships in the interchange model; 2 and 2a are "defined *with reference to* formally organized domains of action, but not as *dependent* upon them" (321). It is in 1 and 1a that Weber's "*loss of freedom*" thesis holds, since the sub-systems of money and power abstract from concrete relations and the communicative sphere, and due to superior forms of social integration are able to dominate the lifeworld. This is not so with the relationship of consumer and citizen, since relationships are tied to lifeworld contexts of communication. That is to say, demand and mass loyalty can be changed and are not economically and politically dependent and legally enforceable.

The loss of individual freedom occurs when individuals are dependent upon organizational roles abstracted form lifeworld contexts. The requisite forces are "monetarization" and "bureaucratization."

Weber's "*loss of meaning*" thesis is also explained with reference to the interchange model between the system and the lifeworld. Monetarization and bureaucratization lead to a "one-sided style of life" within the economic and administrative systems and what Habermas calls the "desiccation of the political public spheres" as serious debate of political issues is side-tracked. Parallel to this is the loss of meaning due to the "cultural impoverishment" of the lifeworld in private and public and the "distance" between the culture of experts and the broader public, which together cause the destruction of communicative structures which maintain the vitality of a culture.

A THEORY OF DISTORTED COMMUNICATION

Habermas first considered distorted communication in the context of the relationship between psychoanalysis and social theory. It followed his critique of science and culture as sources of ideology and rigid forms of thought and practice. In the psychoanalytic relationship, the client has a problem of distorted communication and used the analyst to reanalyze and reevaluate his or her life history in order to overcome distorted, internal communication pointing to the ideal of communication free from such distortion. Freud's theory of the ego, id and the superego is a model of internal conflict due to distorted communication within the narrative nature of self-identity (McCarthy 1978, 193–213).

Ideology is viewed by Habermas as a form of false consciousness. It has a "role in the formation, maintenance and the transformation of a society" (McCarthy 1978, 86). Ideology has a place in the theories of Marx, Freud and Habermas. They viewed ideology as sources of conflict and power. Ideology reflects the existing power relationships in a society which has become hardened into sources of conflict and thus distorted communication, since they are free from critical self-reflection.

Scientific and technical knowledge has become an ideology because such knowledge has become so pervasive in modern culture that values have been excluded from consideration. An example is the fact and value distinction which is an invalid one. Facts and values are connected through feelings. A fact produces a feeling.

THE EMANCIPATION OF MODERNITY

Habermas's critical social scientific theory takes practical knowledge seriously. It also contains a philosophy of history which takes the relationship between the past, present and future as unified so that the past becomes the future. The future is the dimension of concern in this section.

Habermas claimed that modern consciousness is organized around "the three specialized forms of argumentation" based on truth, truthfulness and sincerity and their "corresponding cultural value spheres."

The possibilities of learning in the two neglected spheres of understanding constitute the "learning potential of modern structures." They also represent "an adequate understanding" of the "processes of unlearning" that have accompanied modernization, in particular the subjugation of both "outer" and "inner" nature caused by the neglect of learning potential in the moral/practical and aesthetic spheres of rationality (White 1988, 128).

"Environmental destruction," "the domination of inner nature" and the "atrophying of our aesthetic-expressive capacities" have been caused by the selective "cognitive-instrumental relation with *outer* nature" (White 1988, 134). The modern subject's "way of learning about and relating to the world" (134) has been transformed by modern culture's selective process of rationalization. Rationalization in only the technical sphere has distorted the communicative relationship based on performance, which the modern subject should have with the environment.

The lifeworld of the subject under modern conditions has achieved a "rationalized" lifeworld as the lifeworld is structurally differentiated, and in order to assume its reproductive functions must perform in the communicative sphere. It is the failure of the lifeworld to develop adequately which has unbalanced modern structures of consciousness.

A rational, emancipatory education would be concerned to develop a rational understanding in all three rationality domains equally, since this is where a balanced knowledge and understanding is presented.

The three cultural spheres are "interdependent," not independent. They have arisen historically and not as a result of philosophical reflection; therefore that is the way things are and so they verify Habermas's theory of speech acts (White 1988, 132).

The project of modernity can be redeemed by promoting a balanced reason which can overcome the "deformed" reason of the Enlightenment project. The model of modernity presents the possibilities opened up by the rationality complexes as learning processes which can be promoted through the performance of communicative rationality in daily life. The project of modernity remains to be fulfilled by the "learning potential" in the moral/ practical and aesthetic spheres. The "learning" potential of modernity is an "unfinished project."

A "balanced" modernity would require unlearning the unbalanced model that has produced a deformed, modern consciousness. The understanding is provided by the critique of systems theory and the introduction of hermeneutic, meaningful understanding.

The sphere of moral/practical rationality can be enlightened by evaluating modern society's dominant-submissive relationship to "outer nature," as industrialism has exploited material resources thus upsetting a delicate balance between man and nature (136–143).

The model of balance also provides a framework for evaluating institutions and for the need for a "decentered political practice" to allow alternative ways of doing things differently from traditional practices to be explored (White 1988, 140). The student movement of the 1960s was an effort in this direction. The model demonstrates the "symbolic character" of "social disobedience," since young people who have given up on learning, for example, are expressing a felt dissatisfaction which they can't articulate but which they are responding to in their upbringing; that is, their misbehaviors can be understood from a rational point of view since they are living in an unbalanced culture.

The model conceptualizes the idea of a cultured person and also suggests a modern collective identity of practical possibility (140).

The enhancement of the aesthetic sphere is the mode of rationality in the subjective sphere which has also been neglected in a one-sided development. It could be enhanced through teaching art and music equally with the cognitive-instrumental subjects. This would meet Habermas's critique of knowledge as positivist and make for an education based on reflective and self-reflective needs and how they are interpreted (144–152). It would work by changing the way people interpret their needs as persons, since their understanding of their aesthetic needs would be a significant part of a rounded sense of rationality, which they would need to give time to developing. There is a learning process in the aesthetic sphere (White 1988, 144–152).

In *How We Understand Art* (1987), Michael J. Parsons has produced a cognitive developmental account of aesthetic experience parallel to Piaget's in the cognitive sphere and Kohlberg's in the moral sphere, thus completing Habermas's model of balance in the third sphere and providing empirical evidence appropriate to a reconstructive science. Parsons argued that the aesthetic sphere is sui generis and is concerned with the development of the self in subjective experience. Art objects have to be treated as aesthetic objects. Art opens up to an exploration of the self which takes place in developmental stages from one to five, which Parsons designated as follows:

Stage one: favoritism

Stage two: beauty and realism

Stage three: expressiveness

Stage four: style and form

Stage five: autonomy (Parsons 1987, 1–36)

These stages of aesthetic, cognitive development are the essential third learning component of Habermas's model of balance through which the subjective self can be explored throughout life and interpreted and understood.

Habermas's model offers a "standard" for judging modernity and by implication standards for education, since "normativity" is linked to a balanced view of rationality. Modernity is required to create "normativity out of itself" through communicative action, rationality and ethics. The collective identity of modernity would be tied to the model of balance which would be recognized through the redemption of validity claims in argumentative discourse. Habermas's model of rationality provides a "framework for thinking . . . about institutions" such as schools (White 1988, 140).

Habermas's model also provides a "comprehensive framework for subjectivity" since it views the subject in relation to the three cultural spheres of understanding. It restores the lost sense of unity caused by the existence of "expert cultures" which control critical attitudes. Criticism is returned to the everyday level of culture so that citizens control their cultural values rather than having them externally controlled. Reason is regarded as having a regenerative capacity as critical enquiry and a "probing into the unknown." It is no longer deformed by a one-sided application but can realize the enlightenment project of modernity in the three cultural spheres. The model ensures the "institutional" "transmission" of "differentiated" knowledge arising from the "logics" of the three cultural spheres.

Habermas, in conclusion, offers a new model of the self as subject. Modernity has not realized the possibilities for learning except in a "narrow" domain of reality. The theory of speech acts carves out three domains of communicative relationship with the world in the objective, social and subjective spheres. Modern consciousness has been "deformed" by a reason which has narrowed itself to the cognitive domain of the objective world as systems theory in sociology has exemplified. Weber's theory of rationalization of world views in the cultural sphere has been transferred to the social sphere. Weber's model did not realize its full potential. Habermas has incorporated a theory of communication into a theory of society. His concept of a "rationalized lifeworld" is a concept of the educated person using the full resources of modernity in the three cultural spheres. The structure of the lifeworld in culture, society and personality are ideal structures of development. The pathologies of modernity are due to the power of the system to dominate the lifeworld. Thus, Habermas's model of modernity can illuminate modern educational conditions and problems which have a "symbolic character."

SINGULAR CAUSAL IMPUTATION

Habermas's theory of modernity rests in part on Weber's theory of the causal connection between the Protestant ethic and the spirit of capitalism. The idea of a singular causal imputation connects narrative with explanatory causality. Dray has argued that a causal explanation cannot be reduced to a law but must be in terms of reasons of various kinds. Von Wright has connected cause and reasons by teleological explanation. Teleological explanation is connected with the intentions of agents to act and to change a course of events in a new direction. They are "quasi-causal explanations" and these refer back to "singular causal imputations." These two elements constituted a "singular causal chain" (Ricoeur 1984, 182–192).

CONCLUSION

I have explained in this chapter the problem of domination from a long-term, historical and cultural perspective. The long-term process of modernization has been accompanied by a "paradoxical rationalization." The reason of the lifeworld has been "colonized" and dominated by the reason of functionalism and the characteristic model is the large, formal organization.

This chapter explained a historical framework for understanding the culture and formal organization of a school and its pathologies. My argument is that Habermas's model diagnosed the situation of the case narrative. The system of bureaucracy dominated the lifeworld of communicative interaction. There had been a loss of meaning and a loss of freedom, as Weber diagnosed, and the system did turn back on and colonize the lifeworld, and there was a fragmentation of consciousness and a one-sided development. The conflict in the case history is usefully viewed in a Habermasian perspective which also pictures a future narrative potential for change and development.

I conclude that an understanding of Habermas's theory of emancipation would enhance the understanding of the educational process.

Chapter 9

Narrative Explanation, Validity and Conclusion

Freedom is a necessary condition for individual and social progress, for the expansion and development of a personality or a society. It is not, however, a sufficient condition: we need to add to it communication. It is a failure of communication which results in a vacuum.

—Wilson 1964, 31

The historian Jacob Burckhardt spoke of the tyrants of the modern age as "brutal simplifiers," and the regimes we think of as authoritarian fit this formula.

—Sennett 1980, 165

The aim of this study has been to exhibit narrative, historical understanding of the politics of a school, of resistance to and possibilities for change. I analyzed the school from a practical, "humanly relevant" time perspective and exhibited the importance of concrete, contextual analysis. I exemplified the use and usefulness of social theory for understanding. In this final chapter I synthesize the plot and interpret the meaning of events as a whole, validate the research as "epistemic gain" and draw conclusions. The narrative argument has led to one main practical claim. It is the ignorance and misunderstanding of the "master-science" of politics which partly causes educational failure.

NARRATIVE EXPLANATION

Why did the events I have related unfold? Why did the amalgamation fail to create a recognizable comprehensive school and result in the domination of the Crosslinks values and Crosslinks head teacher?

Let us recapitulate the plot and its origins in time and causation. The appointments made at the amalgamation signaled a policy of continuity with the past and a one-sided continuity rather than real change, and this is one causal factor that runs through the case history. The traditionalists were in charge and responsible. The amalgamation of the Boreham and the Crosslinks schools, described in Chapter 1, resulted in the cultural, ideological and political domination of the Boreham academic, educational and cultural tradition by the Crosslinks tradition, since the Crosslinks house teachers through the house system of organization dominated the entire system and the director of studies was the old Crosslinks head of mathematics. An unarticulated, secretive egalitarian form of education based on Crosslinks common sense was instituted, which dominated the Boreham academic concept of education which had been a strong tradition of a grammar school and a recognized strength of the English system of education. There was no new comprehensive school policy or statement of aims and hence an intellectual vacuum was created. Relations of meaning and power between the Crosslinks and Boreham schools were "systematically asymmetrical." I proposed a change from a house to a year system in the intellectual vacuum which had opened up a creative opportunity. This was the second event in the plot in response to the situation. I chose to represent the academic concept of education in the face of a dominant sociological concept. The staff as a whole supported the logical change. The house teachers resisted change, a committee was set up and I was excluded from it. This was a significant third step in the plot. I had researched the issue of the house and year systems and I conducted a dialogue with Simon Creech, the senior house teacher. This established the ideological power and purpose of the house system as a narrative tradition. Its logic was flawed. The house teachers acted to defend the house system and exclude opposition. They were ideologically attached to the practices of the system and maintained it for eight years against the will of rationally persuasive opposition; and they did not accept political freedom of opposing action as acceptable conduct and practice. The chairman of governors reinforced the exclusive and domineering egalitarian ideology by political means and attempted to introduce mixed-ability teaching and to prevent opposition by force by asking for my resignation. He thus acted to define and dominate the educational philosophy of the school. This was another step in the unfolding plot. He didn't have a true understanding of politics and political activity as legitimate, inevitable and free cultural activity. The common sense system of education constituted practice without articulated theory.

The plot and theme of ideological and authoritarian domination and the expulsion of political culture and "constitutional ethics" runs through the case history. Brian Fellows, the first head teacher, declined to debate the house system with me and supported it by silent, secretive authority and stonewalling inaction. He was "non-political" in public even though his job entailed politics. He exceeded the limits of the "authority of authority" by refusing to communicate about the issues in order to understand them, thus rendering confidence in intellectual debate meaningless. Authority didn't discuss, it ordered. I wrote a confidential letter to the authority in order to inject some thought and educational understanding into the new system. This action concluded with inaction on the problems raised and the swift retirement of the head and the closing up of discussion as "unprofessional." Mr. Stephens, the assistant education officer of the City Education Authority, dominated by dissembling since he didn't recognize the opposition's contribution to initiating change and didn't act to change the system. He didn't accept politics as the "master-science." He refused a relationship of communication with me and caused a communicative "vacuum." He complicated my political situation by non-recognition. Alan Brownley, the administrative head of the City Education Authority, refused a discussion of the issues and supported the internal status quo by silence and inaction. He was "a-political," otherwise he would have accepted a discussion as necessary for cultural innovation and educational development. He accepted the secrecy of scientific bureaucracy as the way to manage an education system. Dennis Moore, the district inspector, rejected discussion of all educational issues as "unprofessional" while conceding the validity of my line of argument on the house system. He had the democratic authority and power to change the system but didn't act. He blamed me that the system was not changed earlier. He didn't accept politics as discussion and was "a-political" or perhaps "non-political." He didn't accept intellectual activity as important in the life of a school. Hence, the system as a whole excluded true politics and had disempowered itself because communicative action takes place in the lifeworld. Thus, a managerial, technological politics dominated rational and cultural politics by argument, as Habermas's theoretical position maintained. The new head teacher was an ex-Crosslinks teacher of long standing and appointed to maintain the old Crosslinks tradition. The governors had appointed someone with no teacher education, which meant they did not attach any importance to it, even in a top position. I had been in continuous in-service training since the amalgamation and believed in its importance and the importance of educational theory. The new head teacher maintained a "non-political" neutrality of secretive silence on the issue of the house system, and managed the school in a silent manner. He didn't attend the first governors' meeting, which was an action politically designed to remain uninvolved and distant from events and history. The governors at the first meeting didn't discuss issues but did pass a resolution recognizing my qualifications and satisfied my desire for change and improvement; it was a victory for rational thought and action. However, Dennis Moore did not implement the governors' resolution, in my view, and changed its meaning as I understood it. The absence of the head teacher at the meeting added to the confusion. I approached the governors a second time because their resolution had not been carried out by Moore. I met Dr. Hall and Dr. Kinship to discuss whether a meeting could take place. They agreed. I was preparing a document for a meeting arranged at short notice. Moore took the document without my permission and circulated it to prevent the governors from discussing it, as he clearly said, and put me on a charge of unprofessional conduct. Dr. Hall and Dr. Kinship recommended a medical inspection to the governors. The governors agreed with Dr. Hall and Dr. Kinship and allowed a charge of unprofessional conduct to go forward without discussion. This enabled Dennis Moore to avoid any questioning or responsibility for not implementing their resolution in the first meeting. I was medically inspected and found mentally fit by a psychiatrist within a short space of time; hence Dr. Hall's and Dr. Kinship's recommendation was without foundation, but politically motivated. The governors didn't follow up after the inspection, which had been hastily implemented, or take appropriate action. The charge of unprofessional conduct was for criticizing a head teacher. Moore initiated the charge but said the real responsibility was the education officer's who didn't appear at the tribunal and had no part in it. Moore's story was confused and unreliable. In my view, Moore took the document to prevent the governors from discussing why he had not implemented the governors' resolution, which was common sense in view of my strong educational qualifications and record of achievement in the school. A second charge appeared at the tribunal, initiated by the head teacher, for illegal corporal punishment. In my view, this action was a violent response to my confidential document which he had not discussed with me. Dr. Hall was a party to the request for a medical inspection but her story lacked any historical perspective and analysis, on her own admission, and was uninformed. Dr. Kinship was a party to the request for a medical inspection on slight acquaintance. I had succeeded in obtaining a meeting with the governors by sticking to my aim, which they did everything to prevent. I think this exhibited political skill, and they didn't like being outmaneuvered by an employee when they were self-important governors with long lists of qualifications. Feeling thwarted, they introduced a charge of mental instability. Tim Atherton, a Cambridge English graduate and independent witness, put sense and perspective into the situation, but when it came to hierarchical authority versus argument, hierarchical authority, without merit, won the day. In written evidence, the intelligent Alan Harkness explained that the situation had arisen because I could not put my ideas into practice. This is the human explanation. What in fact we have seen throughout is an authoritarian government out of touch with practical reality.

The political and biased tribunal board of inquiry recommended my dismissal against reason and evidence of wrongdoing, probably because they couldn't contemplate the political implications of a finding of not guilty, since the situation would have been reversed. The appeal committee changed their decision in a politically significant move but maintained a finding of guilt against evidence and natural justice and recommended I be removed to another school, thus defeating years of work and effort and carrying out a "miscarriage of justice." Finally, the Department of Education and Science, in a test of democratic principles, refused to implement section 68 of the Education Act and ignored constitutional ethics.

Now for the test of the plot in terms of an alternative plot. It would be a mistake to see the conflict in personal terms. It was a battle of ideas embodied in narratives. The authorities of the Borecross school were consistently conservative and the one radical idea of mixed-ability teaching was rejected by the teaching staff as hardly worthy of serious consideration, in part because no one was trained for it. Supposing the governors had appointed a head from outside the school, who might have changed the situation if he had been trained in educational theory, and might have had ideas he wanted to transfer to practice and cause educational change. Supposing that the governors had not been almost consistently behind the Crosslinks ideology and anti-academic, intellectual concept of education. They might have seriously listened and considered ideas to change the path and direction of the school policy. I offered them a genuine alternative and they rejected it. They chose a head teacher who had no teacher education and that was a significant choice, because of his powerful position in the system to prevent change and innovation. They rejected my qualifications as irrelevant to educational improvement despite the fact that I had changed the house system and caused other changes, including the abrupt retirement of the first head teacher.

The causal process might have been changed if Dennis Moore had acted differently. First, consider the statement that "Social relations concern the 'positioning' of individuals within a 'social space' of symbolic categories and ties" (Giddens 1984, 89). That means that individuals, whatever their rank, are positioned in political relations. Authoritarian relationships are illusory. Power is "merely a factual relationship." All actors are positioned and positioned relationally in time and space. Thus, the narrative was caused by individual actors who acted for reasons for which they were responsible. It is these reasons that drove the narrative to its conclusion. If Moore had responded differently on the house and year systems issue, he could have had the system changed. He could have given the amalgamation a fresh start by rethinking the mistakes that had been made and responding to inside information which I had provided. He could have advised against appointing a new head teacher who had been the director of studies when the house system was instituted in the new school. Dennis Moore was a major causal factor in the narrative process. He could have prevented the policy of appointing people of the same frame of mind and simply supporting the authority of the head teacher regardless of the merits of the issues. Moore had alternatives but never chose them. He acted to prevent initiative and change. He even acted illegitimately to stop it.

What was the outcome of the plot? The City Education Authority was abolished in 1989. One of the considerations is likely to have been its poor performance and reputation over the years. It had a great opportunity to implement comprehensive reform but, on the evidence of these pages, had no idea how to do so. Does it matter whether educators do the right thing or merely the expedient thing? It matters a great deal and makes the difference between educational success and failure. The practical outcome of the plot was the triumph of a dominant authoritarian and instrumental view of education in the sense that the view I represented was defeated, since I resigned from the school. The values of a critical education science I have represented in this narrative are those of "rational self-clarity," "collective autonomy" and "happiness" (Fay 1987, 66–83). These are end values of meanings, feelings and states of mind. They are valuable in themselves, not for where they lead. The value of happiness is of a life taken as a whole and is one aim of education. The instrumental view of education is "secular" and "non-teleolgocial," thus it has no interest in ends. In that view, death is the disintegration of the body without meaning, even if it is your own mother. It is a view of a "dehumanized" humanity because good feelings have existence like good cars.

VALIDITY

There are a number of considerations involved in the explanation of the plot and narrative I have constructed (Polkinghorne 1988, 170–178). First, the explanation should answer a "why" question. Second, the explanation should be coherent and should provide a causal explanation which is "appropriately" unified and "intelligible" in human terms. Third, it should explain human action. The explanation of human action relies on "teleological inference" in terms of "intentional understanding" and "singular causal imputation." Fourth, the test of causal significance is a testing of "different plot schemes." If a causal factor had been different, how would the story have changed? Fifth, the explanation should be "well-supported" and "well-grounded." Finally, the validity of the research depends upon "verisimilitude" by scholarly consensus (176). These are the criteria of the above narrative explanation.

First, I will address the criterion of causal relatedness. As the historian of the plot analysis, I was in a privileged position of superior understanding, since I put the plot together and no participant knew it entirely. I have narrative competence and I obtained narrative knowledge and narrative reality. The plot is the causal mechanism which converts events in time into a "configuration" of meanings, in this case the amalgamation of two schools. The end of the story was the political and educational failure to end as a comprehensive school during the time period in question, since the one-sided secondary modern system dominated and the policy of "melting differences" and ideology prevented development. The primary positions of responsibility for the story were the agents of the City Education Authority. My own role, as a protagonist, not a researcher, was from a subordinate position of limited responsibility other than as an advocate of change from a position of opposition.

The research passes a number of tests. I recount the events and actions which led to a particular outcome and I explain the significance of an event in relation to the plot and story. The narrative explanation is based on past facts (Polkinghorne 1988, 175). The facts are organized into a unified story and I explain the links between events and their significance in a plot. It is "detective" work. The interpretative problem is to determine the plot.

How does narrative organization work? The narrative form organizes events and human actions in time by the plot, causal mechanism, and relies on a teleological form of explanation; that is, agents have the ability to act and cause something to happen. I was, for example, the main cause of the change from a house system to a year system, but it was voted on several times by the entire body of staff, who supported it, and when the new deputy head supported the change after it had been resisted for many years by his predecessor, the change was finalized and implemented. The model of narrative explanation mixes "multiple causal explanation" with "teleological explanation." Human action is different from physical action. A causal analysis cannot be reduced to a causal law in the human sciences but is rather connected to the analysis of reasons. Narrative explanation is quasi-causal (Von Wright) in which rational explanation and teleological inference are linked. Teleological inference rests on the prior understanding of the intentional character of action. A causal explanation refers back to a "singular causal imputation." I traced the causal imputation to a rigid educational traditionalism and deep resistance to change (Polkinghorne 1988, 157–184).

Narrative knowing is based on the proposition that you can only know time through the narrative form of organization. Time, plot and narrative are connected (Ricoeur 1984).

I have tested different plot schemes on the actual events of the case narrative. "In order to penetrate the real causal relationships, *we construct unreal ones*" (Polkinghorne 1988, 172). This is a "what if" thought experiment. Supposing Simon Creech and the house teachers had not been emotionally attached to the house system, it would have been changed in

1973 with no friction. The majority of the staff wanted a change because the school was disorganized. When Simon Creech retired, the new head of the house system led a change to the new system and so did the other deputy head who had been loyal to the old system for many years. What if the first head had not been afraid to change the system for fear of upsetting the entrenched house teachers, who regarded it as a sacred Crosslinks tradition? Then the events would have taken a different course. What if the criticisms of the first head had been dealt with in a straightforward manner instead of sweeping things under the carpet? There are many other what ifs. What if Dr. Hall had recognized the history of the situation? She would have judged the circumstances differently. There were so many miscalculations which made the causal sequence inevitable. What if the main witness at the tribunal had appeared? What if the appeal committee had listened to the CEA Lawyer? I conclude that the causal sequence is the only satisfactory explanation and cannot be falsified. An alternative that I was punished for bad discipline amounting to unprofessional conduct wasn't the cause at all, because talking to the governors is not an offense. What if systems theory hadn't been the dominant form of organization and the sociology of organization had not been in such an undeveloped state? The more tests I apply the more my analysis is the correct causal one.

Is the research valid? Valid means "well grounded" and "well supported." Narrative research does not rely on formal logic but on linguistic reality. It is research into the realm of meaning. It aims at "verisimilitude." All knowledge is limited and, according to the philosopher of science, Karl Popper, only the "falsity of statements" can be demonstrated not their truth. Conclusions are open-ended. The "ideal of scholarly consensus" is the "test of verisimilitude," not logical or mathematical validity (Polkinghorne 1988, 196, 197). I am confident my research passes all these tests.

The question of the reliability of the research rests on the details of the procedures. I collected the details of my research over nine years. Important parts of it are extremely detailed; for example, the verbatim report over three days of evidence by a large number of witnesses. The dialogue on the house system was very detailed. I took evidence from different sources and differing interests.

In narrative analysis the data consists of a "collection of stories." "The goal of analysis is to uncover the common themes of plots in the data" (Polkinghorne 1988, 177). A crucial test is whether other researchers of the same evidence would agree. I claim they would and I am willing to open all my research evidence to other researchers.

Finally, the analysis moves between the data and the "emerging description of the pattern," that is, in a "hermeneutical circle." This kind of analysis is supported by the tradition of literary criticism.

CONCLUSION: ORGANIZATION AND AUTHORITY

I wanted to understand at the beginning of this study the problem of how to close the gap between theory and practice in education. I focused on the events of my school situation in "humanly relevant" time and introduced educational theories to illuminate practical problems. I uncovered the real political relationships and concluded that the organized school system dominated the human agent in an authoritarian manner; that is, no individual or individuals controlled the school and no one was responsible. I used the narrative method to uncover accountability and provided a long-term view of one school. This methodology of explanatory plot analysis is a useful aid to school accountability and responsibility, and could be used in any school to find out the political and educational realities with respect to aims, policy, methods and success.

The reading of authority and authoritarianism in one organization has been the significant theme of this study. Martin Albrow, in *Do Organizations Have Feelings?* (1997), has explained the problem of formal organization divorced from feelings. He argued that Weber's "legal-rational authority" has held a "pivotal" position in modern society (74). He called it a "machine-like" concept, noting its close connection with hierarchical organization and obedience without rational evaluation. He explained the "influence" of the concept of authority across a wide range of social life including language, writing, parenting, schooling and the conduct of youth (75); hence, the formidable influence of an authoritarian misconception of authority. This case history has witnessed legal-rational authority's "authoritarian imperative force" and "authoritarian imperative control." The concept of authority in organizations requires reconceptualization.

There is a better alternative concept of authority for organizations. An individual carries authority when others respect it (82). This gives rise to a "chain of authority" (82). The essence of authority is "professional authority" based on the knowledge capacity of the authority figure. Authority is linked to rightness which makes it acceptable (82). Authoritarianism makes normal social interaction in society "exceptional" rather than "normal." The legal-rational concept of authority excluded "personal influence, attraction, emotional bonds, faith, commitment, initiative and excitement" (84). Albrow remarks that it "occasions a certain sense of astonishment that the twentieth century could have divorced humanity of its feelings for so long" (108). "Authority . . . inheres in the quality of relationships" (87).

Richard Sennett has implied that there is nothing more serious almost for the culture of a school organization than the relationship between authority and those related to it (Sennett 1993). Authority should recognize that differences in society exist and therefore people are free. The problem of authoritarianism is "brutal" "simplicity" hiding complexity (165). Educators need "visible" and "legible" authority (165–190). They need a "structure of power" and authority which those in a subordinate position can respond to. Authority with caring can fulfill the needs of young people. Authority relationships "between" persons in a "chain of command" should be "disruptible" so that beliefs can be allowed to change and develop (175–190). Authority should not be feared but should allow its recipients to come up close. It should be caring. "Fallible" not "infallible," "legitimate" not "omnipotent" authority is what subordinates need. Subordinates to authority need to understand its influence and power and know how to "disengage" by internalizing their relationship to authority figures (134). Authority should not embrace "deception" and "illusion" (191–197). It should not create "distance and control" by silence. Authority should seek a "non-embedded" authority rather than a self-serving security at the cost of liberty. The problem of authority in situation requires further research.

Bibliography

Albrow, Martin. 1997. *Do Organizations Have Feelings?* Routledge.

Austin, J. L. 1962. *How to Do Things with Words.* Oxford.

Ball, Stephen J. 1987. *The Micro-Politics of the School: Towards a Theory of School Organization.* Methuen.

Ball, Stephen J. 1990. *Politics and Policy Making in Education: Explorations in Policy Sociology.* Routledge.

Ball, Stephen J. 1994. *Education Reform.* Open University Press.

Bendelow, Gillian and Williams, Simon J. 1998. *Emotions in Social Life: Critical Themes and Contemporary Issues.* Routledge.

Bernstein, Richard. 1985. *Habermas and Modernity.* Basil Blackwell.

Billington, Michael. 1996. *The Life and Work of Harold Pinter.* Faber and Faber.

Blau, Peter. 1974. *On the Nature of Organizations.* John Wiley and Sons.

Bok, Sissela. 1989a. *Secrets: On the Ethics of Concealment and Revelation.* Vintage Books.

Bok, Sissela. 1989b. *A Strategy for Peace.* Vintage Books.

Bratman, Michael. 1987. *Intentions, Plans, and Practical Reason.* Harvard University Press.

Bruner, Jerome. 1986. *Actual Minds, Possible Worlds.* Harvard University Press.

Bruner, Jerome. 1990. *Acts of Meaning.* Harvard University Press.

Calhoun, Craig. 1995. *Critical Social Theory.* Blackwell Publishers.

Carr, David. 1986. *Time, Narrative, History.* Indiana University Press.

Carr, Wilfred and Kemmis, Stephen. 1986. *Becoming Critical: Education, Knowledge and Action Research.* The Falmer Press.

City Education Authority. 1980. *Verbatim Notes of Proceedings of a Disciplinary Hearing.* Tennyson and Company.

Cooper, David E. 1980. *Illusions of Equality.* Routledge and Kegan Paul.

Cooper, David E. 1983. *Authenticity and Learning: Nietzsche's Educational Philosophy.* Routledge and Kegan Paul.

Cooper, David E. 1990. *Existentialism*. Blackwell.

Corwin, R. G. 1983. *The Entrepreneurial Bureaucracy*. JAI Press.

Crick, Bernard. 1962. *In Defence of Politics*. University of Chicago Press.

Crossley, Nick. 1998. "Emotion and Communicative Action: Habermas, Linguistic Philosophy and Existentialism." In *Emotions in Social Life*. Gillian Bendelow and Simon J. Williams, eds. Routledge.

Dearden, Robert. 1968. *The Philosophy of Primary Education: An Introduction*. Routledge and Kegan Paul.

Downie, R. S., Loudfoot, Eileen M., and Telfer, Elizabeth. 1974. *Education and Personal Relationships*. Methuen.

Dreyfus, H. L. and Rabinow, P. 1982. *Michel Foucault: Beyond Structuralism and Hermeneutics*. Harvester Press.

Dunlop, Francis. 1984. *The Education of Feeling and Emotion*. George Allen and Unwin.

Eagleton, Terry. 1976. *Marxism and Literary Criticism*. Methuen.

Ewert, Gerry D. 1991. "Habermas and Education: A Comprehensive Overview of the Influence of Habermas in Educational Literature." *Review of Educational Research* 16(3), pp. 345–378.

Fay, Brian. 1987. *Critical Social Science*. Cornell University Press.

Fromm, Eric. 1960. *The Fear of Freedom*. Routledge and Kegan Paul.

Geertz, Clifford. 1973. *The Interpretation of Cultures*. Basic Books.

Geertz, Clifford. 1983. *Local Knowledge: Further Essays in Interpretive Anthropology*. Basic Books.

Giddens, Anthony. 1984. *The Constitution of Society*. University of California Press.

Giroux, Henry. 1988. *Teachers as Intellectuals*. Bergin and Garvey.

Habermas, Jürgen. 1970. *Toward a Rational Society: Student Protest, Science and Politics*. Beacon Press.

Habermas, Jürgen. 1973a. *Legitimation Crisis*. Beacon Press.

Habermas, Jürgen. 1973b. *Theory and Practice*. Beacon Press.

Habermas, Jürgen. 1979. *Communication and the Evolution of Society*. Heinemann.

Habermas, Jürgen. 1985. "Questions and Counterquestions." In *Habermas and Modernity*. Richard Bernstien, ed. Polity Press.

Habermas, Jürgen. 1986. *The Theory of Communicative Action, Vol. 1: Reason and the Rationalization of Society*. Thomas McCarthy, trans. Heinemann.

Habermas, Jürgen. 1987a. *Knowledge and Human Interests*. Polity Press.

Habermas, Jürgen. 1987b. *The Theory of Communicative Action, Vol. 2: The Critique of Functionalist Reason*. Thomas McCarthy, trans. Polity Press.

Habermas, Jürgen. 1991. *The Structural Transformation of the Public Sphere*. The MIT Press.

Hargreaves, David H. 1972. *Interpersonal Relations and Education*. Routledge and Kegan Paul.

Hargreaves, David H. 1982. *The Challenge of the Comprehensive School: Culture, Curriculum and Community*. Routledge and Kegan Paul.

Harré, Rom. 1979. *Social Being*. Blackwell.

Held, David. 1980. *Introduction to Critical Theory: Horkheimer to Habermas*. University of California Press.

Hepburn R. W. 1972. "The Arts and the Education of Feeling and Emotion." In

Education and the Development of Reason. R. F. Dearden, P. H. Hirst and R. S. Peters, eds. Routledge and Kegan Paul.

Hirschmann, A. O. 1970. *Exit, Voice and Loyalty.* Harvard University Press.

Hirst, Paul H., ed. 1983. *Educational Theory and Its Foundational Disciplines.* Routledge and Kegan Paul.

Hoagland, Jim. 1997. "Lessons from LBJ." *Washington Post,* 4 December.

Hobsbawm, Eric. 1997. *On History.* The New Press.

Hodgkinson, Christopher. 1978. *Towards a Philosophy of Administration.* Basil Blackwell.

Hodgkinson, Christopher. 1983. *The Philosophy of Leadership.* Basil Blackwell.

King, R. 1968. "The Head Teacher and His Authority." In *Headship in the 1970s.* B. Allen, ed. Basil Blackwell.

Kogan, Maurice. 1978. *The Politics of Educational Change.* Fontana.

Langford, Glenn. 1973. "The Concept of Education." In *New Essays in the Philosophy of Education.* Glenn Langford and D. J. O'Connor, eds. Routledge and Kegan Paul.

Lawrence, Ian. 1992. *Power and Politics at the Department of Education and Science.* Cassell.

Lukes, Steven. 1974. *Power: A Radical View.* Macmillan.

McCarthy, Thomas. 1978. *The Critical Theory of Jürgen Habermas.* Polity Press.

Mezirow, J. 1981. "A Critical Theory of Adult Education and Learning." *Adult Education* 32(1), pp. 3–24.

Minow, Martha. 1996. "Stories in Law." In *Law's Stories: Narrative and Rhetoric in the Law.* Peter Brooks and Paul Gewirtz, eds. Yale University Press.

Musgrove, Frank. 1971. *Patterns of Power and Authority in English Education.* Methuen.

Parsons, Michael J. 1987. *How We Understand Art: A Cognitive Developmental Account of Aesthetic Experience.* Cambridge University Press.

Pedley, Robin. 1963. *The Comprehensive School.* Penguin Books.

Perkins, David. 1986. *Knowledge as Design.* Lawrence Erlbaum Associates.

Peters, R. S. 1965. *Education as Initiation in Philosophical Analysis and Education.* Reginald D. Archambault, ed. Routledge and Kegan Paul.

Peters, R. S. 1966. *Ethics and Education.* George Allen and Unwin.

Peters, R. S. 1972. "The Education of the Emotions." In *Education and the Development of Reason.* R. F. Dearden, P. H. Hirst and R. S. Peters, eds. Routledge and Kegan Paul.

Peters, R. S. 1974. *Psychology and Ethical Development.* George Allen and Unwin.

Polkinghorne, Donald E. 1988. *Narrative Knowing and the Human Sciences.* State University of New York Press.

Ricoeur, Paul. 1984. *Time and Narrative, Vol. 1.* University of Chicago Press.

Rogers, Carl. 1961. *On Becoming a Person.* Houghton Mifflin.

Rosaldo, Renato. 1989. *Culture and Truth: The Remaking of Social Analysis.* Beacon Press.

Scheff, Thomas J. 1990. *Microsociology: Discourse, Emotion, and Social Structure.* University of Chicago Press.

Scott, James C. 1990. *Domination and the Arts of Resistance.* Yale University Press.

Searle, J. R. 1965. "What Is a Speech Act?" In *Philosophy in America.* M. Black, ed. Cornell University Press.

Sennett, Richard. 1993. *Authority*. W. W. Norton.

Sergiovanni, Thomas J. and Corbally, John E., eds. 1984. *Leadership and Organizational Culture: New Perspectives on Administrative Theory and Practice*. University of Illinois Press.

Sheridan, Alan. 1980. *Michel Foucault: The Will to Truth*. Routledge.

Simon, Brian. 1991. *Education and the Social Order*. St. Martin's Press.

Simon, Brian. 1994. *The State and Educational Change: Essays in the History of Education and Pedagogy*. Lawrence and Wishart.

Stenhouse, Lawrence. 1975. *An Introduction to Curriculum Development*. Heinemann.

Straughan, Roger. 1982. "What Is the Point of Rules?" *Journal of Philosophy of Education*.

Taylor, Charles. 1985. *Philosophy and the Human Sciences*. Cambridge University Press.

Thompson, John B. 1981. *Critical Hermeneutics: A Study in the Thought of Paul Ricoeur and Jürgen Habermas*. Cambridge University Press.

Thompson, John B. 1984. *Studies in the Theory of Ideology*. University of California Press.

Thompson, John B. 1990. *Ideology and Modern Culture*. Polity Press.

Thompson, John B., ed. and trans. 1981. *Paul Ricoeur: Hermeneutics and the Human Sciences*. Cambridge University Press.

Turner, Johnathan H. 1974. *The Structure of Sociological Theory*. Dorsey Press.

Warnock, Mary. 1973. "Towards a Definition of Quality in Education." In *The Philosophy of Education*. R. S. Peters, ed. Oxford University Press.

Warnock, Mary. 1988. *A Common Policy for Education*. Oxford University Press.

White, John. 1982. *The Aims of Education Restated*. Routledge and Kegan Paul.

White, Stephen K. 1988. *The Recent Work of Jürgen Habermas: Reason, Justice and Modernity*. Cambridge University Press.

Wilson, John. 1964. *Aims of Education*. Manchester University Press.

Wrong, H. Dennis. 1988. *Power: Its Forms, Bases, and Uses*. University of Chicago Press.

Wuthnow, Robert, Hunter, James Davison, Bergesen, Albert, and Kurzweil, Edith. 1984. *Cultural Analysis*. Routledge and Kegan Paul.

Index

Action, political, for change, 18, 36
Acts of Meaning (Bruner), 18, 98. *See also* Symbolic analysis
Albrow, Martin, 73, 167, 211
Amalgamation, symbolic meanings: appointment of Fellows, 2; avoidance of conflict, 7; "bright tie day," 5, 6; "critical reality definer," 2–4; cultural differences, 5; culture of Borecross, 5; day of amalgamation, 7; decisions, 3; democracy or not?, 10; Gardner, analysis, 10–11; historical background, 1, 2; house or year system, 8; house system, Crosslinks, 4; ideology, 4; match, putting symbolism, 9; micro-political model, 6; name of new school, 9, 10; "nasty political battle," 5; nature of politics, 6; newspaper situation, 10; policy of "melting differences," 6; political power of head, 3; retrospective conclusions, 11; summary and conclusion of story, 31–32; symbolic walk, 7; symbolism, absence of, 8; teachers of history, 8; void of policy, 5
Armitage, Peter: action by letter of criticism, 36–38; approach to Creech, 18; characteristics of Habermasian practi-
cal discourse, 24; choice of voice option, 77; confidential report to the governors, 92–93; consequences of first governors' meeting, 91–92; communication with the DES, 181–183; critique of Stephens's letter, 42–48; distribution of house and year system, critique, 15–17; "egalitarian" remark, 12; exclusion from house committee, 17; first meeting with governors, 78; Habermasian discourse with Creech, 19–23; head's absence from meeting, 90; meeting with chairman, 13; opposition by house teachers, 16–17; political action, 15; protagonist and historian, 35–36; reaction of colleagues to letter, 47–48; reeducation of, 73; request for resignation, 13; response to meeting with head, 41; review committee, 16–17; second meeting with governors, 92–94; style of teaching, 126; Tottenham's assessment of, 147; transcript to head, 24; unbelievable judgment to Stephens's letter, 44. *See also* Atherton, Tim; Bright, city disciplinary inspector; Buckley, Brian; Creech, Simon; Hall, Dr. Ca-

About the Author

PETER B. ARMITAGE is an independent writer and researcher and lives in Annandale, Virginia.

ISBN 0-89789-690-4

90000>

EAN

9 780897 896900

HARDCOVER BAR CODE